# NEGOTIATING RELIGIOUS FAITH
## *in the Composition Classroom*

*Edited by*

*Elizabeth Vander Lei*
*and*
*bonnie lenore kyburz*

D1557239

Boynton/Cook
**HEINEMANN**
Portsmouth, NH

*For Paul and twenty*
*—EVL*

*For Mike, proof*
*—blk*

**Boynton/Cook Publishers, Inc.**
A subsidiary of Reed Elsevier Inc.
361 Hanover Street
Portsmouth, NH 03801–3912
www.boyntoncook.com

*Offices and agents throughout the world*

**Library of Congress Cataloging-in-Publication Data**
Negotiating religious faith in the composition classroom / edited by
Elizabeth Vander Lei and Bonnie Lenore Kyburz.
    p.   cm.
  Includes bibliographical references.
  ISBN 0-86709-576-8 (alk. paper)
  1. Christian literature—Authorship.   2. Religious literature—Authorship.
3. English language—Composition and exercises.   4. College students—Religious life.
I. Lei, Elizabeth Vander.   II. Kyburz, Bonnie Lenore.   III. Title.

  BR44.N44 2005
  200'.71—dc22

                                                                        2005016930

*Editor:* Charles I. Schuster
*Production:* Patricia I. Adams
*Typesetter:* TechBooks
*Cover design:* Joni Doherty Design
*Manufacturing:* Louise Richardson

Printed in the United States of America on acid-free paper

09   08   07   06   05   DA   1   2   3   4   5

# Contents

# Acknowledgments

Everyone says it because it's always true: So many people have had a hand in shaping this book. We are grateful for the graciousness and keen intelligence of the chapter authors. They have introduced us to new scholarly voices and helped us think new thoughts about religious faith and the writing classroom. We are glad to call them friends as well as colleagues. We are especially grateful, too, to the students who willingly shared their voices and their essays with the chapter authors. Chuck Schuster took an active interest in this project from the beginning, and we are grateful for his encouragement. Everyone at Heinemann has been kind and helpful as well; we'd like to thank Lisa Luedeke, especially, and Patty Adams. Melissa Van Til and Leslie Harkema deserve high honors for their dedicated attention to editing and formatting details.

Elizabeth writes: My colleagues in the English Department at Calvin College have been better to me than I deserve; it was they who first pressed me to consider the topic, and they helped me throughout this project. They asked about the work-in-progress, suggested scholarly resources, posed difficult questions, and listened carefully as I tried to frame answers. With homemade treats they enticed me away from the work; best of all, they made me laugh. This project was bonnie's at the beginning, and I am glad for her generosity in inviting me to join her. Keith Miller, Lauren Fitzgerald, and Jeff Cain have collaborated with me on other scholarly presentations on this topic; their incisive thinking has honed my own. Working on a project that sometimes overlapped this one, Tom Amorose, Beth Daniell, Anne Gere, and David Jolliffe have sustained me, body and soul. To Paul, who goes out of his way to find time for me to write, my love forever. For Andrew, Bryant, Maria, and Josephine, who sometimes leave me to my work and other times lure me away from it, I am eternally grateful.

bonnie writes: Nothing is of importance without my patient, supportive, and delightful husband, Mike Kyburz, who deserves every good thing for marrying me. And talk about patience! Many thanks to my parents, Gerald and Mary Surfus, and my sisters, Amy, Emily, Carrie, and Daphne. For unconditional support and love, I am grateful to my mother- and father-in-law, Helmut and Leni Kyburz. Thanks also to our dear friends Rick, Jenny, Nick, and Zoe McDonald. For making sure this project made it to completion with good will and fabulous advice, thanks to Elizabeth Vander Lei. For their support and generosity, thanks to Christa Albrecht-Crane; Mark Crane; John Goshert; Jeanne Gunner; Joe Moxley; Duane Roen; Ryan, Barb, and Claire Simmons;

Brian Whaley; and Kathi Yancey. Thanks to the membership of the WPA list-serv for enduring my rants. Thanks to Utah Valley State College, Arizona State University, and the University of South Florida. And for reminding me of the spirit of creativity, beauty, and expansive possibility, I want to thank the Sundance Film Festival and Institute, both of which make my life in Utah something truly special, something that feels like a calling.

# Part I

# Teachers and Students Negotiate

# 1

# Coming to Terms with Religious Faith in the Composition Classroom
## *Introductory Comments*

### Elizabeth Vander Lei

Negotiating. When I reflect on the scholarship represented in this volume, I think this word sums up our work well. From the outset we tried to negotiate in the business sense of the word—our goal has always been an optimistic one—to search for ways in which academic scholarship and religious faith might work together to accomplish the stated outcomes for our composition courses. We did not blithely root that optimism in the nature of religious faith—it's too easy to point to the damage that has been done in the name of religion; in fact, several chapter authors describe specific kinds of harm that religious faith can cause in the writing classroom. Rather, we are optimistic that by acknowledging the presence of religious faith in our classrooms—maybe even by inviting it in—we can do a better job of helping students recognize and respond to inappropriate rhetorical uses of religious faith in both academic and civic discourse. Furthermore, we are optimistic that when we seize opportunities to teach students about the potential for religious faith to inspire and nurture effective rhetorical practice, we might help them become more engaged students and more effective citizens. As we worked, we found ourselves negotiating in another sense of the word, too: we confronted challenges; some we traversed, while we skirted others. To negotiate these challenges, we sought out new ways to think about the relationship between religious faith and the teaching of writing, brought new voices to the conversation about teaching writing, and proposed frames for imagining the work we do in the classroom.

Some of the challenges we faced were inherent in the relative novelty of the topic: what did we need to talk about? In answering that question, we looked to the scholarship of our field, choosing to attend to the topics teachers of writing most often discuss: the theories that shape our teaching, the curriculum we teach, the people (students, faculty, administrators) who teach and learn, and the institutions that credential student learning and pay our salaries. These topics grew to serve as the organizing principles for the book.

Other challenges resulted from the hesitancy many still feel when considering private issues in a public space—a hesitancy that's only heightened when the private issue in question is religious faith. What's legal? What's ethical? What's wise? In our work, we built on the claim Holdstein and Bleich make in their introduction to *Personal Effects*: ". . . humanistic inquiry cannot develop successfully at this time without reference to the varieties of subjective, intersubjective, and collective experience of teachers and researcher" (2001, 1). We expanded on their scope by adding the experience of students and the history of institutions while narrowing our focus to religious faith. For many students, teachers, theorists, and administrators, religious faith is a significant part of their private lives; it permeates, animates, perhaps haunts their thinking. To press such writers into denying the effect that faith has on them and their writing is to pressure them, in Stephen Carter's words, "to be other than themselves, to act publicly, and sometimes privately as well, as if their faith does not matter to them" (1993, 3).

A little story from my past illustrates this point. When I taught at Arizona State University, campus policy demanded that students lock their weapons in their vehicles before they came to class. The policy did not cover holsters, however, so one semester a student, Mike, showed up in class every day with an empty gun holster on his belt. (To get the full effect of this story you must realize that it was only a short walk from my building to the parking lot.) Probably Mike wore that holster for dramatic effect only at the beginning of the semester: to remove the holster as well as the gun would have required him to remove his belt, too. And to leave both the gun and its holster at home would have denied who he was—a proud Arizona gun owner. Nevertheless, you can imagine that even though I never saw the gun, its presence signaled by that empty holster shaped my relationship with Mike for the entire semester. Like Mike, some people find it impossible to neatly extract themselves from their faith. Were they to try to leave it in the car, so to speak, signals of its existence would nevertheless accompany them into the classroom, shaping their relationships with the people and ideas they meet there.

What's the effect of our asking students to keep their faith at home or lock it in the car? It suggests to students that to succeed in our composition courses, they must deny who they are; as a result, they may find little reason to engage with either the writing or the other individuals in the composition classroom. Priscilla Perkins describes writing classes that had successfully locked away the fundamentalist Christian faith of the students and, in the process, failed to teach them much at all about the rhetorical power of writing.

> Because of its ability to contain digression and force closure, the five-paragraph essay was the favored genre, and . . . students rarely read any text longer than five pages. . . . Though many instructors practiced only what Paulo Freire called "banking methods" of education, some who were familiar with more student-centered pedagogies became "depositors" out of desperation. These teachers insisted that their students were incapable of critical thinking, but I saw no evidence that the teachers regularly offered opportunities for problem-posing education. (2001, 587)

By excising that which they believe to be at best outside the academic realm or at worst anti-intellectual, teachers risk creating not a neutral space but a sterile place where learning is safe from ideas that are potentially community-shattering, such as those regarding gender roles or environmental responsibility. Composition classrooms become safe, true, but for some students these classrooms also become so disjointed from their lives that they would prefer not to engage the teacher or the course at all. They leave at home the "ingenuity," to use Perkins' term, that enlivens their extracurricular lives.

Academic institutions, both public and private, can also carry holster-like traces of religious faith. At some places, like Calvin College where I teach, the religious ways of thinking are obvious. The college is owned by a Christian denomination and, as an institution, attempts to enact its motto, "My heart I offer, Lord, promptly and sincerely." For a variety of historical, cultural, and theological reasons, faculty and administrators at Calvin carefully articulate theological rationale for the things that happen at institutions of higher learning—curriculum, to be sure, but also pedagogy and even admissions. At other universities, the ways that religious faith shapes institutional practice are less obvious; time and circumstance have smoothed the rough edges of religion's influence, polishing away its distinctive features. In *The Soul of the American University*, historian George Marsden notes that in the United States "most major universities evolved directly from nineteenth century [evangelical protestant] colleges. As late as 1870, the vast majority of these were remarkably evangelical" (1994, 4). But according to Marsden: "within half a century the universities that emerged from these evangelical colleges, while arguably carrying forward the spirit of their evangelical forbears, had become conspicuously inhospitable to the letter of such evangelicalism" (4). What produced such a radical transformation? Marsden claims that the vices of liberal Protestantism, its self-promotion as *the* normative worldview (rooted in its vilification of Catholicism) and its absorption of Enlightenment assumptions regarding the universality of science, assured not only the exclusion of all other faiths but also its own eventual exclusion from the academy.

> Unlike some other Western countries which addressed the problems of pluralism by encouraging multiple educational systems, the American tendency was to build what amounted to monolithic and homogeneous educational establishment and to force the alternatives to marginal existence on the

periphery. Almost from the outset of the rise of American universities, such universality was attained by defining the intellectual aspects of the enterprise as excluding all but liberal Protestant or "nonsectarian" perspectives. . . . Eventually, however, the logic of the nonsectarian ideals which the Protestant establishment had successfully promoted in public life dictated that liberal Protestantism itself move to the periphery to which other religious perspectives had been relegated from some time. (5)

So, according to Marsden, the real story of the relationship of religion and the academy is one of love and hate, like the child who grows up to repudiate his parents. What was once a "disestablishment of religion has led to the virtual establishment of nonbelief" (6). All that remains of Protestant domination is "cultural hegemony under the rubric of consensual American ideals" (6), vestigial limbs or ineradicable habits of being, at best useless and at worst potentially damaging.

Religious faith shapes civic discourse as well. Stephen Carter reminds us that religious faith has always been an aspect of human culture in general, and since the founding of our country it's been a particularly notable feature of American society.

> The battle for the public square is already over. The rhetoric of religion is simply *there*; it is far too late in America's political day to argue over "shoulds." The important question is not whether religions can act as autonomous, politically involved intermediary institutions or whether religious people should have access to the public square. Those questions history has already decided.
>
> The question crying out most vitally for resolution, given the presence of religions in the public square, is whether and how to regulate that presence. (1993, 101, emphasis his)

Regardless of the nature or intensity of our own religious faith, we all, students and teachers alike, encounter the religious faith of others; if we hope to prepare our students to write effectively as citizens, we must help them understand the ways that religious faith shapes public institutions and influences civic arguments. Doing so will allow us to negotiate religious faith in the composition classroom in the third sense of the word that *Webster's Third New International Dictionary* offers: "to encounter and dispose of a problem with completeness and satisfaction" (1967, 1514). Beyond accommodating religious faith, we believe that by negotiating religious faith in our composition classrooms, we better teach our students how to analyze and respond to the arguments they encounter every day in political speeches, civic debate, and scholarly discussions.

Why did we choose to focus on religious faith rather than institutional religion? Because religion, while it may shape the practice of academic institutions, doesn't enter most of our classrooms—personal faith does. Faith comes in with the people who populate a composition class, and they carry faith in a variety of ways. Some carry faith as unexamined warrants. Some bring faith as a skeleton in their psychological closet, one they'd rather not acknowledge but can't quite seem to escape. Some bring faith as an acknowledged and well-developed worldview that shapes the claims they make and the goals they set for their writing. For some, faith is a set of nagging questions or haunting suspicions. For others, it registers most strongly as doubt or vilification of particular religious dogmas or religion in general. Religious faith for some functions as a self-imposed filter, a safeguard against "damaging" or "corrupting" ideas or maybe against change of any kind at all. While it may be more or less affiliated with theology or a religious community, religious faith is inherently personal and spiritual. It is how people live out theology or religion, whether they're embracing it, challenging it, fleeing from it, or only suspecting that it affects their lives.

So why not focus instead on spirituality? It's time now, I suppose, to acknowledge the trouble that the term *faith* causes. First, it's a word most commonly associated with Protestant Christianity, and thus carries the potential to disenfranchise those from other religious traditions or to limit our thinking to Protestant concepts. Second, for some the word connotes mindless adherence to religious dogma, a surrender of independent thought and the silencing of skepticism. Third, the word *faith* can denote a static set of principles or doctrines rather than the dynamic process of believing, of "having faith in," or of living faithfully. Recognizing these difficulties, we might have been tempted to accept "spirituality" as an alternative, but we chose to stick with "faith," despite its flaws, for two reasons. First, while it's true that some scholars have worked with a much broader definition of spirituality (see, for example, Carlton and Emmons 2000 and Miller 2000), most recent work has focused on student writers who are members of organized religions. For example, Amy Goodburn (1998), Lizabeth Rand (2001), Priscilla Perkins (2001), and Ronda Leathers Dively (1997) consider the composition experiences of students who define themselves as Christians, particularly Christian fundamentalists or evangelicals (many scholars use these terms interchangeably). Second, the term *religious faith*, at once corporate *and* personal, allows us to explore the connections between the social and personal aspects of faith. Such exploration is important because of a curious dichotomy that has developed in the scholarship on faith and the teaching of writing, particularly in the scholarship that focuses on Christian fundamentalist students.

Reviewing Dively's essay, Rand notes this curiosity, finding a "lingering assumption that we'd naturally think it constrictive for God to be at the center of someone's universe" (2001, 362). Considering ways to help students counter the presumably constrictive effects of Christian belief, Dively turns to literary theory, in particular Spivak and Lacan as appropriated by Paul Smith:

> In that Spivak and Smith's theories may lead students to recover aspects of
> self that they have denied in accordance with certain appropriations of

religious doctrine, students who read such theory may come to understand
that the "easy answers" provided by those belief systems are not adequate for
addressing the complexities of human existence. (Dively 1997, 97)

This impulse to promote a particular literary or rhetorical theory as an acceptable substitute for students' religious faith pervades the scholarship on the role
of faith in the teaching of writing as seen in Handelman, Goodburn, and Perkins.

While it seems that composition teachers are interested in accommodating students of faith (how can we not?), we're less interested in accommodating the religion that shapes their faith. We might willingly accept religions and
religious views that can cohabit with our literary and rhetorical theories or
with our pedagogical goals, but we are likely to reject those that contradict
them, or we might attempt to substitute religions we find more attractive for
those we abhor. Such pedagogical inhospitality does not invite students to
bring their religious faith to their writing nor does it encourage them to
respond effectively to the religious faith they encounter in the public square.
Ultimately, this is what we really hope for our students: not that they alter what
they believe but that they learn to use tension between faith (their own or that
of others) and academic inquiry as a way of learning more and learning better.

In general, we believe that fostering a healthy tension between faith and
academic work is productive, but what about particular cases? What of the
Bartelby students, those like Melville's scrivener, who would prefer not to?
Should we demand that both students and teachers acknowledge their religious
allegiances in the writing classroom? When considering this question, it is
worth remembering Anne Gere's compelling argument for a student's right to
silence. In her essay "Revealing Silence: Rethinking Personal Writing," Gere
argues that it's helpful to think of silence as a productive counterpart to speech:
"Seeing silence in continuity with speech invests it with qualities of affirmation
and fullness" (2001, 207). Gere notes that silence allows the writer the dignity
to "shield portions of one's life from public view" (208); it creates an ethical
stance that allows writers to refuse to betray the trust of others (214), and
teaches a way of resisting the urge to colonize students' experiences or writing
(216–19); it can serve as a "white space" around speech, actually enhancing
what is written (212). When we ask students to open their private lives in the
public classroom, we must also respect some students' desire to keep their religious faith a private issue, one about which they prefer to remain silent.

To be sure, inviting the topic of religious faith into the composition classroom is risky business for teachers, students, and institutions. But is a risk
worth taking. As Jan Swearingen has argued, "Among the many cultures of
today's multicultural academy are the cultures of religion and spiritual values
whose insistent voices are beginning to be heard. We ignore these self-
understandings, these convictions, and their intellect at very great peril to us
all" (2000, 150). We hope that the essays in this book will contribute to an
open and vibrant discussion about religious faith and the teaching of writing.

*little about assumptions*

# Framing the Questions

We open this collection of essays with three chapters that frame the questions authors return to throughout this volume. In her essay, Juanita Smart provides three important correctives to previous research on the religious faith in the composition classroom. First, the focus of this scholarship has rested almost exclusively on the religious faith of students; the religious faith of instructors has, until now, received scant attention. In describing how a student's essay evoked strong memories from her religious past, Smart demonstrates the powerful ways both her religious heritage and her current religious faith shape her reading of a student's writing. Second, Smart reminds us that religious faith sometimes operates as a negative force—haunting students' and teachers' responses to their academic work. And third, Smart offers her own experience as evidence that religious faith does not exist as an autonomous identity issue; it shapes and is shaped by other factors of identity such as gender and sexual orientation. In her conclusion, Smart offers a challenge that is met by other chapters in this collection: "we need to interrogate the beliefs we espouse in both the real and rhetorical situations we share with our students."

One of the basic assumptions that writing teachers must interrogate is the presumption that it is probably unconstitutional and potentially unethical for teachers to allow religious faith into the writing classroom. In her essay, Kristine Hansen provides a robust overview of both American political history and contemporary arguments regarding the acceptable roles for religious faith in academic inquiry. Recognizing how difficult it can be to envision ways to enact these roles, Hansen outlines a writing course based on Pratt's concept of the contact zone, offering hope that "both prudence and civility will migrate from the classroom to the public square." Given the imprudent and uncivil ways that religious faith has been put to argumentative purpose in the public square recently, such curriculum offers the potential to accomplish much good.

While Kristine Hansen convincingly argues for inviting religious faith into the writing classroom, Doug Downs helpfully analyzes the "mutually exclusive and negating epistemologies" that bedevil our attempts to help students bring their religious beliefs to their academic writing. In the writing classroom, Downs concludes, the teacher's first allegiance must be to academic inquiry. Downs suggests ways that teachers can help students "reconcile the irreconcilable" and, in so doing, accomplish the objectives of our composition courses.

# Works Cited

Buley-Meissner, Mary Louise, Mary McCaslin Thompson, and Elizabeth Bachrach Tan, eds. 2000. *The Academy and the Possibility of Belief: Essays on Intellectual and Spiritual Life*. Cresskill, NJ: Hampton.

Carlton, Karen, and Chalon Emmons. 2000. "Every Moment Meditation: Teaching English as Spiritual Work." In *The Academy and the Possibility of Belief: Essays on Intellectual and Spiritual Life*, edited by Mary Louise Buley-Meissner, Mary McCaslin Thompson, and E. Bachrach Tan, 17–38. Cresskill, NJ: Hampton.

Carter, Stephen. 1993. *The Culture of Disbelief: How American Law and Politics Trivialize Religious Devotion*. New York: Basic Books.

Dively, Rhonda Leathers. 1997. "Censoring Religious Rhetoric in the Composition Classroom: What We and Our Students May Be Missing." *Composition Studies* 256 (1): 55–66.

Gere, Anne Ruggles. 2001. "Revealing Silence: Rethinking Personal Writing." *College Composition and Communication* 53: 203–23.

Goodburn, Amy. 1998. "It's a Question of Faith: Discourses of Fundamentalism and Critical Pedagogy in the Writing Classroom." *JAC: A Journal of Composition Theory* 18: 333–53.

Handelman, Susan. 2001. " 'Knowledge Has a Face': The Jewish, the Personal, and the Pedagogical." In *Personal Effects: The Social Character of Scholarly Writing*, edited by D. Holdstein and D. Bleich, 121–44. Logan, UT: Utah State University Press.

Holdstein, Deborah, and David Bleich, eds. 2001. *Personal Effects: The Social Character of Scholarly Writing*. Logan, UT: Utah State University Press.

Marsden. George. 1994. *The Soul of the American University: From Protestant Establishment to Established Nonbelief*. New York: Oxford University Press.

Miller, Hildy. 2000. "Goddess Spirituality and Academic Knowledge-Making." In *The Academy and the Possibility of Belief: Essays on Intellectual and Spiritual Life*, edited by Mary Louise, Buley-Meissner, Mary McCaslin Thompson, and E. Bachrach Tan, 69–84. Cresskill, NJ: Hampton.

Perkins, Priscilla. 2001. " 'A Radical Conversion of the Mind': Fundamentalism, Hermeneutics, and the Metanoic Classroom." *College English* 63: 585–611.

Rand, Lizabeth. 2001. "Enacting Faith: Evangelical Discourse and the Discipline of Composition Studies." *College Composition and Communication* 52 (3): 349–67.

Swearingen, C. Jan. 2000. "The Hermeneutics of Suspicion and Other Doubting Games: Clearing the Way for Simple Leaps of Faith." In *The Academy and the Possibility of Belief: Essays on Intellectual and Spiritual Life*, edited by Mary Louise Buley-Meissner, Mary McCaslin Thompson, and E. Bachrach Tan, 137–152. Cresskill, NJ: Hampton.

*Webster's Third New International Dictionary of the English Language, Unabridged*. 1967. Springfield, MA: G. & C. Merriam.

# 2

# "Frankenstein or Jesus Christ?"
## *When the Voice of Faith Creates a Monster for the Composition Teacher*

Juanita M. Smart

I reach for the last essay from my Writing About Literature course. But when I read the title, "Frankenstein or Jesus Christ?" my stomach tightens and my feet shift uneasily underneath the chair. The title catches me off guard. My assignment asks students to "write a thoughtful, critical response to Mary Shelley's *Frankenstein*." This writer's use of Jesus to examine the subject of Frankenstein strikes me as an inappropriate response to the analytical essay I assigned. Moreover, the phrasing of the student's title asks me to position myself at either end of an uncomfortable extreme: Given the choice that the writer poses, do I situate myself on the side of the Monster or the Messiah, with the devil or the divine?

The dualistic prompting of this essay's title sounds an alarm for me. While my own spirituality draws deeply from the ingrained teachings of an evangelical Christian upbringing, I have nevertheless been progressively engaged in a strong effort to sustain a life of faith that does not preclude my vital consciousness and life as a lesbian. The student's rhetoric invokes the church language I associate with the anti-gay curses of my youth, distancing me and threatening to cloud my evaluation of the essay. Complicating that dilemma is an insistent summons that I want to ignore—one that goads me to once again revisit and reconcile my own professions of faith with the emerging professions of my sexuality.

The student's language chafes a vulnerable place inside of me, but while I acknowledge my personal resistance to his text, my sense of responsibility as teacher compels me to read on. The paper begins:

11

Frankenstein's monster, a creation forsaken by his master and left alone to face a cruel and unforgiving world. He has no friends, no family, and no one to take care of him. His life is a direct reflection of his loneliness. From his attempt to befriend the De Lacy family to his revengeful murders we find that the sole motivation for the monster's actions is his solitude. Yet the same words that describe one man's forsaking can also be associated with another—Jesus Christ. He also was forsaken by everyone—even His Creator—as well as suffering complete humiliation at the hands of people who did not accept Him. Frankentein's [sic] monster and Jesus Christ, two beings who experienced similar persecution as a result of their creator's choice to forsake them.

I note the opening and ending sentence fragments. Fragments typically signal impulsiveness rather than care in the construction of meaning. However, these bookend fragments and the use of hyphens engage my attention. The sentence fragments impart a stylistic emphasis that seems more intentional than careless. The cadence of that dualistic reiteration, "Frankenstein's monster and Jesus Christ," combined with the larger-than-life images it projects, is not unlike the effect of a popular movie trailer urging me to see the film. I envision two superheroes stomping across my visual screen as the words "Frankenstein or Jesus Christ" belt out with the combative urgency of a T.V. promotional clip that roars: "Monster Garage—Where Ordinary Vehicles Are Changed Into Extraordinary Machines!"

I wonder what will follow, but echoes from my fundamentalist past make me resist this writer's appeal. The language is familiar, and I am wary of where it might lead—to a sermon or an altar call, I suspect. Still, I am curious to discover this paper's locus of meaning and the pattern of logic that the writer will use to develop it. The analogy he formulates between Frankenstein's monster and the biblical persona of Jesus poses some fruitful possibilities, and I am wondering how this writer will develop his argument.

Following his opening claim that Frankenstein's monster and Jesus represent "two beings who experienced similar persecution," the writer's focus shifts abruptly in the next two paragraphs as he names "loneliness," "child abandonment," "abortion," and "infanticide" as dominant cultural maladies that precipitate the kind of social estrangement and alienation experienced by Frankenstein's monster. Although he identifies a potentially meaningful parallel between "people [who] are killing their creations through abortions and infanticide because their child is either born or will be born with an abnormality," and Victor's attempt to "leave his monster for dead," his reading strikes me as stereotypical scapegoating and leads directly to fundamentalist moralizing. The student's comment, "[t]his appalling reality concerns me and as I read Frankenstein this was one of the things the story made me think about," is itself an aborted strand of thought that leaves me wondering what other "things" in the novel "made [him] think."

The student's writing lures me into a familiar trajectory of introspection. As I scan the writer's inventory of crimes against God's "creation," I wonder why feminism and homosexuality are so conspicuously missing from the list. That lacuna in the student's text—one makes me curious. I am a "feminist" who is also "homosexual." Although I do not come out to my classes, at various times throughout my teaching career a handful of gay and lesbian students have found their way into my office and disclosed their identity to me. I think about the pink paperback catalogue of gay and lesbian websites that sits in plain view above my desk: *Gay and Lesbian Online: Your Indispensable Guide to Cruising the Queer Web.* I think about the personal conferences I schedule with my writing students. Did this writer notice that pink book on my office shelf and leap to his own conclusions? Aware of the slippery dynamic of power that circumscribes teacher and student relationships, I wonder if he has purposely or even subconsciously avoided naming what he construes to be my own "Frankenstein" culpability. I wonder if he hopes such an omission will save his paper from unfavorable review, despite his concluding disclaimer, "now this isn't an issue about Christians versus non-Christians."

At the bottom of page two the writer repeats his opening argument: "Shelley's story also causes me to think about another man who was destined to be forsaken: the Lord Jesus Christ." Following that pronouncement, the writer notes the injustices that both suffered. "Jesus also received physical torture just as Frankenstein's monster did yet the extent of the torture that the Son of God had to endure far exceeds that of the monster." In language that brings to mind the bloody spectacle of Mel Gibson's *The Passion of the Christ,* the writer details the brutalities inflicted upon Jesus prior to his death on the cross. "As they strike the body [of Jesus] they dig into the flesh tearing out large chunks as they are ripped back for another strike." Underscoring the torture suffered by Jesus, the essay subsequently elaborates on the crucifixion rather than fulfilling the conventions of literary analogy that the paper had earlier promised. The language urges readers to "picture a crown of thorns being pounded into someone's skull," leading finally to the writer's concluding admonition: "If a person truly looks at the graphic details of what Jesus went through it would probably drive him/her to tears, yet Jesus did go through all of those things so that we wouldn't have to." Reading on, I experience tent-meeting talk, pulpit testifying, and the fervent appeal of a type of religious discourse that was silencing for me growing up in the church.

Writing about his own conflicted experiences with students' faith-oriented discourse, Chris Anderson calls "Jesus" papers like this one "description[s] of an embarrassment" (1991, 22), a term he borrows from theologian Karl Barth. According to Anderson, faith writing is "embarrassing" when it enacts "foolishness that is unaware of itself" (1991, 20)—what Anderson identifies as a superficial assumption of personal authority—one that lends itself to an "either/or, dogmatic," and "unexamined" posture of argument. My student's essay with its dualistic thinking (Frankenstein or Jesus Christ?) and explicit disregard for the complexities and ambiguities that constitute faith embodies a type of writing that Anderson might characterize as "superficial foolishness."

While Anderson's own "description" of certain faith writing may seem pejorative (see Rand 2001, 357–58), he nonetheless understands what other academics write off as nonsense—that the constraining discourse of faith-oriented students is partly a consequence that language itself imposes on our attempts to translate religious experience into words because, "religious experience is like a difficult language" (Anderson 1991, 26). Faith embarrasses our attempts to articulate it because it is otherworldly and thus other-word-ly: Faith asks us to explain the unexplainable, to describe "a leap that cannot be justified to anyone who hasn't made that leap" (22). Anderson challenges writing instructors to help faith-oriented students move from "embarrassment" to engagement by asking students to examine their religious assumptions and the language they use to articulate those assumptions. Although Anderson stops short of providing heuristics for writing about faith, his insights legitimize the faith-centered voices of our students.

Despite the awareness of academics like Anderson, however, what frustrates students like my *Frankenstein* writer is an academic community that too often silences voices of faith, effectively prohibiting students' efforts to integrate faith and learning into the cultural discourse of the university. Writing about that prohibition as it relates to student diversity and education, Maxine Hairston observes that while "religion plays an important role in the lives of many of our students," those religious values remain "a dimension almost never mentioned by those who talk about cultural diversity and difference" (1997, 672). Arguing from a similar perspective, Lizabeth Rand observes the postmodern academy's response to faith-centered writing that "in the name of 'diversity' an entire subculture [of Christian-identifying students] often gets silenced" (2001, 351). Acknowledging that difficulty, Anderson (1991) contends that effective educators must examine the assumptions and absolutes that govern our epistemologies as academics, beginning with our need to "understand that academic language is not the only language" (22); we must admit that "transcendence" may manifest itself "way outside or in excess of language" (22), that it is ineffable, that faith itself may be unspeakable. We must examine the values we profess, the sacred "faiths" that we insist on in our classrooms as we help our students learn to write (24–26).

More typically within the academic community, however, the student's profession of faith is perceived as a kind of ill-formed, if not illegitimate, monster—a rhetoric that offends and threatens rather than instructs or enlightens other members of the composing community. More often than not, faith talk from students elicits a derisive and pejorative response like the bumper sticker glued to a colleague's door: "Jesus, Save Me from Your Followers." Mindful of those postures, and of my own complicated response to my *Frankenstein* writer's essay, I do not want to perpetuate a similarly dismissive response to my student's writing. Still, the essay troubles me. In part I am experiencing what Susan McLeod refers to as an "affective bump" (1997, 4)—the feelings the essay has aroused are thwarting my intellectual readiness to respond. McLeod invokes the cognitive theory of psychologist George Mandler to explain how the delicate relationship between affect and cognition governs our response as teachers: "we experience the feelings of emotion when the expectations of some schema are violated—when there is a discrepancy in what we think will happen and what actually happens, when some action is interrupted, when ongoing plans are blocked" (30). I asked for an analytical essay about *Frankenstein* but received something resembling a sermon instead. In the end, even the attempt at literary analogy is subsumed by the writer's hortatory voice of faith.

More problematic for me than this student's conversion of the assignment into a personal profession of his beliefs, however, is my resistance to the rhetoric of his faith. Knowing that the writer sees himself as a principled and moral individual, I nevertheless experience his text as a kind of disappointing salesmanship. His repeated invocation of the name of Jesus—with nineteen references to "Jesus," the "Son of God," and "Christ" recurring throughout the five-page document—is familiar and alienating. As a young person much like this undergraduate writer, I too had practiced a religious ethos that compelled me to profess my faith publicly. Within my church community, witnessing was customary and expected—the litmus test of our commitment. "Testifying" in the name of Jesus was part of a sacred, verbal code; as believers, we called it, approvingly, "taking a stand." As an eighteen-year-old, my own act of taking a stand had cost me the opportunity to deliver the graduation address to my high school class of four hundred students, all because I had staunchly refused to remove a line from my handwritten speech that asserted that "Jesus" was "the only way," the only "bridge" for developing a meaningful future among my generation of peers.

While I am thus well acquainted with the religious stance that my student is taking in his paper and can identify with the spiritual consciousness that risks that stance, I feel cornered by the nonnegotiable terms of his rhetoric. Twenty years later, "taking a stand" no longer signifies for me the enactment of spiritual conviction and compassionate invitation. Now those words invoke an intolerant and exclusionary stance—not an invitational one.

I recall my teenage participation in a program called Blueprint for Evangelism, which was adopted enthusiastically by my homogenously white, working-class youth group. Our local Blueprint for Evangelism called on us to "take a stand" every Tuesday evening by knocking on the doors of an inner-city housing project to share the gospel with the low-income and ethnically diverse residents who lived there. I recall one African American woman from the project, a single mother who invited my evangelism partner and me into her apartment for sweet potato pie. We were caught off guard by her reciprocity, hesitating awkwardly before stepping across the threshold into the dwelling of her life and belief. The memory of her hospitality serves as a rich reproof for me now and speaks much more profoundly about Christian charity and grace than any of the things I stood for as I sputtered formulaic phrases to her about her need to trust in Jesus.

Yet another image that the phrase "taking a stand" evokes for me is of an itinerant preacher and his small band of followers who visited my graduate university campus every year, waving giant poster-board placards inscribed with bold phrases: "GOD HATES FAGS!" and "ABORTIONISTS BURN IN HELL!" Surely they too were taking a stand, professing a faith, and insisting on a certain way of believing—but that kind of stance, and the hateful and ecclesiastical language that it appropriates, compels me now to turn away from such presumptions of spiritual privilege and power. Ultimately I have come to experience that stance as an unexamined assent to injustice rather than the courageous assertion of a moral ideal.

Ironically, I consider, my reformed faith and tolerance seem to render me equally intolerant toward my *Frankenstein* writer and the articulation of faith he embraces.

Theorizing the mutable nature of language and its powerful influence on our perceptions of reality, Mikhail Bakhtin observes that "language . . . lies on the borderline between oneself and the other. The word in language is half someone else's" (1981, 293). But borderlines, like language, are mutable too, and as I ponder the borderlines that lie contested between my student and me—the meanings and idioms that complicate our faith—what had earlier struck a dissonant chord for me in the tenor of my student's language subsequently transposes into a galvanizing realization. The word *abomination*, though absent from this paper, nonetheless asserts a powerfully inferred presence there for me as reader. In my religious lexicon, "monster" is synonymous with "abomination," which invokes a powerful censure from my past.

Years before, I received a verbal indictment from my youngest sister after I disclosed my lesbian identity to my family. "You are an abomination," she had written, "believe me, your prayers aren't getting past the ceiling." She banned me from her home and from spending time with her three young children. Her sanctions against me were bolstered with the standard scripture references, most notably the Levitical stricture against same-sex relations, "thou shalt not lie with mankind, as with womankind: it is abomination" (Leviticus 18:22), and the passage from the book of Romans, which denounces the expression of "vile affections" between women (Romans 1:26). My family no doubt believed that they were taking a stand, "speaking the truth in love," but their reproach, waved beneath the banner of biblical Christianity, inflicted a monstrous bruising that persists in alienating me today.

During graduate school that sense of alienation was aggravated by my knowledge of another incident. At the state land-grant institution where I taught and studied, the student gay, lesbian, bisexual, and transgendered (GLBT) organization had struggled vigorously to gain constitutional approval by the student governing body. As has been the case in so many other settings, recognizing the GLBT as a legitimately sanctioned university organization was highly contested. At one public forum, members of a local Christian fundamentalist congregation (cheekily nicknamed "the ziggurat" because of the way its multiple stories dominated our agricultural landscape) had materialized as the most vocal opponents of the GLBT's endorsement, disparaging the GLBT and its allies with the same kind of rhetoric that my sister had used to disparage me. Much has been written about the mutual relationship between life and literature, and even though the problematic episodes I write about have no specific connection to my Writing About Literature class, they are nonetheless real and rhetorical exigencies that shadow my response to my *Frankenstein* writer's text.

In her groundbreaking essay, "Enacting Faith: Evangelical Discourse and the Discipline of Composition Studies" (2001), Lizabeth A. Rand revalues the  religious discourse of our students and offers practical insight into the ways in which writing instructors might respond more effectively to the discourse of faith. Rand infuses new meaning into academia's casual reading of our students' faith-centered texts by insisting that evangelical subjectivity is a radical and "critically resistant stance" (363). "[F]or many Christians," Rand contends, "a declaration of faith in Jesus is far from being pious cliché or a sign of dull conformity. Witnessing talk does involve a complex interrogation of the self; it can in fact be thought-provoking" (363). Indeed, the verbal prompts that Rand invents are thoughtful writing heuristics for provoking the kind of faith-based, self-interrogation that she wants to invite. Rand questions her students, for instance, about how resistance to "mainstream values and culture" has "shaped their lives" and how it impacts their relationships with those who are not members of their faith communities (363).

But when Rand asks parenthetically, "[h]ave [Christian, evangelical students] faced rejection from family members, friends, coworkers, classmates, etc.?" (363), I, who am both Christian and lesbian, mouth an immediate, affirmative response, discovering that the lesbian cog of my consciousness resonates much more saliently with Rand's reference to "rejection" than my Christian consciousness does. While I do not want to undervalue the kinds of struggles her question seeks to validate for faith-oriented students, I also feel compelled to cite the "critically resistant stance" of uncounted gay and lesbian students who have traditionally been disfranchised from faith communities and who in many cases lead the ranks of those whom Christian culture would cast out. While Rand inquires of her faith-minded students "[h]ow . . . [do] those in the secular world react to their religious identity?" (363), I cannot help but entertain a paradoxical revision to her question: "How do those in the church community react to gay and lesbian students' sexual identity?" Rightfully, Rand recognizes that academic discourse "at times trivializes and misrepresents faith-related expression" (350). Responding to that discrepancy she recommends that writing instructors should approach our students' faith-related texts, "with more knowledge" (and presumably more respect) "about

their religious identities," arguing that that approach "might be the most effective and inviting way to connect with them as people and as writers" (353). But
what happens when "identity" and the rhetoric that embodies it is the very
thing that occludes the likelihood of "invitation"?

Compelled by that question I return to my student's *Frankenstein* essay
and discover an island of insight that I had earlier overlooked. Drawing a parallel between the cultural ostracism of Frankenstein's monster and the orthodox culture's ostracism of Jesus, the student writes:

> Where as the monster *looked* different, Jesus *acted* different from the other
> Jews [emphasis in original]. Two different reasons for hatred but the same
> results nonetheless. In both cases people found a reason to dislike them and,
> out of that dislike, attempted to purge the problem.

The student's commentary, "[t]wo different reasons for hatred but the same
results nonetheless," brings me pause. Encoded in that language I discover a
crossroad of meaning with my *Frankenstein* writer—a fragment of possibility
where the circumstance of our "difference" is the distinguishing condition that
marks us as the "same." Writing about the freakishness of life and our own
"demon[s] of fear," Mary Clearman Blew notes "*monster*, from the Latin *mon-
strum*, means a prodigy or a portent" (1999, 55–56). Sandwiched within the
borderlines of my student's writing I discern that portentous prodigality—
where the culture's intolerables, monsters and messiahs, share a mutuality as
sacred as it is profane.

Writing about the conflicted possibilities of another portentous place—the
"hard place" of deciding whether or not to disclose the "secret" of our sexual
identity to our students—Mary Elliott (1996) claims "many of us cannot avoid
seeing ourselves as we have been taught to imagine that others see us" (696).
Elliott's insight is instructive for me as I wrestle with my student's *Frankenstein*
paper. Elliott's description of the false imaging that shapes gay and lesbian consciousness, the familiar depictions of gays and lesbians as social perverts and
abominable monsters, for instance, enlarges the meaning for me of James
Berlin's theory that "only through language do we know and act upon the conditions of our experience" (1996, 82). What seems so clear to me, but what my
student may not yet understand, is that much of the religious discourse he
invokes is verbal code that can be estranging to an audience not conversant in
that code, or whose identification with it is something "other" than what the
writer values. In particular, the writer's recurring use of phrases like "the Lord
Jesus Christ," "Son of God," and "the truth of God's word" polarizes readers
who have experienced those references as threatening incantations, words
invoked to bolster the stereotypical, ostracizing, and "monstrous" charges that
too often misrepresent and nullify the ethos and identity of [an]other.

Harriet Malinowitz notes that "people may share a word with which they
define themselves, but the condition signified by that word does not seem to be
shared" (1995, 14). Her observation aptly depicts the delicate contingencies

that govern the "Christian" affiliation I share with my student. Undeniably my student's purpose is passionate and ambitious—no doubt he had hoped to move his reader toward his own bountiful vision of faith. But his fraught language eclipses that possibility for some: I had encountered the mute apparition of a monster, and the monster resembled me. Just as I had done in my high school graduation speech, this student had erected a barrier where he had intended to ✓ build a bridge. Making that connection with him now requires of me a different leap of faith: While on one level a part of me isn't sure whether to respond with a verbal thrashing or a prayer vigil, on another level, as writing teacher, I wonder how I can draw on my own faith experience and knowledge to facilitate a more successful fulfillment of the writing assignment by this student.

Lizabeth Rand contends that "in order to respond more effectively to those who write about religion," composition teachers would "benefit from extended conversation of the ways that faith is 'enacted' in discourse and sustained through particular kinds of textual and interpretive practice" (2001, 350). Considering the ways in which that conversation must ultimately include the student, where might I begin a dialogue with one whose ethos seems so dedicated to silencing the ethos of voices like mine? How might that unpredictable exchange be instructive and transforming not only for my student but, more important, for me? What might the shared value of our rhetorical process be?

Rand's comment invites me to consider faith as discourse from the perspective of my own "enacted" interpretive practices and the intricate gestalt that informs those practices. I recall a curious scene I once witnessed while riding a transit bus in downtown Portland, Oregon. Staring out the window of the bus, I noticed a large contingent of multigenerational men swarming through a public parking arena and strolling along the street together. What caught my attention was the way in which their posture and body language communicated their obvious love of one another's company. Strolling alongside each other, they conversed and made light body contact; some openly embraced. These men struck me as intimates rather than acquaintances. Their affective stance toward one another marked them for me as decidedly "gay." As the bus lumbered along and turned the corner, I read the large marquee that juts out from Portland's downtown stadium—"Welcome Promise Keepers."—just in time to make the startling discovery that what I just witnessed was not a fraternity of gay men, but rather a Christian, evangelical-sponsored "fellowship" for (presumably) straight men. I rolled my head back. The irony of the powerful role that my own references of meaning played in my reading of that ambiguous situation was not lost on me.

The "evangelical discourse" enacted by the Promise Keepers brought me a revelation. My misreading of their situational cues demonstrates how the highly contested constructs of spirituality and sexuality resist cultural codification, maintaining the unpredictable and rich valence of possibilities that constitute human experience and consciousness. Alternatively, my reading of the Promise Keepers behavior metaphorically empowers me as a gay believer with an inclusive vision of faith, enabling me, in Carolyn Heilbrun's words to "take [my] place in whatever discourse is essential to action" and claim "[my] right to have [my] part matter" (1988, 18).

The charge that I face regarding my student's evangelical discourse seems clear: Somehow I both need and want to help him claim "[his] place," and "the right to have [his] part matter," without disallowing his profession of faith. Within the immediate context of my Writing About Literature class, I want to give him the opportunity to rehearse the kinds of scholarly strategies that will allow him to think more critically within the scheme of his rhetorical purposes as he seeks to integrate faith and learning in his writing assignment. Within a larger educational context, I hope that my student will begin to cultivate fruitful strategies for integrating the discourse of his faith with the discourse of the academy, strategies that will recommend him to, rather than alienate him from, an eclectic audience of academic mentors and peers.

During our initial conference I explain that he is responsible for fulfilling the assignment. I also ask him to consider his rhetorical situation and the need to address his purpose and audience appropriately by composing a paper for a literature class, not a sermon for church. Four weeks later, my student submits his revision, a paper which he renames "Crime and Punishment"—a title that clings to the moralistic positioning of his "Frankenstein or Jesus Christ?" paper, but one that also grounds the writer's work within the context of literary explication by invoking the title of Dostoyevsky's novel.

In his opening paragraph the writer asserts an explicit comparison between Victor von Frankenstein and the Ancient Mariner in Samuel Coleridge's "The Rime of the Ancient Mariner." He also enacts the discourse of his faith through his interpretation that "[b]oth of these men . . . committed a spiritual crime against God and both were punished with a strong sentence." In his revision of the writing assignment, the writer asserts the biblical adage "we reap what we sow," but uses illustrations from each text to demonstrate the ways in which that adage manifests itself through plot structures and character development, rather than insisting on biblical conduct codes as the standard against which the value of each narrative should be rehearsed.

While the writer maintains a dualistic logic, and while there are still noticeable leaps in the logic that he applies, certain constructions of meaning do demonstrate that he is beginning to explore the ambiguities of good and evil, and his writing demonstrates a more intentional interrogation of the text. He writes,

> [Victor von Frankenstein] was a man who was more into science than he was into religion because of his hunger for knowledge. Mary Shelley seems to be showing in her story that this hunger for knowledge and desire to take the authority of God into man's hands is a mistake that brings a penalty alongside of it.

My requirement in the writing assignment that students "demonstrate [their] understanding and application of at least one of the critical theories [included in the Bedford edition of *Frankenstein*]" was a detail that the writer hurriedly glossed over in his first draft. In the revision, however, the writer grapples with the Marxist criticism given in the book, finding it useful to support his reading that the willful acts of both Frankenstein and the Ancient Mariner were driven by each protagonist's desire for material control and power:

> It seems as if the two men were after the same thing—control and change. They wanted to have control over their circumstances because of the feeling of power that comes with it. The Marxist critics agree with this interpretation as they equate the story of Frankenstein with the French and British revolutions and their desires for change: "Mary Shelley's work is incontestably interwoven in this history: it bears witness to the birth of that monster, simultaneously the object of pity and fear . . . (Montag 303).

Although the writer wobbles somewhat as he incorporates critical theory into his own thinking and writing, that sophisticated maneuver nevertheless demonstrates his ability to respond to the rhetorical conventions required of him by the writing assignment.

While my student's revision bears witness to his success in the assignment, I experience some shades of doubt as I reflect on that tentative process with him: what cost do such acts of re-vision exact on the privately intuited, epistemological registries of the student? Aside from the conflict I have about my own culpability in my student's abandonment of his original idea, I wonder, as many of us do, what he learned from his composition process. Was his reincarnation of the *Frankenstein* paper just another perfunctory exercise in delivering what the teacher wants? Early on in my relationship with this student he had shared with me that he hoped eventually to earn his Ph.D. He wanted to become an English professor. At the time, his comment made me revalue what he stood to gain from investing in his writing. Some months after he had successfully completed my Writing About Literature course we crossed paths again and he told me that he had changed his major to business.

As I continue to replay my own negotiation of the *Frankenstein* scenario, the student's blunt declaration, "[t]wo different reasons for hatred but the same results nonetheless" returns to me again and again. If a parallel referent for "faith" exists within the intellectual orthodoxies of academia, that referent must be the word *persistence*. Mary Elliott has written, "if we cannot see the source of our fear or measure the effects our actions will have, then the power of these unknown causes and consequences can assume unlimited proportions" (1996, 696). I wonder if my student learned, as I did, about the value of persistence in facing unknowns?

Faith-centered discourse is a recurring theme in many of our composition classrooms. Responding to that voice of faith challenges those of us who are unwilling or unable to engage a way of learning and knowing that seems so deeply embedded in the student's privatized, intuitive constructs

of meaning. While we may be willing to acknowledge that religious belief, or its absence, significantly relates to the nature of learning, we resist the voice of faith in an effort to prevent alienating and exclusionary rhetorics from dominating the discussion. We do not want our learning communities to be disrupted by the "one way" thinking of the student who feels that she owns a monopoly on the truth. But as Sue McLeod advises, "as teachers we need to know more about how our students' beliefs and attitudes are formed and how we can help students understand them as they interact with their writing processes" (1997, 74). And, I would add, we need to interrogate the beliefs we espouse in both the real and rhetorical situations we share with our students.

Such knowledge is hard won. As I persist in the struggle to learn how reasons for hatred are formed, I cross the brink to a prodigal place where I confront and reconcile my own fears about the faith-generated monsters of my past.

# Works Cited

Anderson, Chris. 1991. "The Description of an Embarrassment: When Students Write About Religion." In *Balancing Acts: Essays on the Teaching of Writing in Honor of William F. Irmscher*, edited by Virginia A. Chappell et al., 19–27. Carbondale: Southern Illinois University Press.

Bakhtin, M. M. 1981. *The Dialogic Imagination: Four Essays by M. M. Bakhtin*. Edited by Michael Holquist. Translated by Caryl Emerson and Michael Holquist. Austin: University of Texas Press.

Berlin, James A. 1996. *Rhetorics, Poetics, and Cultures: Refiguring College English Studies*. Urbana, IL: NCTE.

Blew, Mary Clearman. 1999. *Bone Deep in Landscape: Writing, Reading, and Place*. Norman: University of Oklahoma Press.

Elliott, Mary. 1996. "Coming Out in the Classroom: A Return to the Hard Place." *College English* 58 (6): 693–708.

Haggerty, George E., and Bonnie Zimmerman, eds. 1995. *Professions of Desire: Lesbian and Gay Studies in Literature*. New York: The Modern Language Association of America.

Hairston, Maxine. 1997. "Diversity, Ideology, and Teaching Writing." In *Cross-Talk in Comp Theory*, edited by Victor Villanueva Jr., 659–75. Urbana, IL: NCTE.

Heilbrun, Carolyn G. 1988. *Writing a Woman's Life*. New York: W. W. Norton.

Malinowitz, Harriet. 1995. *Textual Orientations: Lesbian and Gay Students and the Making of Discourse Communities*. Portsmouth, NH: Heinemann Boynton/Cook.

McLeod, Susan H. 1997. *Notes on the Heart: Affective Issues in the Writing Classroom*. Carbondale: Southern Illinois University Press.

Montag, Warren. 1992. "'The Workshop of Filthy Creation': A Marxist Reading of *Frankenstein*." In *Frankenstein*, by Mary Shelley, edited by Johanna M. Smith, 300–311. Boston: Bedford Books of St. Martin's Press.

Morrison, Melanie. 1995. *The Grace of Coming Home: Spirituality, Sexuality, and the Struggle for Justice.* Cleveland, OH: The Pilgrim Press.

Rand, Lizabeth. 2001. "Enacting Faith: Evangelical Discourse and the Discipline of Composition Studies." *College Composition and Communication* 52 (3): 349–67.

# 3

# Religious Freedom in the Public Square and the Composition Classroom

## Kristine Hansen

Today's teachers of writing—whether they acknowledge it or not—constitute part of the 2,500-year-old rhetorical tradition that, during most of its long history, prepared young people to participate in civic life. As Robert Connors has shown, this tradition metamorphosed during the nineteenth century into the composition course, where one of its remnants is the argumentative essay, usually about some controversial aspect of public life (see Connors 1997, 1–12, 210–40). Often students choose or are assigned to write about controversial political issues such as abortion, capital punishment, gun control, gay marriage, or preemptive war. Because such issues are contested in our society, it makes sense that students learn how to represent their opinions effectively in these debates. Yet I have often heard writing teachers express dismay—I have done so myself—when students' papers for or against a particular position on an issue are grounded mainly in their religious beliefs and are more in the genre of sermonizing or witnessing than of political argument. "Don't these kids know," we lament, "that you just can't do that? You're not going to persuade any audience that doesn't already share your beliefs." At the same time, we feel a twinge of guilt because it seems wrong to tell students they can't use as reasons for their position the very beliefs to which they feel most deeply committed.

With our own commitment to academic freedom, we recognize that students should be able to voice the religious reasons for their positions. We feel conflicted because we want to be tolerant, yet we recognize that, as arguments, some students' papers will miss their audiences. For their part, students may feel that we are demeaning their faith when we attempt to show them why and where their arguments are ineffective. They may think they have to choose

24

between saying what they believe and getting a good grade (see Rebecea Nowacek's essay, Chapter 13). I have known students to resolve this dilemma by supporting their positions either with reasons that they don't really believe in or with reasons offered by others that they don't fully understand—a good first step, perhaps, but not a satisfactory final one. Some students change topics to something easier and safer. A few teachers I know have simply stopped assigning papers about controversial public issues because they don't want to confront the dilemmas such assignments raise.

But are any of these good solutions to the problem? I think not. My reasons for this answer are partly personal, so I spell those out first. Next, I explain why I believe writing teachers must come to grips with students' desire—indeed, their right—to express their religious views in the writing classroom. Finally, I explore some possible answers to these two questions: How can we teach students with strong religious convictions to write about controversial public issues so that they can learn and practice the rhetorical arts that will prepare them for citizenship in a pluralist society? And how can we do this without making them feel they must deny or trivialize their religious beliefs?

## The Personal Is Political

First, I want to provide some personal context since it certainly influences what I have to say here. I belong to a distinct minority in the state of Utah, being a Democrat who is also an active, devout member of the Church of Jesus Christ of Latter-day Saints (often called the Mormon Church, hereafter referred to as the LDS Church). Well over seventy percent of Utahns are members of the LDS Church, and, though I don't know the percentage, more than half are Republicans. Currently, no Democrats hold statewide office, and the numbers of Democrats in both houses of the state legislature are too small to block any legislation the majority determines to pass. Many races for statewide offices and seats in the legislature are uncontested because no Democrat is available or willing to run, and Republicans usually win the contested elections by lopsided margins. Of Utah's five members in the U.S. Congress, only one is a Democrat, and the 2001 state legislature gerrymandered his district in an obvious—and barely unsuccessful—attempt to unseat him (Harrie 2002, A1).

Because the Republican Party dominates a state that is also dominated by the LDS Church, many people inside and outside Utah assume that membership in the church goes hand-in-glove with membership in the party. Although the LDS Church's leadership has gone to some pains to disavow connections to any political party—a high-ranking member of one of its presiding councils gave a lengthy front-page interview to the *Salt Lake Tribune* explaining why a two-party system is desirable and why Mormons can be Democrats—the belief that "good" Mormons are Republicans remains popular (see Fraughton

1998). It is not uncommon for Republican state legislators to justify their positions on political issues with veiled or open references to LDS doctrines; for example, legislators opposing bills to make child car seats and seat belts mandatory complained that such laws would violate people's God-given agency to choose between right and wrong. Every day, letters to the editor of the two statewide newspapers are filled with arguments connecting political views to religious teachings. Occasionally in church meetings I am subjected to teachers whose political leanings—usually Republican—color their interpretations of the scriptures.

Readers from other regions where one religion and one party predominate probably recognize the situation I describe. Frankly, I am not surprised by the extent to which politics and religion intermingle in my state or elsewhere. It would surprise me if they did not: Those who are inclined to be deeply religious and also interested in politics no doubt view religion and government as the two things that have the power to affect their daily lives the most. It would be surprising if those who are religious did not seek to bend political decisions in a direction congruent with their beliefs. And it is understandable when the reverse happens and people attempt to shape religious organizations to mirror their political desires. I admit that I want public policy to mirror my deeply felt religious convictions. Like many who are religiously minded, I can interpret scripture to support my stances on political issues, so I tend to feel that my political positions are not only right but righteous.

Yet it's radiantly clear that members of my church who don't share my political views feel just as strongly that their positions are divinely inspired. This sometimes presents a problem for me in my professional life, particularly whenever my courses veer toward political issues. I teach at Brigham Young University, which is owned and operated by the LDS Church. Some 32,000 students from all fifty states and more than 130 foreign nations are enrolled there. Approximately ninety-eight percent of them are members of the LDS Church; and, although diversity seems to be increasing, the majority are politically conservative. No doubt they have come by their politics just as I did, by growing up in a family where their parents discussed their political views as they taught their children religious precepts, making it seem as if the two were one and the same. Some of my students are aghast when they discern my political leanings. I seem so orthodox in the faith, it's hard for them to imagine how I could be—gasp!—so liberal, a word most have heard used mainly as a term of derision. Despite knowing that I share their religious beliefs, students can find it unsettling if I question something they have written about political issues, prompting them to state the point better, support it more fully, or earn rather than assume the reader's agreement. Sometimes students seem to think I have questioned their understanding of God's truth. And when I attempt to explain my own positions, I find that I have to choose my words carefully so as not to offend my students, who think their political positions are right in almost the same way they think their religious beliefs are right.

Many of us have sensed this kind of student reaction or have faced inter-esting politico-religious challenges. Whether the teacher, the student, neither, or both are religious, and whether they are at a private or a public institution, instances of misunderstandings and conflicts are bound to arise with regard to the expression of religious and political views—particularly when religion and politics intersect. We must deal openly and effectively with those occasions to further both our students' learning and the future of our democratic polity.

## Why We Should Tolerate Religious Expression in the Writing Classroom

*[handwritten annotation: Almost all literature is from a Christian-Judeo perspective]*

I offer four reasons why teachers should permit students to talk and write about their religious beliefs, particularly in connection with the political stances they take on issues that confront society. First, the First Amendment to the U.S. Constitution allows freedom of expression, and that freedom does not end when students enter the classroom. The classroom is an extension of the public square, particularly at public institutions of higher education. And while private institutions may limit the amount and nature of expression (e.g., my university prohibits disparagement of the sponsoring church), in general on private campuses, freedom of religious and political expression is also safe-guarded by the Constitution. Although some interpret the establishment clause of the First Amendment to mean that religion has no role to play in the politi-cal realm and that public discourse ought not to be inflected by the idiom of religion, the courts have consistently ruled that individuals may express their religious views freely. The clause means only that government is barred from favoring the religious views and practices of some citizens over those of oth-ers. The famous "wall of separation" between church and state does not mean that religion must be banned from the public square; it means only that gov-ernment cannot establish preferences among religions.[1] Furthermore, it means that government cannot prefer non-religion to religion. As Supreme Court Jus-tice William O. Douglas wrote in a 1952 opinion, no clause in the Constitution requires that "government show a callous indifference to religious groups. That would be preferring those who believe in no religion over those who do believe" (quoted in Eastland 1993, 107–108).

The second reason we should allow freedom of religious expression in the discussion of political issues is that we have inherited from the founders of our nation a language that is no longer adequate for conducting our political affairs. This language, often called the discourse of philosophical liberalism,[2] is inade-quate because it does not allow for the expression of particular religious beliefs, which are, for many people, the basis for some important political decisions. Philosophical liberalism is the product of eighteenth-century Enlightenment ideals propounded by John Locke and others, who taught the separation of pri-vate and public, of subjective and objective knowledge. According to these ideals, objective knowledge is that which is universally available through the application of rational methods of discovering truth (see Elshtain 2001, 50–53). These methods are basically scientific and mathematical; they are favored because, in theory, they produce knowledge that is objective, or knowledge that can be quantified and reproduced. Quantification is desirable because it seems solid and factual, and the rhetoric used to present numbers is thought to be transparent, objective, and rational. Reproducibility is desirable because, if knowledge is reproducible, it can stake a greater claim to universality. Objective knowledge became favored as the basis for political action in the eighteenth century for, as Kant said, a law can be a law only if the people can understand it and would impose it on themselves (1986, 266–67). People across generations and across time must be able to understand why it is a law. Succeeding generations would not understand laws, in Kant's view, unless they were built on universal reason. Philosophical liberalism has been mostly successful as a basis for governing a diverse nation like the United States because it appears to promise that disagreements can be solved with recourse to the proper rational methods, thus regulating public affairs in a way that is neutral and fair.

But philosophical liberalism, because it separates public and private knowledge, also effectively separates public and private spheres. Religious knowledge is consigned to the realm of the private because it is not obtained through the application of rational methods, but rather through divine revelation, from sacred texts and sanctioned authorities. Moreover, religious knowledge is apparently not universal, or else all would have the same religious beliefs. The presumed advantage of consigning religion to the private realm is that deliberation about a political course of action can then proceed without the interruptions, impasses, and violence that sometimes occur when different religious beliefs come into conflict. Given the increasing pluralism of our society, some argue, political debate is not well served by the introduction of religious ideals and language into its give and take.

In response to these arguments, however, others claim that our political discourse would be enhanced if it included more references to religious teachings. For example, Robert Bellah and his coauthors of *The Good Society* state that "philosophical liberals . . . have tended to define politics as narrowly concerned with procedural justice, with, as they put it, matters of the right rather than of the good. In [their] reading, religious groups, with their strong visions of the good, tend to disrupt democratic politics by bringing into public life matters that should remain essentially private" (1991, 180). However, Bellah and associates worry that in its aim to use only an unbiased, secular political vocabulary, philosophical liberalism risks promoting an incomplete and impoverished public discourse by excluding the rich ethical vision that religion can bring to public deliberations. They have no fear that what they call the "public church" might steamroll nonbelievers into a theocratic system because "few if any issues in the history of the United States have pitted the churches against the secularists; usually we find different denominations on different sides, disagreement within denominations, and religious and secular people joined on one side or the other" (181). Because the alignment of various groups and the consensus on various issues is "ever fragile and changing," there is no reason to exclude religions from public debate. In fact, "The importance of the discussion, and of the religious contribution to it . . . cannot be overestimated. The public church has almost never spoken with a single voice; that does not diminish its significance in our common life" (181).

Likewise, Jean Elshtain argues that taking philosophical liberalism to its logical conclusion would mean the triumph of liberal monism. Liberal monism is the belief that the institutions of a democracy act in accordance with "a single authority principle" as well as "a single standard of what counts as reason and deliberation" and "a single vocabulary of political discussion." As a result, liberal monism defines reason "in such a way that faith is discounted as irrationalism" (Elshtain 2001, 54). Liberal monism underlies the doctrine of "strong separationism," which interprets the First Amendment to mean that church-state separation requires a "thoroughly secularized society stripped of any and all public markers and reminders of religion" because religion is entirely private and therefore must be invisible in public life (53). To press for strong separation, thus enthroning liberal monism as the ruling ideology, would be to undermine the vitality of the American polity, claims Elshtain, for American social pluralism is constituted "by the history and presence of diverse faith communities" (54). In our system, "religion and politics have always mutually constituted one another in ways direct and indirect" (40). It would be painfully ironic if a nation that emerged in part as a reaction to religious intolerance were itself to become intolerant of religion.

Similarly, Stephen Carter argues that the religiously devout should not have to disguise their moral convictions and translate them into a language that philosophical liberalism accepts. Carter dismantles the distinction between facts and values that philosophical liberalism uses to describe religious knowledge as simply a set of values that believers hold. Believers know what they do because their epistemology is not limited to methods accepted by eighteenth-century rationalists. Therefore, says Carter,

> What is needed is not a requirement that the religiously devout choose a form of dialogue that liberalism accepts, but that liberalism develop a politics that accepts whatever form of dialogue a member of the public offers. Epistemic diversity, like diversity of other kinds, should be cherished, not ignored, and certainly not abolished. What is needed, then, is a willingness to listen, not because the speaker has the *right voice* but because the speaker has the *right to speak*. Moreover, the willingness to listen must hold out the possibility that the speaker is saying something worth listening to; to do less is to trivialize the forces that shape the moral convictions of tens of millions of Americans. (1993, 230–31, emphasis his)

This trivialization of religion has also been noted by Stanley Fish, who calls on academics to actually listen to religious voices and take them seriously.

Fish notes that while religious views are usually tolerated on campuses as *expressions*, the content of those expressions is often vilified. But this vilification makes religious views "just like other views" because the only thing valued about them

> is that they have been freely produced (no one forced you to utter them) and that they are freely broadcast (no one has censored them). What is not valued about them is the content of what they urge. As instances of a favored category—expression—religious utterances are cherished; as something you are asked to take seriously, they are feared and condemned. (1999, B4)

In this way, Fish says, "liberalism, in the form of academic freedom, gets to display its generosity while at the same time cutting the heart out of the views to which that generosity is extended" (B5). If academic freedom allows religion to be a part of university life only "so long as it renounces its claim to have a privileged purchase on the truth"—which is, of course, the very thing that makes a religion a religion and not just an opinion—then it is asking those who are religious to "inhabit their moral convictions loosely and be ready to withdraw from them whenever pursuing them would impinge on the activities and choices of others" (B5). Fish claims that our society is morally "thinner" when individuals' moral stances are turned simply into individual preferences and their moral assertions become mere opinions. The salient point is this: If we allow free expression in the public square and on the college campus, we have to take seriously not just people's *right* to assert their beliefs. We must also take seriously their *beliefs*.

The third reason writing teachers should allow religious expression in the classroom derives directly from the second: When religious voices are not only tolerated in the public square but listened to, good things may happen. Stephen Carter points out that some of the most important accomplishments in the history of the American polity—the abolition of slavery, the enacting of fair labor laws, and the civil rights legislation of the 1960s—came about largely because religious people worked tirelessly to advocate and realize their vision of a more just society, a vision inspired by their beliefs (2000, 4). The Reverend Martin Luther King Jr. made no apologies for his use of Bible-based rhetoric to earn the right for African Americans to eat at lunch counters, use restrooms, sit in the front of the bus, attend any public school, and vote. According to Carter, "King and other religious leaders showed no reluctance to claim for their positions an 'exclusive alignment with the Almighty.'" Likewise, Carter notes, much of the antiwar effort during the Vietnam conflict was inspired and led by members of the clergy, who "freely invoked God's name" (1993, 48–49). In its day, each of these efforts was opposed, even by other religious voices, but the majority prevailed, in part because of the ability of religious discourse "to fire the human imagination, and often the conscience, even of nonbelievers" (232).

No doubt my readers agree that the abolition of slavery, fair labor laws, the extension of civil rights, and the end of the Vietnam conflict are praiseworthy milestones in the nation's history, so it is worth pointing out that these were movements of which the political left would approve. And it is also worth noting, as Carter has shown, that the use of religious rhetoric in behalf of those movements was not criticized to the same extent that religious rhetoric is criticized today, when most of it comes from the political right. The fact that religious rhetoric is now more identified with the right should not be a reason to condemn the invocation of religious beliefs in political causes. If one disagrees with a platform, conservative or otherwise, one should condemn the platform, not attempt to stop its supporters from using religious reasons to support it. Whatever cause the religious raise their voices to support, they are "only doing what communities of faith around the world have always done: advocating and working for the world they believe God prefers" (Carter 2000, 69). Without their voices insisting that laws and policies be informed by what the people believe is ethical, moral, and right, democracy would be the poorer. Again in Carter's words,

> A democracy that lacks the moral force of religious understanding is likely to be a democracy without purpose, in which politicians promise to allow citizens simply to satisfy their own wants, whether for money, power, or sex, with little regard for the needs of others; in which the measure of success in war is how small a sacrifice the nation's citizens are called upon to make, as the enemy's dead, including civilians, pile up unmourned, at least by Americans—they are, after all, merely the enemy; in which the worst off are allowed to languish and often die in their segregated urban prisons, while the elite live in safe high-rises and safer suburbs. (2000, 31)

None of the foregoing is intended to mean, of course, that only religious persons can or should seek to influence the course of politics in ways that reflect their moral convictions. I acknowledge that secularists also have a sense of right and wrong and their own codes of morality and ethics; therefore, they too should speak up. But if unbelievers can freely do so, believers can too.

The fourth and final reason we should allow religious expression in the classroom is that it seems to be increasing in the public square, not only in volume but in diversity. That suggests a rhetorical situation is developing that we need to help students address, if we see part of our aim as preparing them for citizenship in a diverse society. Political discourse in this nation since the days of George Washington has always included what Alexis de Tocqueville called our "civil religion." Civil religion has been defined by Frederick Gedicks as "faintly Protestant platitudes which reaffirm the religious base of American culture despite being largely void of theological significance" (1991, 113). This civil religion is the reason that "In God we trust" is printed on our money and the reason our presidents intone "May God bless America" at the end of speeches. The widespread acceptance of civil religion fifty years ago is probably why "one nation under God" seemed an innocuous addition to the Pledge of Allegiance. Each of these expressions has come under fire in recent times from those who believe such phrases promote government's establishment of religion, but I doubt they will disappear. If anything, I believe we are likely to see more evidence of what Lee Albert calls "God talk"—"public expressions of piety" and "bland assertions of faith in a generic deity that most believers (and some non-believers) can embrace" (2000, F1). Many observers have pointed to the 2000 presidential election as an interesting example of this, particularly vice-presidential candidate Joseph Lieberman's frequent references to his faith, perhaps as a way of indicating that the political right had no exclusive claim on spirituality.

But even beyond the "God talk," I think we are likely to see more serious, specific, and denominationally related religious discourse in politics. Michael Novak not only foresees but celebrates this possibility.

> We should be glad that the old pluralism of give-no-offense, lowest-common-denominator mumble is giving way to a new and more mature pluralism: frank public discussion of the diverse convictions that move us. In the next century, religion is likely no longer to be "believed in without discussion" [de Tocqueville's phrase]. Arguments in public will be many and hot. We are becoming confident enough of each other's bona fides to say who we are, each of us; to listen respectfully to those who differ; and to argue with one another civilly. (1998, 37)

If Novak is right, then I believe it is incumbent on us as teachers to explore how religious and political discourses intersect. The changing landscape of American politics and the diversity of our society will require rhetorical sensitivity and dexterity if we are to engage religiously motivated arguments while promoting understanding and sufficient national unity to prevent prejudice, divisiveness, rebellion, or opting out of the political process altogether. We and our students need to know more about the origins, nature, and purposes of religious political discourse; how to create such discourse if it seems necessary or desirable to do so; and how to receive and evaluate it.

## Teaching Students to Give and Take Religious Arguments Responsibly

In a previous essay about politics in the writing classroom, I have stated that I don't believe teachers should try to change students' politics. I won't here depart from that stance (Hansen 2002). But I do claim that politics—including the religious convictions that might inform a person's politics—can legitimately be the focus of a composition course. In such a course, the teacher should make every reasonable effort to work with students of any political and religious or nonreligious persuasion to help them develop their rhetorical powers, even when the teacher personally dislikes some or all of the beliefs those students espouse. What I am suggesting here is that, rather than set religion aside as irrelevant or inadmissible in the teaching of rhetorical arts, we confront the fact that religion matters to many students. It follows that we need to help students find the language that will allow them to bring religious values into public discourse without crippling the dialogue that a democracy depends upon.

To that end, I sketch below some pedagogical activities for a course centered on politics and religion for sophomores or advanced first-year students. This outline is suggestive, not exhaustive. The final form of any course based on this pedagogy would be determined in the teaching, and it would change each time it was taught because it would evolve out of the exchanges between student and teacher, student and student. The premise for the course would be that the United States is not a melting pot in which citizens are homogenized, but a salad or a stew in which the components retain their identity. A familiar way of describing the nation is as a set of contact zones, defined by Mary Louise Pratt as "social spaces where cultures meet, clash, and grapple with each other, often in highly asymmetrical relations of power" (1991, 34). Contact zones form wherever diverse ethnic, racial, and socioeconomic groups meet, but also where different religions meet. Because religion intersects all ethnicities and social strata, it simply makes contact zones more complex. Writing classes at public institutions and some private ones are likely to be, in many ways, a microcosm of national contact zones, so this concept can be fairly well exemplified within the classroom walls. By introducing volatile political topics into a class of students whose cultural, ethnic, class, and religious identities differ, the clashing and grappling Pratt identifies would no doubt appear, as they do in the group interview Nowacek describes in this volume[3] (see Chapter 13).

In fact, Pratt describes her roller-coaster experience when she first taught the Cultures, Ideas, Values course at Stanford, after the traditional Western Civilization course was changed to include more non-Western and minority texts and experiences:

> This course attracted a very diverse student body. . . . The classroom functioned not like a homogeneous community or a horizontal alliance, but like a contact zone. Every single text we read stood in specific historical relationships to students in the class, but the range and variety of . . . relationships in play were enormous. Everybody had a stake in nearly everything we read, but the range and kind of stakes varied widely. . . .
>
> All the students in the class had the experience of . . . hearing their culture discussed and objectified in ways that horrified them. . . . All the students experienced face-to-face the ignorance and incomprehension, and occasionally the hostility, of others. . . . Along with rage, incomprehension, and pain, there were exhilarating moments of wonder and revelation, mutual understanding, and new wisdom—the joys of the contact zone. (39)

Pratt's course sounds like what sometimes happens in the public square when people set forth their religious or their secular reasons for their political positions—except for the part about "exhilarating moments of wonder and revelation, mutual understanding, and new wisdom." I wonder how often those moments of wonder and revelation, mutual understanding, and new wisdom occur. Are there more frequently moments of tuning out, indifference, anger, and polarization? In the course I propose, the goal would be to get past the ignorance, the incomprehension, the objectification, the hostility, and the pain to the mutual understanding and the wisdom. The reading and the talking in this course would be calculated to bring about the clashing of the contact zones; the further discussion and the writing would be aimed at the under-standing and the wisdom.

To that end, I would employ some of what Pratt calls the pedagogical arts of the contact zone to encourage students to become skilled in what she calls the literate arts of the contact zone. The first pedagogical art is exercises in sto-rytelling. Students would produce an autoethnography, wherein writers "describe themselves in ways that engage with representations others have made of them" (Pratt 1991, 35). So, for example, Catholic or LDS or Jewish or Muslim students might look in encyclopedias or history and anthropology texts to see how they have been represented to readers who are not of their faith, and they would then describe themselves "in response to or in dialogue with those texts" (35). I would have students share their autoethnographies orally, in order to enact the "redemption of the oral," another pedagogical art of the contact zone (40). And I would have them comment orally on each other's stories in as detached and objective a fashion as possible, accepting each other's represen-tations for what they are, not praising or blaming. In this way, students would examine their own identities from new angles and get to know every other member of the class more than superficially. The goal would be that this famil-iarity should breed not contempt but understanding and respect.

A second pedagogical art consists of exercises in "identifying with the ideas, interests, histories, and attitudes of others" (Pratt 1991, 40). In these exer-cises students would role-play and impersonate. They might role-play one of their classmates, not in parodic fashion, but seriously, attempting to use the ideas and words of that person. They might impersonate a historical figure or a type. For example, I might ask my LDS students to identify with the ideas, interests, and attitudes of the non-LDS minority in Utah by impersonating a member of that group and writing a letter to the editor about some facet of LDS culture or religion that would be strange or unsettling to the minority member. As another example, students might research the way Jews, Catholics, Mus-lims, or Buddhists have been treated as they have immigrated into this country and then write a narrative of a day in the life of a fictional person in a minority group. In my experience, taking seriously the requirement to step into the shoes of a person you don't understand creates empathy for that person.

Another pedagogical art Pratt calls "experiments in transculturation and collaborative work and in the arts of critique, parody, and comparison" (40). Transculturation is defined as "processes whereby members of subordinated or marginal groups select and invent from materials transmitted by a dominant or metropolitan culture" (36). In such an exercise, students might identify an aspect of their own beliefs that they consider to be marginalized by some strand of dominant culture and then criticize that domination either straight-forwardly or in a parody, using the language of the dominant culture. The critique might take the form of a dialogue between the dominant and the subordinate viewpoints, or it might set them side by side. Asking two students whose backgrounds are rather different to collaborate on such exercises might deepen their understanding for each other while both find a mutually satisfying way to contend against the dominator. Another form of collaboration might be for a student who understands the dominant culture to mediate it to the one who feels marginalized. For example, a student who is new to the ethos of rugged individualism in the West might need to have an insider mediate an understanding of why gun ownership is considered almost a sacred right by so many rural Westerners. Another form of mediation might be translating a dominant belief from the peculiar language of an in-group to the vernacular, so that an outsider student would understand it.

Still another pedagogical art Pratt mentions is "ways to move *into and out of* rhetorics of authenticity" (40, her emphasis). Since Pratt offers no further explanation, let me describe how I interpret "authenticity." It obviously implies that some rhetoric is inauthentic, and perhaps one kind of inauthentic rhetoric is the "God talk" that Lee Albert speaks of in political campaigns, which often "constitutes pandering, hawking of faith and marketing of God in a manner that insults, demeans and trivializes both religion and political discourse." In addition, Albert deplores "religious jingoism, the portrayal of America as the special object of God's blessing and the special recipient of God's mission" (2000, F1). There seem to be plenty of instances of pandering and jingoism during political campaigns, a fruitful time to ask students to identify authentic and inauthentic uses of religion in speeches. This would be a tricky assignment because two students might bring in the same example, one declaring it pandering and the other declaring it sincere. But the very difference in reception could lead to valuable discussions of the rhetorical concepts of ethos, situation, and audience. The one who identifies it as pandering might be asked to indicate under what circumstances, if any, such discourse might be authentic. The one who identifies it as sincere could likewise identify the circumstances and audience for which the discourse would be inauthentic.

All of these pedagogical exercises are potentially explosive. It would take a skilled teacher to keep the students on track, and it would take commitment from the students to continue to engage in the dialogue even when they have been misunderstood or hurt. The final outcome of some dialogues might be that students agree to disagree. Students would find themselves sometimes in the majority, sometimes in the minority. But at least they would feel they had been heard. I hope that the outcome of such a course would be the forging of what Pratt calls "ground rules for communication across lines of difference and

hierarchy that go beyond politeness but maintain mutual respect" (1991, 40).
Such rules are not now clearly defined. As Albert puts it, the Constitution does
not interdict or qualify religious expression in the public square, but it also
gives no principles or rules to follow in such expression. Where principles are
lacking, we have to rely "on the dictates of prudence and civility" (2000, F1). I
think that prudence will come from the classroom experiences I am proposing
here, and I believe that greater civility of tongue and pen will be the natural outgrowth of the talking and writing required. My fondest hope is that both prudence and civility will migrate from the classroom to the public square. In this
way, we might reclaim for the composition classroom the rhetorical tradition's
serious purpose of preparing the young to participate effectively in civic life.
What is more, we might contribute to renewing the vitality of the dialogic
processes that sustain democracy.

# Notes

1. See Carter's *God's Name in Vain* (2000), especially Chapter 5, "The Single-
Sided Wall," for an enlightening discussion of the history of separation of church
and state in the United States. Briefly, the origin of the metaphor of a "wall of separation" is not in Thomas Jefferson's 1802 letter to the Danbury Baptists, but in the
seventeenth-century writings of Roger Williams, who conceived of the wall as pro-
tecting the garden of the church from the menacing wilderness of the secular state,
not the other way around. Williams' idea was that people would tame the wilderness
by using their religious beliefs to shape the political realm. Carter adds, "No serious
historian disputes the proposition that the antiestablishment provision in the First
Amendment was included *solely* to prevent the Congress from either establishing a
national church or interfering with those states that had established churches" (217,
emphasis his). In other words, the separation was not meant to stop people from
expressing their religious views in public and using them as motivations for political action.

2. Philosophical liberalism is the name given to the tradition of thought and practice that undergirds Western forms of political democracy and notions of individual freedom. It is not the same as espousing liberal or left-of-center positions on public policy.

3. Geoffrey Sirc's *English Composition as a Happening* (2002) seems implicitly
to criticize Pratt's description of the college classroom as a potential contact zone by
criticizing at length David Bartholomae's (1996) article "What Is Composition and (If
You Know What That Is) Why Do We Teach It?" in which Bartholomae writes approvingly of the style of Pratt's travel narratives, holding it up as a model for students to
aspire to. By proposing that writing courses aspire to be more like "happenings" on the
"Campus of Interzone University" (2002, 40), Sirc imagines a new space (between
zones?) in which boundaries and genres dissolve. Sirc asserts that Bartholomae would
have students imitate Pratt, urging them "to retrace a became" instead of "tracing a
becoming" (61) so that their writing will have the "literary aesthetic of the Contact
Zone" (52). The goal of such imitation, Sirc says, is "museumification" of student writing. My goal in the pedagogical sketch I offer, following Pratt's suggestions, is not to
have students write like Pratt, nor yet to have them create beautiful objects worthy of a

museum. In fact, I agree with Sirc that there is a great "need to address deep, basic humanity in this modern, over-sophisticated age" (31). Thus, I believe the possible assignments I propose (and they are by no means prescriptions), would answer Sirc's call for writing that is "new, interesting, and transformative," because they are assignments that "experiment with new materials and forms, blur disciplines and boundaries, and subsume the whole with a life-affirming humor." I believe that the writing I would want students to do in the kind of course I propose "might," to use Sirc's words, "in some small way, change the world" (31).

# Works Cited

Albert, Lee. 2000. "God in the Public Square." *Buffalo News*, 15 October: F1.

Bartholomae, David. 1996. "What Is Composition (and If You Know What That Is) Why Do We Teach It?" In *Composition in the Twenty-first Century: Crisis and Change*, edited by Lynn Z. Bloom, Donald A. Daiker, and Edward M. White, 11–28. Carbondale: Southern Illinois University Press.

Bellah, Robert N., Richard Madsen, William M. Sullivan, Ann Swidler, and Steven M. Tipton. 1991. *The Good Society*. New York: Knopf.

Carter, Stephen. 1993. *The Culture of Disbelief: How American Law and Politics Trivialize Religious Devotion*. New York: Basic Books.

———. 2000. *God's Name in Vain: The Wrongs and Rights of Religion in Politics*. New York: Basic Books.

Connors, Robert. 1997. *Composition-Rhetoric: Backgrounds, Theory, and Pedagogy*. Pittsburgh: University of Pittsburgh Press.

Eastland, Terry, ed. 1993. *Religious Liberty in the Supreme Court: The Cases That Define the Debate over Church and State*. Lanham, MD: Ethics and Public Policy Center.

Elshtain, Jean. 2001. "Faith of Our Fathers and Mothers: Religious Belief and American Democracy." In *Religion in American Public Life: Living with Our Deepest Differences*, edited by Azizah Y. al-Hibri, Jean B. Elshtain, and Charles C. Haynes, 39–61. New York: Norton.

Fish, Stanley. 1999. "Academic Freedom: When Sauce for the Goose Isn't Sauce for the Gander." *Chronicle of Higher Education* 26 (November): B4–B6.

Fraughton, Paul. 1998. "GOP Dominance Troubles Church." *Salt Lake Tribune*, 3 May: A1, A20.

Gedicks, Frederick. 1991. "The Religious, the Secular, and the Antithetical." *Capital University Law Review* 20: 113–45.

Hansen, Kristine. 2002. "Second Thoughts on 'Diversity, Ideology, and Teaching Writing.'" In *Against the Grain: A Volume in Honor of Maxine Hairston*, edited by David Jolliffe, Michael Keene, Mary Trachsel, and Ralph Voss, 227–47. Cresskill, NJ: Hampton.

Harrie, Dan. 2002. "Backlash Vote May Propel Matheson." *Salt Lake Tribune*, 23 October: A1.

Kant, Immanuel. 1986. "What Is Enlightenment?" In *Philosophical Writings Immanuel Kant*, edited by Ernst Behler, 263–69. New York: Continuum.

Novak, Michael. 1998. "Faith in Search of Votes." *The New York Times Magazine*, 31 March: 37.

Pratt, Mary Louise. 1991. "Arts of the Contact Zone." In *Profession 91*, 33–40. New York: MLA.

Sirc, Geoffrey. 2002. *English Composition as a Happening*. Logan: Utah State University Press.

# 4

# True Believers, Real Scholars, and Real True Believing Scholars

## *Discourses of Inquiry and Affirmation in the Composition Classroom*

Douglas Downs

"Congratulations! You've just written the most indoctrinated, close-minded, uncritical, simplistically reasoned paper I've ever read!" Thus began the harshest response I've ever written on a student's paper, one that made me sound like a jerk. I was frustrated, of course, in this case with a student engaging in dogma rather than inquiry. One of the greatest challenges in negotiating religious faith in writing classes is helping students whose faith precludes inquiry learn to be inquiringly faithful. Often in giving that help, though, teachers who receive dogmatic arguments struggle with impatience, disagreement, and even dejection with those arguments. Recognizing the source of these reactions is one key to handling them.

The student in this case, whom I'll call Keith, had taken for his researched argument the issue of gay adoption, mostly because debate over a state law prohibiting it was in the Utah news. The state's gay lobby was fighting the prohibition, a battle that in this most conservative, Republican, Mormon (LDS), Western state might optimistically be described as "uphill." The issue was fit for academic inquiry at the University of Utah, where I taught, but Keith had not approached the assignment in this spirit. My response framed the problem thus: "Remember all that high-minded stuff about academic argument at the beginning of the semester? About *honest* inquiry? About trying to understand opposing positions in order to reach *agreement*? In a debate, you'd look good. In this game, this paper makes you look silly because you haven't played by the rules."

Keith stuck to orthodox LDS doctrine, assumptions, and language, contradicted by much of his research (which he thus ignored), about "the gay lifestyle" and the certainty that gay parents turn their children into gays. He took at face value an anti-gay group's claim that gay men average fifty partners per year and then assumed that claim applied to gay fathers (he seemed unaware that women can be gay, too). He cited biblical injunctions against "men lying with men," explained that people choose to be gay because they don't fit in socially, and blithely warranted the perfect nuclear family of family-values talk. He insisted that gay parents would not let their children choose to be straight and predicted mass pedophilia by gay parents. He also predicted increased suicide among the inevitably gay children of gay parents because of teasing they would receive at school—but gave no indication he thought such teasing would be wrong. He spotted bias in studies undermining his position but found none in those supporting it, ensuring that his received knowledge about gay adoption would not be challenged.

Most of my students would confirm I don't yell at them on paper, but Keith got a Howler:

> You haven't deeply examined the situation. You've gone and found the evidence . . . that would support your long-held preconceptions. You didn't talk to any gay people; never met any gay parents; never got critical of straight parents; never sought to see the good things in gay parenting and the problems with the "nuclear" family; never questioned all the assumptions you have about homosexuality (how do you picture gays living, for instance?); never questioned why it's okay to make fun of gay kids in school. They're freaks, right? But I thought "the children" were important to you. Not if they're gay? That's very consistent of you, Keith.

My revision suggestions to Keith demonstrate my thinking at the time that it was simply his arguments and logic that pushed my buttons so uncharacteristically: "You've got to introduce some opposing views *from sources sympathetic to those views*, discuss them, and *then* explain why you choose not to accept them. No academic argument is complete without these, and the stronger your preconceived notions on your topic, the more you need to do it."

Yet other students' poor arguments and weak logic did not provoke such an intolerant response from me. In later semesters, I have come to recognize a different source for my frustration, one which instructors must account for in negotiating faith in the composition classroom. I believe that my frustration was actually rooted in the functional conflict of discourses I'll call Inquiry and Affirmation, which are constituted in part by mutually exclusive and negating epistemologies. For some students such as Keith, the never-easy transition to college and academic inquiry valued there is complicated by an existing discourse of affirmation which finds inquiry threatening. For these students, an entire way of knowing and being is on the line. We could call it the conflict between "real scholar" and "true believer."

This chapter makes my case somewhat speculatively. Using the discourse and cultural theory of James Gee, I theorize these adversarial discourses, Inquiry and Affirmation. Then, drawing on my experience with Keith and on composition literature that deals with students of religious faith in the writing classroom, I analyze the most intense points of conflict between the two discourses. Finally, I speculate on ways this discursive conflict can help a teacher achieve pedagogical goals and adopt classroom stances. I write from a perspective consciously favoring Inquiry, believing that discourses have contextual rather than essential value. In a context where inquiry is the *raison d'etre* of higher education, it seems reasonable to value discourses of inquiry and question those that undermine it. There is worth in exploring what other discourses can add to inquiry, or how they can support it, but in an academic setting if inquiry and another discourse prove incompatible, inquiry earns a certain priority in lying at the heart of the academic mission. Hence I privilege it in this discussion.

## Discourses, Epistemologies, Values

According to James Gee, Discourses are "ways with words, feelings, values, beliefs, emotions, people, action, things, tools, and places that allow us to display and recognize characteristic *whos* doing characteristic *whats*" (1999, 19). (The capital *D* differentiates them from "discourse" as a particular instance of language use.) In other words, a Discourse is "a sort of 'identity kit' which comes complete with the appropriate costume and instructions on how to think, act, talk, and write, so as to take on a particular social role that others will recognize." Discourses are the "saying-doing-being-valuing-believing combinations" that tell people how to *be* in given situations (1989, 7). Gee says that when we recognize a performance of a Discourse, we are identifying an individual as a "real" *X* (e.g., doctor, bachelor, student) and accepting him "in" that Discourse (1999, 18).

There is in Gee's concept of Discourses something of Foucault's notion of "discursive formations"—"regulations and structures grounded in power relations that covertly shape our perspectives and insidiously mold our constructions" (Kincheloe 1993, 111). But where Foucault describes rigid structures, Gee's Discourses are fuzzy and malleable by the subjects inhabiting them. In the example this paper focuses on, LDS doctrine would constitute a discursive formation and Keith's performance of it would constitute a Discourse. Discourses, as performed activity-identities, need not be large scale, are always defined against other Discourses, and are limitless and uncountable. Individuals participate in any number of them, and each is inflected by all the others.

Individuals can also perform multiple Discourses simultaneously and have them all recognized (Gee 1999, 21–22). Discourses are, of course, still more or less compatible: The Discourses of "learned scholar" and "medical doctor" are distinct but similar enough to be easily enacted simultaneously. "Medical doctor" and "windsurfer" are a greater distance apart but not mutually exclusive. "Computer geek" and "Luddite" are sufficiently opposed in values and purpose that we might assume anyone enacting them simultaneously would need psychological attention. "Inquiry" and "affirmation" are not so incompatible, but as we will see their underlying values are in strong conflict and enacting them simultaneously is neither easy nor intuitive.

Given these "fuzzy" characteristics, Gee's notion of Discourses is also divergent, in important ways for my project, from the concept of "discourse community" that many writing instructors teach. By genre analyst John Swales' definition, discourse communities have common public goals, methods of member intercommunication, and specific genres and lexis (1990, 24–26). Such rules, helpful for defining small groups, preclude analysis of large heterogenous groups that share only broadly similar goals. Swales' categories cannot be satisfied by claiming a broadly academic "discourse community," because it would not share genres and lexis. Yet there is undeniably an object and activity of "scholarly inquiry" shared by those associated with higher education. Thus, where my project would fail if it relied on analyzing a specific discourse community, it is enabled by identifying a Discourse of inquiry, a way of believing-valuing-being, shared by a broad and amorphous group of participants.[1]

My proposition is that Keith and I were enacting two Discourses, and that my hostile reaction to his work stemmed from his embrace of an affirming Discourse that negated the inquiring Discourse I was trying to help students perform. Discourses of inquiry embody ways of behaving, habits of mind, values and beliefs, epistemologies, and dispositions that favor questioning, pursuit of new knowledge and understanding, desire to analyze and synthesize, curiosity, and "negative capability" (Keats' term for deliberate tolerance of long-term cognitive dissonance stemming from not having one's mind made up). In Gee's terms, one embodying a Discourse of inquiry might be recognized as a "real scholar." Many writing programs and teachers of first-year writing courses envision helping students become "real scholars," preparing them for active intellectual participation in college, a variety of writing tasks, and a lifetime of critical inquiry as citizens. "Real scholars" do, of course, affirm beliefs (not least the belief that inquiry is preferable to dogma), but they affirm through inquiry rather than through initial affirmation of received knowledge followed by total deflection of inquiry.

The latter description characterizes Keith's Discourse of affirmation. Such Discourses embody behaviors, epistemologies, values, beliefs, dispositions, and habits of mind by which one affirms given knowledge and overtly resists critical inquiry into it. Because this distinction is largely epistemological,

Affirmation is not necessarily dependent on particular beliefs: how one *arrives* at a belief is as important to embodying the Discourse as what one chooses to believe. Therefore, injunctions against doubt or insistence on the rightness of received wisdom are hardly limited to religious expression. For instance, some "patriot" Discourses, particularly jingoistic ones, are affirming: for those who interpret patriotism as unquestioning loyalty, the act of questioning undermines the values of the Discourse itself in a logically paralyzing contradiction. Nor can writing teachers expect that all students who express religious faith embody Discourses of affirmation. Many if not most religious faiths disavow the universalism, absolutism, and fundamentalism that Discourses of affirmation seem to demand, centering instead on *mystery* of one kind or another, an "unknowable" quality that undermines Affirmation.[2] While Discourses of affirmation cannot be neatly equated with religious expression, though, writing teachers can also expect to regularly work with students whose object of affirmation, as in Keith's case, is a particular religious doctrine and culture.

There are a number of alternative explanations for the interaction between Inquiry and Affirmation that I have considered but not accepted. It might be suggested that Keith was merely poorly performing Inquiry. But both Gee's theory and Keith's performance suggest that Affirmation is autarkic, its own entity, not a pale or immature version of Inquiry. An immature performance of a Discourse of inquiry is what Gee calls "mushfake." Keith's work was not mushfaked Inquiry; the strategy of his argument was to reject out-of-hand knowledge that clashed with received doctrinal wisdom. He was not poorly performing Inquiry, as I thought at the time, but positively performing Affirmation. It might also be argued, as James Kincheloe does in analyzing problems fundamentalist students face in college, that affirmation is a lower level of cognitive development than inquiry (1993, 51, 159). But as Discourses with distinct behaviors, objectives, epistemologies, dispositions, and habits of mind, Affirmation and Inquiry are not a hierarchy of cognitive virtuosity such as William Perry's dualism and commitment (1968, 58). One does not "grow out of" Affirmation and into Inquiry as if growing "up" from dualism into relativism. Nor are "Affirmation and Inquiry" versions of Peter Elbow's (1982) doubting and believing game. Elbow shows how we can alter our reading stance in doubt of or belief in a writer—but always in a framework of inquiry. Conditional belief (negative capability) in pursuit of inquiry does not equal unconditional and uncritical embrace of received knowledge.

## Points of Conflict Between Inquiry and Affirmation

Discourses, then, tell us "what it means to be a good X." Being a good "true believer" requires values, beliefs, habits of mind, assumptions, and dispositions that oppose those required of a good participant in Inquiry—a "real scholar." I complete my case for that assertion through analysis of the conflict of Discourses revealed in Keith's work and my response.

## Epistemology

That these Discourses work from opposing sources of knowledge is clear in their labels: Inquiry suggests questioning as a valued source of knowledge, while Affirmation suggests a pre-existent source of knowledge to be valued. What "true believers" value as closed, fixed, permanent, and absolute, "real scholars" value as a subject to be opened. What "real scholars" value as knowledge creating, "true believers" find threatening to existing knowledge. Affirmation's final answer is Inquiry's opening question. Some enacting Discourses of inquiry might accept some received knowledge; what distinguishes such "real scholars" from "true believers" is that the received knowledge is not exempt from critique, and a "real scholar" works to fit received knowledge and inquired knowledge into a coherent framework. A Discourse of affirmation, on the other hand, avoids questioning received knowledge (or defers questioning to superiors) and subordinates new knowledge to received knowledge. Again, the loose connection between religion and "true believer" Discourses means people of the same faith can easily enact different Discourses. Keith demonstrated a "true believer" Discourse while LDS "real scholars" embody Discourses of inquiry.

In his writing course Keith found himself stretched between Inquiry and Affirmation: the context demanded Inquiry that his Discourse of affirmation precluded. In LDS theology, wisdom comes from three sources: the Church's Prophet, scripture, and felt spiritual experiences. The first two are infallible, though God may reveal, directly to the Prophet, new knowledge that supercedes old. This infallibility favors acceptance and discourages questioning. The third source is a spiritual urging toward truth that saints experience as a confirmatory feeling. Miriam Horne, a compositionist who is Mormon, explains that "specific feelings and experiences . . . were identified by my religious training as 'spiritual.' These 'spiritual' experiences are given to somehow testify of God, or some aspect of God. Therefore, any occurrence of these particular feelings that had been defined as spiritual was a manifestation of the truth of God" (2004). Horne's account of this doctrine of spiritual urging demonstrates a certain passivity of knowledge seeking: even experience or felt sense comes from God. No space is left for religious knowledge gained through active inquiry rather than active acceptance of revelation.

Keith affirmed scriptural truths he had received and wrote with felt conviction of the godliness of his views. Amy Goodburn describes similar students' beliefs as "stable, unitary, universal, and revealed by God" (1998, 344), the essence of Affirmation. Such Discourses are incongruent with two widely used epistemological theories of inquiry, positivism and social constructionism. Positivism sees spiritual-received knowledge as nonrational (Stark, Iannaccone, and Finke 1996, 1) in its dependence on the supernatural, mysticism, and historically and materially transcendent sacred texts (Brummett 2000, 128–29). In Hildy Miller's words, "spiritual belief is seen not simply as another way of knowing, but instead as a way of not-knowing" (2000, 70). Concomitantly, Discourses of affirmation usually conflict with social constructionist inquiry. Horne again:

> I grew up with an absolutist position on life. Right and wrong were supposed to be black and white, and the nature of God was clearly defined and true. . . . Not until life began to happen to me as an adult did I begin to understand the concepts of social constructionism which are so antithetical to the absolutist community to which I belong. (2004)

Social construction, the notion that communities of humans create their own truths and naturalize them as received truths, undermines the received knowledge that grounds Discourses of affirmation such as Keith's. For these reasons, "real scholars" are unlikely to find truth in the same places and ways as "true believers" are. In a college context that privileges inquiry, students' Affirmation ways of knowing will conflict with the critical thinking asked of them in writing courses.

## Responding to Order, Authority, and Power

While members of one set of "true believer" Discourses, fundamentalist religions, often revere individualism and personal agency (Bleich 1990, 168), usually they simultaneously worship orderly, absolute hierarchy (Brown and Olson 2000, 164). George Lakoff's foundational "strict father" metaphor seems applicable here:

> [C]hildren must respect and obey their parents; by doing so they build character, that is, self-discipline and self-reliance. Love and nurturance are, of course, a vital part of family life but can never outweigh parental authority, which is itself an expression of love and nurturance—tough love. Self-discipline, self-reliance, and respect for legitimate authority are the crucial things that children must learn. (1996, 33)

Authority and hierarchy are dominating principles of this metaphor, which describes ideals many students such as Keith embrace. In the absence of corporeal authority, self-discipline and self-reliance enable respect of received (often spiritual) knowledge.

"True believers," therefore, predictably find it difficult to accept another presumption of "real scholars": the autonomy and power of the inquirer. We should not underestimate the authority one must take upon oneself in order to question the existing (revealed) order. It should not come as a surprise if some students in Discourses of affirmation refuse our invitations to question God, instead asking what right they have to do so and also challenging the teacher's purpose. In Discourses of inquiry, the right is taken for granted; "real scholars" of religious faith may, in fact, see it as a responsibility. "True believers," though, are likely to find such questioning

disloyal and arrogant. The difference is important: if I had imagined Keith
writing from such a perspective, my response would have been different
than when I imagined him shirking his responsibility as a "real scholar."
Had he pointed out that questioning church doctrine was not his place or
right, I would have recognized a different set of epistemological assumptions than the paper otherwise conveyed.

## The Role of Culture

Stemming from reliance on revealed knowledge and skepticism regarding
social construction, "true believers" limit culture's role in shaping knowledge.
For them culture can reinforce or undermine existing truths, but Truth exists
independent of culture. "Real scholars," on the other hand, even if they accept
some revealed knowledge, will likely be open to recognizing cultural influence
on its interpretation.

In Keith's case, the clearest site of this conflict was his acquiescence to
teasing gay children. Because in a "true believer" Discourse he recognized
such teasing as the inevitable status quo, there was no sense in speaking
against it. (In Utah LDS culture, openly gay church members are routinely
excommunicated and frequently disowned by their families.) From an Inquiry
perspective, I was outraged that a supposedly morals-based argument would
be used to support an immoral and obviously culturally originated practice. I
take this conflict of opinion as evidence that a "true believer" Discourse precludes inquiry when revealed knowledge not only is intolerant of questioning
but stifles the *need* to question.

## Tolerance for Change and Instability

Given their nature of questioning received knowledge, Discourses of inquiry
destabilize the status quo. To embody "real scholar" is to invite and create
change. Discourses affirming revealed knowledge, in contrast, tend to discourage instability and resulting change. In some religious versions of Affirmation, for example, the transcendent, universal, unchanging nature of the
faith is not only believed but celebrated. LDS doctrine allows for change
through divine revelation to its Prophet, subsuming change to revelation, so
the principle of received knowledge itself is never threatened.

This difference in how change is valued and enabled creates another conflict between "real scholars" and "true believers." "Real scholars," particularly teachers of writing, often seek to increase students' recognition of complexity and help students reposition themselves in relation to their
surroundings. Yet "true believers" have a powerful disincentive for such
change, as it is likely to be interpreted as undermining stability, a key value
of the Discourse they embody. Particularly among "true believer" students
whose Discourses are religious, including Keith, there is a defensive certainty

that college professors will attack and attempt to change students' values. Such students come to college with their guard already raised against change (cf. Perkins 2001).

## Encountering Challenge and Doubt

Challenge and doubt are antithetical to the Discourse of affirmation, threats to be avoided when possible and conquered when necessary. Religious Discourses of affirmation may even encourage their disciples to believe "beyond a shadow of a doubt." While "true believers" have no trouble challenging opponents, sources of received knowledge are placed beyond challenge. Priscilla Perkins describes a class of "Bible-reading Christians" as happy to argue with their instructor, but "even the appearance of 'talking back' to the text might have jeopardized those identities" as believers (2001, 594). This aspect of Affirmation is too certain, too dogmatic, too sure of itself for Inquiry. "True believer" Discourses appear to quell wonder, curiosity, suspicion, and other counterparts, at least around subjects of inquiry that "real scholar" Discourses find interesting.[3] James Moffet argues against pedagogies that reinforce monolithic culture and heritage precisely because students learn from pluralism and difference that raise their awareness of their values as socially constructed (1990, 116). By raising such awareness, many writing teachers hope to bring students into a Discourse of inquiry from whatever home Discourses they might inhabit. Keith did demonstrate his ability for doubting and challenging ideas he already doubted and challenged, but his "true believer" Discourse actively disallowed him from inquiry into his own values.

## Interpreting Complexity and Multiplicity

Perhaps the most frequent difficulty "real scholars" have with the thinking of "true believers" is absolutism. "True believers" frequently have One Right Answer, often based on purportedly literal reading. Goodburn's explanation of her student Luke's beliefs captures this well: For students like Luke and Keith, "there are clear cut positions that one can take on every issue and thus a research paper is an exercise in persuasion. . . . To present multiple perspectives is to acknowledge and legitimize their validity, a move [Luke] was unwilling to make based on his beliefs about the nature and authority of knowledge" (1998, 345). Perkins describes students so literalist that as football fans they were flummoxed by an Old Testament injunction against touching pigskin (2001, 593). As Jeannette Lindholm and Lizabeth Rand both demonstrate, such students are engaging conventions lived by adults in their home cultures, conventions as natural to them as breathing. As with doubt, Discourses of affirmation profess to banish subjective and multiple interpretations and thus complexity.

Discourses of inquiry typically favor the opposite, frequently to a fault. The writers I cite in the last paragraph all testify that many "real scholars" react less than patiently to claims for the One True Literal Answer, some even making my response to Keith look compassionate. Inquiry has concluded that literal reading is physically impossible (see Anderson 1977 or Tierney and Pearson 1983), so some "real scholars" see "true believer" claims to literalism as naive at best and devious at worst, sometimes treating simplicity and obviousness with derision or suspicion, labeling them parochial, narrow-minded, simpleminded, obstinate, immature, or stupid (Perkins 2001, 608). In Lindholm's telling, some students have therefore even come to think of themselves as "'thickheaded Christian[s]'" (2000, 55). Many "real scholars" try to broaden students' horizons or "shake" them out of "complacency"—and in so doing demand that students park their religious Discourses of affirmation at the edge of campus. This category of complexity is thus a clear example of how Discourses of both inquiry and affirmation include potentially useful qualities in the abstract, with context determining how each will value a given quality. All these reactions help explain the difficulty "real scholars" have with relating to "true believer" Discourses whose participants seek college degrees (a talisman of Inquiry) yet rule out the interpretation, multiplicity of perspectives, and complexity that mark that Inquiry.

## Composition Instructor Stances for Productive Use of Discursive Conflict

I take one of the goals of college writing instruction to be making students inquirers with us. Given the conflicts between Discourses of inquiry and affirmation, students embodying the latter will predictably have special difficulties understanding, desiring to embody, and justifying embodying the former. This means we need to teach such students how to be both "real scholars" and "true believers" in response to the demands of context, inflecting each with the other as Gee argues individuals do when embodying multiple Discourses. Yet the evidence suggests that composition instructors are at least as likely to ignore or belittle students, ban religious faith from the classroom, try to teach rationality, or just suffer through religious papers, grading as fairly as possible but never addressing the underlying problem.

In contrast to such reactions, Kurt Spellmeyer (1993) speaks of the importance of letting students write from and to their lifeworlds so as to build learning on private knowledge. Thomas Newkirk similarly argues for pedagogy centered on students' non-school lives and the ensuing possibility of "whole-hearted" discourse (1997, 103). For Spellmeyer (2000, 193) and Newkirk (1997, 202), college must guard against serving students slivers of "education" unconnected to their lifeworlds. Given those lifeworlds, another motivation for engaging "true believers" might be the desire to help them say what they have to say. As Virgina Chappell eloquently asserts, "my work, it seems to me, is to enliven in students the rhetorical and linguistic ability with which they can articulate their commitments and write about the somethings for which they stand" (2000, 41). This is all to say that education should engage students' lives rather than ignoring them. Such a principle suggests a heartfelt desire for our students' best interests. In her article "Narratives of Literacy: Connecting Composition to Culture," Beth Daniell reminds us that Paolo Freire was as concerned with saving his students' souls as with their physical welfare (1999, 402). Daniell's identification of such love echoes Newkirk's request that we "demonstrate an alternative—extend a repertoire" but not "try to eradicate a 'lower' form of consciousness" (1997, 102). That is, our motivation for engaging our "true believer" students could be the desire to show them what we understand of their situation in an attempt to expand their options. In Karen Carlton and Chalon Emmons' terms, "We hope to bring passionate and loving attention to every classroom experience. . . . We would strive to cultivate 'God's perspective' in ourselves and our students—that is, a perspective that sees infinite value in each person, each moment" (2000, 36–37). In short, we would seek to affirm our students if not Affirmation itself. This desire can motivate us to adopt the stances I describe in closing this chapter—stances that can help us help students reconcile the irreconcilable.

## *Guide*

A writing teacher who calls attention to the discursive conflict between Inquiry and Affirmation will both help students better understand discourse and writing and frame the challenges that "true believers" face in learning to embody Inquiry. Guiding in this sense means to define the problem rhetorically and frame it in discourse theory. Instead of teaching Keith from the stance of "we do academic argument here, which means inquiry, which means critical questioning," as a guide I would have taught that "we come to knowledge in different ways, and it's possible that our customs for reaching knowledge in college are different than those you're comfortable with. Let's talk about that." What I did not know to say to Keith was "we're working in two different Discourses, and it's creating problems." Lessons that affirm rather than exclude students of religious Discourses of affirmation may require a Rogerian telling their values back to them in ways they will recognize, and then contrasting those values with those of "real scholars" and showing students where the opposing Discourses can be reconciled. Rather than yell on paper at Keith about his failings as a "real scholar," I would have begun by saying, "So it sounds to me like you're advocating a very narrow definition of family; for many of your audience on a college campus, that's going to contradict some deeply held values, so we should strategize some ways of addressing that problem."

### *Translator*

Such reconciliation will require a bridging of "real scholar" and "true believer" for students. As with any other home Discourse, we would not necessarily wish students to leave Affirmation behind. If our project is teaching Discourses of inquiry, then, our task is to help translate, both in the spatial sense of travel between Discourses and in the linguistic sense of moving between dialects or idiom. One essential task in this translation is identifying common ground between "real scholars" and "true believers"—a strategy of which Perkins is a master. She reminds "true believers" (in my terms) that truth is the object of both Affirmation and Inquiry, and notes that Affirmation is not the only Discourse dependent on the absolute power of a sacred text: "Many writing teachers believe just as intensely in the life-changing power of textuality; our task, then, is to help students to see their Bible reading as inherently interpretive and to look at their academic reading as a positive, potentially faith-affirming extension of their more culturally central reading practices" (2001, 595). While the Discourses are still at odds (over the role of interpretation, for instance), Perkins reminds us that engaging the received knowledge of Affirmation is an effective way to move students toward Inquiry.

A "translator" response from me would have been to explain to Keith more about the audience he faced and what sorts of support for his case they would value. I could have shown him how "real scholars" probably wouldn't accept a "the Bible tells me so" argument on its face but might accept similar arguments framed in cultural terms, or how to reframe his question more usefully for them, or how "real scholars" who are unable to accept a "true believer's" received knowledge of spiritual experience might be more sympathetic to "felt sense" (Perl and Egendorf 1986). So I might have shown him how the preference he expressed for two heterosexual parents could be supported not only by the Biblical creation story but by careful analysis of cultural expectations, which "real scholar" readers might be more sympathetic to.

### *Mentor*

Writing teachers who adopt a mentoring stance create a safe, understanding space for students and serve as a positive role model of Inquiry for students. It is helpful, I think, to have embodied a Discourse of affirmation in order to empathize with students who have little experience embodying anything else. Ideally, we would have Burkean consubstantiality with students, but, as Perkins notes, "our students' and our own constant awareness of all that we do *not* share greatly limits our Burkean identification with each other" (2001, 596). Nonetheless, we can express an attitude of sympathy and willingness to listen—something like Elbow's "believing game" in reading. By failing to adopt this attitude with Keith, I precluded the possibility of mentoring him as a "real scholar." An alternative would have been to speak from sympathy or empathy with his position and values: I could have said, "I share your value of concern for children's welfare. If I were trying to drive that home for readers, I would work on a consistent message by being concerned both with their welfare at home with their parents and at school with their peers, and I would make other arguments about how to stop gay kids or kids with gay parents from being teased." Needless to say, the tone and substance of my actual response obstructed such mentoring.

Role-modeling a Discourse of inquiry is another mentoring role. Recall Gee's description of Discourses: we are showing students not a set of rote skills or a specific, isolated attitude, but an entire way of being. Showing "true believers" the look of "real scholar" demands a conscious, self-reflexive embodiment of Inquiry; we must narrate our "walking the walk" to help students see that, for instance, questioning received truth does not immediately render one a servant of Satan. In Keith's case, this sort of mentoring could have looked like an extended conversation about rationales and values in which I could have said, "Here's what I would be thinking and how I would be working if I were investigating your question. Let's talk about our different approaches and I'll try to explain what I'm doing and why I think it's an effective approach." As Keith did his research, for instance, I might have modeled seeking a range of perspectives on gay adoption, specifically searching for work that would counterpoint my initial hypothesis. While doing so I would have narrated the values of Inquiry and demonstrated genuine openness to changing my mind.

## *Coach*

If the mentor invites students to watch another Discourse at work, the coach pushes students to put that Discourse to work in their writing. We might work, for instance, on the problem of "true believers" imagining their beliefs as universal, a problem Stanley Hauerwas addresses at length in *The Peaceable Kingdom* (1983). He argues that an ethical Christianity is contextualized rather than universal, and that narrative—a characteristic of the religion—is powerfully contextual. Particular stories of faith, therefore, are bound by context and do not become overbearing, universalized accounts that George Marsden labels "Christian imperialism" (1997, 32). A coaching strategy based on this principle would be to ask students uncomfortable with the notion of nonuniversal knowledge (Truth) to tell a story exemplifying the knowledge in question and then to see how the story limits the knowledge to a particular context. I might, for example, have asked Keith to examine the specific context supporting his story of the "normal" nuclear family, pointing out all its contingencies and other contexts it excluded (such as families with grandparents instead of parents as primary caregivers). Through such exercises, Hauerwas' thinking can help students examine Affirmation from a perspective of Inquiry.

Coaching also involves kicking butt on occasion. I've identified some strategies that would have been better approaches to responding to Keith, but it's also fair to say that a strategy as weak as the one I chose would have been to say nothing at all. If I *didn't* care to engage Keith, I could have simply assessed his research (good enough by freshman standards) and "objective" aspects of his writing (a nice ten-page paper with the required number of sources, a clear point, a strong voice, grammatically correct sentences, and good unity and cohesion) and while noting some weakness in his arguments given him a respectable grade on the paper. But that obviously wouldn't be teaching writing. I regret the *way* I called Keith out, but I don't regret calling him out.

## Coda

I failed Keith in part because he failed me. I created a safe space for him by supporting his research question on gay adoption, empathizing with his moral discomfort at gay adoption, and helping him in his research. For me it was an unspoken bargain: I'll give you the tools and space to perform inquiry from within the context of your faith; for your part, your argument, grounded in both affirmation and inquiry, will give neither a black eye. My indignant response when his paper blackened both eyes was precisely wrong: I should have become *more* engaged, understanding, patient. Failing that, I failed him, as we fail all our "true believer" students if we do not see the influence of their Discourses of affirmation on how they come to and learn Discourses of inquiry. "True believer" and "real scholar" are not logically or easily reconcilable roles, but the fact is that, more or less well, many of us find ways to be real scholars inflected by true belief. Our students can learn to "cast their nets on the other side" sooner and better if we teach them to. The writing classroom is an ideal site for such learning when teachers show the way.

## Notes

1. I hear an echo of activity theory here too. Cultural-historical activity systems, which David Russell describes as "any ongoing, object-directed, historically conditioned, dialectically structured, tool-mediated human interaction" (1997, 510), can parallel Gee's description of Discourses.

2. Thanks to my friend, poet, and priest-at-heart Sarah Read for calling the role of mystery in this distinction to my attention.

3. A major center of Mormon culture, Utah County—the home of Brigham Young University and the church's Missionary Training Center—is commonly referred to as "Happy Valley" for the sunny, accepting, noncritical outlook on life characteristic of its residents. Discourses of affirmation can create such serenity, which we might recognize as desirable unless the context demands the skepticism attendant on Discourses of inquiry.

# Works Cited

Anderson, Richard C. 1977. "Frameworks for Comprehending Discourse." *American Education Research Journal* 14: 370–83.

Bleich, David. 1990. "Literacy and Citizenship: Resisting Social Issues." In *The Right to Literacy*, edited by Andrea A. Lunsford, Helene Moglen, and James Slevin, 163–69. New York: MLA.

Brown, Robert L., Jr., and Michael Jon Olson. 2000. "Storm in the Academy: Community Conflict and Spirituality in the Research University." In *The Academy and the Possibility of Belief: Essays on Intellectual and Spiritual Life*, edited by Mary Louise Buley-Meissner, Mary McCaslin Thompson, and Elizabeth Bachrach Tan, 153–69. Cresskill, NJ: Hampton.

Brummett, Barry. 2000. "Rhetorical Epistemology and Rhetorical Spirituality." In *The Academy and the Possibility of Belief: Essays on Intellectual and Spiritual Life*, edited by Mary Louise Buley-Meissner, Mary McCaslin Thompson, and Elizabeth Bachrach Tan, 121–35. Cresskill, NJ: Hampton.

Buley-Meissner, Mary Louise, Mary McCaslin Thompson, and Elizabeth Bachrach Tan, eds. 2000. *The Academy and the Possibility of Belief: Essays on Intellectual and Spiritual Life*. Cresskill, NJ: Hampton.

Burke, Kenneth. 1989. *On Symbols and Society*. Chicago: University of Chicago Press.

Carlton, Karen, and Chalon Emmons. 2000. "Every Moment Meditation: Teaching English as Spiritual Work." In *The Academy and the Possibility of Belief: Essays on Intellectual and Spiritual Life*, edited by Mary Louise Buley-Meissner, Mary McCaslin Thompson, and Elizabeth Bachrach Tan, 17–38. Cresskill, NJ: Hampton.

Chappell, Virginia A. 2000. "Teaching—And Living—In the Meantime." In *The Academy and the Possibility of Belief: Essays on Intellectual and Spiritual Life*, edited by Mary Louise Buley-Meissner, Mary McCaslin Thompson, and Elizabeth Bachrach Tan, 39–53. Cresskill, NJ: Hampton.

Daniell, Beth. 1999. "Narratives of Literacy: Connecting Composition to Culture." *College Composition and Communication* 50: 393–410.

Elbow, Peter. 1982. "The Doubting Game and the Believing Game." *Pre/Text* 3: 339–51.

Foucault, Michel. 1972. *The Archaeology of Knowledge*. New York: Harper.

Gee, James Paul. 1989. "Literacy, Discourse, and Linguistics: Introduction." *Journal of Education* 171: 5–17.

———. 1999. *An Introduction to Discourse Analysis: Theory and Method*. London: Routledge.

Goodburn, Amy. 1998. "It's a Question of Faith: Discourses of Fundamentalism and Critical Pedagogy in the Writing Classroom." *JAC: A Journal of Composition Theory* 18: 333–53.

Hauerwas, Stanley. 1983. *The Peaceable Kingdom: A Primer in Christian Ethics*. Notre Dame, IN: University of Notre Dame Press.

Horne, Miriam. 2004. "Learning to Inkshed: Learning to Belong." *Inkshed: Newsletter of the Canadian Association for the Study of Language and Learning* 21.1: np. Online at www.stthomasu.ca/inkshed/nlett604/horne.htm (accessed 23 June 2004).

Kincheloe, Joe L. 1993. *Toward a Critical Politics of Teacher Thinking: Mapping the Postmodern.* Westport, CT: Bergin & Garvey.

Lakoff, George. 1996. *Moral Politics: What Conservatives Know That Liberals Don't.* Chicago: University of Chicago Press.

Lindholm, Jeannette M. 2000. "Listening, Learning, and the Language of Faith." In *The Academy and the Possibility of Belief: Essays on Intellectual and Spiritual Life*, edited by Mary Louise Buley-Meissner, Mary McCaslin Thompson, and Elizabeth Bachrach Tan, 55–67. Cresskill, NJ: Hampton.

Lunsford, Andrea A., Helene Moglen, and James Slevin, eds. 1990. *The Right to Literacy.* New York: MLA.

Marsden, George M. 1997. *The Outrageous Idea of Christian Scholarship.* New York: Oxford University Press.

Miller, Hildy. 2000. "Goddess Spirituality and Academic Knowledge-Making." In *The Academy and the Possibility of Belief: Essays on Intellectual and Spiritual Life*, edited by Mary Louise Buley-Meissner, Mary McCaslin Thompson, and Elizabeth Bachrach Tan, 69–84. Cresskill, NJ: Hampton.

Moffet, James. 1990. "Censorship and Spiritual Education." In *The Right to Literacy*, edited by Andrea A. Lunsford, Helene Moglen, and James Slevin, 113–19. New York: MLA.

Newkirk, Thomas. 1997. *The Performance of Self in Student Writing.* Portsmouth, NH: Boynton/Cook Heinemann.

Perkins, Priscilla. 2001. "'A Radical Conversion of the Mind': Fundamentalism, Hermeneutics, and the Metanoic Classroom." *College English* 63: 585–611.

Perl, Sondra, and Arthur Egendorf. 1986. "The Process of Creative Discovery: Theory, Research, and Implications for Teaching." In *The Territory of Language: Linguistics, Stylistics, and the Teaching of Composition*, edited by Donald A. McQuade, 251–68. Carbondale: Southern Illinois University Press.

Perry, William G. Jr. 1968. *Forms of Intellectual and Ethical Development in the College Years: A Scheme.* New York: Holt.

Rand, Lizabeth A. 2001. "Enacting Faith: Evangelical Discourse and the Discipline of Composition Studies." *College Composition and Communication* 52: 349–67.

Russell, David R. 1997. "Rethinking Genre in School and Society: An Activity Theory Analysis." *Written Communication* 14 (4): 504–54.

Spellmeyer, Kurt. 1993. *Common Ground: Dialogue, Understanding, and the Teaching of Composition.* Englewood Cliffs, NJ: Prentice-Hall.

———. 2000. "The Arts of Compassion and the Instruments of Oppression: James Agee, Lionel Trilling, and the Semiotic Turn." In *The Academy and the Possibility of Belief: Essays on Intellectual and Spiritual Life*, edited by Mary Louise Buley-Meissner, Mary McCaslin Thompson, and Elizabeth Bachrach Tan, 171–95. Cresskill, NJ: Hampton.

Stark, Rodney, Laurence R. Iannaccone, and Roger Finke. 1996. "Religion, Science, and Rationality." *American Economic Review Papers and Proceedings* (May): 433–37. http://lsb.scu.edu/econrel/Downloads/RelScience-D.PDF (accessed 5 June 2003).

Swales, John M. 1990. *Genre Analysis: English in Academic and Research Settings.* New York: Cambridge University Press.

Tierney, Robert J., and P. David Pearson. 1983. "Toward a Composing Model of Reading." *Language Arts* 60: 568–80.

# Part II

# Negotiating Pedagogies

# 5

# Liminal Performances, Discursive Practices
## *Introductory Comments*

bonnie lenore kyburz

I shall define action or agency as the stream of actual or
contemplated causal interventions of corporeal beings in the
ongoing process of events-in-the-world.
—Anthony Giddens,
*New Rules of Sociological Method*

Giddens' work in "structuration theory" seems to me both sensible and hopeful.
He concerns himself with questions of agency because he sees that "the production and reproduction of society" must be considered in terms of "a skilled performance on the part of its members" (1993, 168). Jon McKenzie articulates the
stakes in this game, recognizing the ways in which a cultural performance of
efficacy carries with it the command that inspires his book *Perform or Else*:
*From Discipline to Performance* (2001). McKenzie's notion of performance
"carries theory-builders into a distinctive mode of existence and realization" (37)
within which infinite variables operate dynamically as "assemblage[s] of liminal
processes; reflection and definition, alternative embodiment, transgressive
transformation" (37). While these dynamics may seem difficult to comprehend,
I like the ambiguity inherent in McKenzie's notion of cultural performance. In
preparing students to function successfully within public discourse (to negotiate
scholarly, professional, and media texts)—especially in the post-9/11 discursive
scene that wants to name "good" and "evil"—we must motivate and value performances that avoid (linguistic) acts of disambiguation.

Valuing ambiguity in the context of work that wants to define, classify, and maintain structure is important cultural work that complicates our ideas about "society" as any sort of unified or especially coherent phenomenon. Messy, inexplicable, complex human action shapes the dynamic fabric of society. Often, the teaching of rhetorical knowledge and skills involves attempts to understand (linguistic) motive and action, purpose and direction (audience). Sometimes, we disambiguate these complicated notions as if purpose or audience concepts existed in a state of homeostasis that denies their fuller complexity. Speaking more generally of motive and direction, Giddens clearly realizes the ambivalent nature of human action. He argues that to recognize the production and reproduction of (social) structure as performance "is definitely not to say that actors are wholly aware of what these [performative or rhetorical] skills are, or just how they manage to exercise them" (1993, 168). Nor, he intimates, do human actors necessarily recognize the social and transformative nature of their performances: "[h]uman beings transform nature socially, and by 'humanizing' it they transform themselves" (168). It seems to me that these notions inform our work in Composition Studies as we attempt to teach the particular, ambiguous, and/or alternative ways in which various textual performances operate. We examine, *critically*, the ways in which textual performances are structured, what ends they serve, whose interests are attended, and how such performances affect our lives in ways that matter.

With regard to these hopeful goals, Giddens' work is appealing because of his insistence that change is possible, that individual human actors are capable of generating change, and that social structures move to accommodate intervention and correction, intention and desire. What's more, these moves are available for analysis in both realistic and hopeful terms: "[s]tructure must not be conceptualized as simply placing constraints upon human agency, but as enabling" (169). Giddens calls this notion "the duality of structure" (169). For Giddens, meaningful analyses of structuration hinge on the clear observation that "[p]rocesses of structuration involve an interplay of meanings, norms and power" (169). Teachers and scholars in Composition Studies are likely to find value and direction in Giddens' awareness. We find in the Council of Writing Program Administrator's Outcomes Statement for First-Year Composition a compelling articulation of the goal of teaching this complexity, an expectation that students will come away from the course with an understanding of "relationships among language, knowledge, and power."

But while we may agree on the goal(s), we experience conflict over the methods for teaching these complicated concepts. Do we engage the personal? Discourse, literary, textual, or rhetorical analyses? Three to five sources? And what sort(s) of discourse are we attempting to motivate and/or produce through this work? Do we want to limit the scope and structure of such work by circumscribing the textual shape of student writing? Or do we embrace alternative discourses and those theories and practices that may encourage teachers "to help their students deal with the full range of discursive practices they will need to succeed in college and beyond" (Bizzell 2002a, x). Do we promote alternative discourses (not traditionally academic, expository) in order to "enable scholarship to take account of new variables, to explore new methods, and to communicate findings in new venues, including broader reading publics than academics"? (3).

Questions regarding agency, outcomes, and the nature of discourse(s) we want to privilege and/or encourage our students to produce complicate our work as teachers of composition. We negotiate. And these negotiations matter, for it seems to me that they make possible the kinds of analyses Giddens finds useful as we consider social structuration, as we consider relationships between language, knowledge, and power.

The authors of the essays in this section all find value in negotiating through dual-authorship and multiperspectival textual analyses on matters of faith, teaching, and learning. The work of Miller and Santos may ring familiar; many of us work with media myths and structures toward a kind of critical analysis/intervention through which students may come to recognize the power of institutional discourses and ways in which they are shaped and affected by familiar media narratives. Miller and Santos complicate this work by articulating several media narratives or "plotlines" that operate recursively and appear to be invested with particular interests (beyond "objectivity"). Concerned about the ways that students write from culturally supported faith-based assumptions, Miller and Santos suggest specific assignments that writing teachers can use to help students recognize the religious assumptions and "plotlines" that shape media texts. These assignments encourage students to explore religion's appreciably dynamic power as cultural performance. Thus, Miller and Santos offer both sophisticated analyses and specific classroom possibilities that may encourage useful negotiations between teachers and students as they learn to write their differences and understand how power, knowledge, and language emplot within various textual (cultural) performances.

Roen and Montesano share a mentor-novice dialogue through which they seek to negotiate concerns regarding the ways in which faith enters the classroom; this is a conversation many of us have had—in hallways, offices, over lunches, in private. We know these conversations, and it's time, we believe, to share the knowledge(s) we discover together. Considering our shared knowledges and pedagogies (on matters of faith, teaching, and learning) as performance long in production, we may come to think of them in terms of "liminal rites of passage," which apparently serve several ends, not the least of which is that they become themselves, according to McKenzie, performative "objects of study" (2001, 37). With a sensitivity likely shaped by teaching argument courses in a Department of Religious Studies, Mark shares his particular experiences working with students of faith as they seek to argue from faith-based positions. Duane reflects on Mark's concerns and offers advice that proves productive for Mark's negotiations in the classroom.

Whether we engage in textual analysis or informal conversation as we seek to negotiate appropriate pedagogies that attend to matters of faith in composition classrooms, the important suggestion we want to make is that these negotiations matter. As Giddens argues, our textual performances shape and rewrite culture; we need to attend to the ways in which our performances—even when, maybe especially when, they respond to institutional commands—matter. We need to attend to how our complex identities, our selves—liminal, uncertain, boundless, and full of potential—carry potential to alter culture, often unwittingly, sometimes with intention, and sometimes as a kind of performance that motivates new forms of faith in human (or other) potential.

## Works Cited

Bizzell, Patricia. 2002a. Preface to *Alt Dis: Alternative Discourses and the Academy*, edited by Christopher Schroeder, Helen Fox, and Patricial Bizzell. Portsmouth, NH: Boynton/Cook.

Bizzell, Patricia. 2002b. "The Intellectual Work of 'Mixed Forms' of Academic Discourses." In *Alt Dis: Alternative Discourses and the Academy*, edited by Christopher Schroeder, Helen Fox, and Patricial Bizzell. Portsmouth, NH: Boynton/Cook.

Giddens, Anthony. 1993. *New Rules of Sociological Method*. 2d ed. Stanford, CA: Stanford University Press.

McKenzie, Jon. 2001. *Perform or Else: From Discipline to Performance*. New York: Routledge.

WPA Outcomes Statement for First-Year Composition. www.english.ilstu.edu /Hesse/outcomes.html.

# 6

# Recomposing Religious Plotlines

## Keith D. Miller and Jennifer M. Santos

Students often write and rewrite their own cultures without realizing that they are doing so. They are, perhaps, especially inclined to maintain unreflectively the perspectives about religion that are, in their various circles, socially normative assumptions that shape many of their views regarding gender, sexuality, family, law, race, ethics, art, science, government, patriotism, international affairs, and war. Students constantly investigate these related topics during their undergraduate years. But, unless they take courses in Religious Studies—and at most universities only a small fraction of them do—they rarely, if ever, formally explore views and presumptions about religion that undergird (or, at a minimum, are concomitant with) their perspectives on these topics. It is as though faculty prod students to explore the many floors in the multistory dwellings that students call home without ever asking them to examine the foundations of the building. But if students don't analyze the foundation, they may never understand how to design and furnish their own houses or, more importantly, grasp how other richly designed and elegantly furnished homes can rest on decidedly different foundations.

Consider American civil religion, which seamlessly fuses Judeo Christianity with intense nationalism. Seldom do teachers and students seriously probe or critique American civil religion, even though it buttresses the entire worldview of many Americans and informs and bolsters virtually every speech of virtually every important American politician.

Consider also that students cherish highly standardized plots of Hollywood celebrities, athletic achievers, and politicians—plots often found, for example, in *People* magazine and on both front pages and sports pages of newspapers—including such narratives as Cinderellas, Cinderfellas, and Horatio Algers who find true love while surmounting impossible hurdles as they ascend from hovels to McMansions (or White Houses); nobody Davids conquering unbeatable Goliaths; unblemished innocents fighting a once-and-for-all cosmic battle of good versus evil; invulnerable Napoleons collapsing in utter and grotesque defeat (often a Waterloo occasioned by drug or alcohol abuse) while losing true love; and cultural icons magically and permanently resurrecting themselves from total loss and disgrace (often occasioned by drug and alcohol abuse) to a state of renovated innocence (only to fall again a year or two later). These same plots animate many students' favorite movies and television programs—from *Shrek* (an ogre as Romeo) to *Seabiscuit* (a horse as Cinderella) to *Star Wars* and *Harry Potter* (unsullied young people wrestling unspeakable evil) to *Buffy the Vampire Slayer* (wholesome versus satanic forces with the whole world at stake) to the *Star Trek* canon (all these plots isolated or combined in one episode or another) to reality TV (wannabe Cinderellas and Cinderfellas competing on islands). Inasmuch as these plots, even at their most simplistic, address questions about the meaning of life, they are, we would argue, religious narratives. Further, many students' devotion to these plots is so unshakable and so total that that devotion itself can only be called religious.

Yet faculty and students have good reasons for avoiding talk about religion. Often conversations on that topic, in the classroom and elsewhere, prove highly unproductive. An obvious problem is that, by expounding well-rehearsed views about religion that they gleaned from their parents, their communities, their peers, and the media, students can expound loudly and platitudinously while refusing to listen. Or their dialogues can become extremely freewheeling and unfocused. Discussing arguably religious plots in television and film can also prove fruitless: alas, in our experience, students often love their favorite TV shows and movies so much that they protest any attempt to examine the plots, no matter how predictably codified those narratives might be.

The question then becomes this: How can teachers approach religion in a way that does not yield predictable, polemical debates and resistance to analysis but rather enables students to appreciate many varied perspectives on religion and to enrich and complicate their views about it, whatever those views happen to be? Here, we address this question by proposing that teachers prod students to study the rhetoric of religion by focusing not on metaphysics but on textual constructions. While students can obviously explore the rhetoric of religion in many, many ways, we suggest one particular set of possibilities, hoping that this suggestion might spawn further thought.

Specifically, we propose that teachers and students examine perspectives on religion that appear regularly in American journalism since, in our experience, students have little or no emotional investment in the generally bland and highly standardized news accounts of religion that appear in the press. We do so by asking students to examine, scramble, dismantle, and recompose common forms of reporting on religion that appear repeatedly in the mass-market press. By testing the adequacy of standard journalistic forms in communicating the complexities of religious experiences and institutions, both orthodox and unorthodox, students can begin to interrogate religion intelligently and dispassionately while simultaneously expanding their critical thinking skills, reading and writing abilities, and grasp of audiences and rhetorical situations—all prominent goals in the Council of Writing Program Administrator's (WPA) Outcomes Statement for First-Year Composition—in a well-focused, thematic course that introduces them to rhetoric.

To facilitate an analysis of the new through the familiar, we propose that teachers use a framework derived mainly from Mark Silk's *Unsecular Media: Making News of Religion in America* (1995), an astute treatment of press accounts of religion. Silk observes that, not unlike reporters in general, journalists who write about religion emplot their accounts in a small number of predictable ways. These topoi (his term) or plotlines (our term) include:

1. Worthy religious people and institutions perform "good works," especially aiding the needy. Religious groups who help the poor deserve public recognition and praise for behaving properly. Those who fail to do so deserve public disapprobation. For example, the press consistently uplifts former president Jimmy Carter as a "good Christian" who works to ameliorate poverty.

2. Everyone should practice religious tolerance. For example, in 1960 the press generally criticized explicitly anti-Catholic arguments against the election of John Kennedy, a Roman Catholic, to the White House. In 1992, the news media labeled the Republican alliance with the Christian Right as an embrace of religious intolerance.

3. Hypocritical religious leaders deserve unmitigated condemnation. For example, during the late 1980s, reporters repeatedly skewered Jim Bakker and Jimmy Swaggart, two leading Protestant fundamentalists and television evangelists, for their adulterous escapades. More recently, journalists have excoriated Roman Catholic priests who practiced pedophilia and the bishops who protected them from legal consequences.

4. False religious prophecy warrants unalloyed scorn. Reflecting the Protestant bias of the entire nation, early American newspapers sometimes identified and blasted Catholicism as false prophecy. Throughout much of the nineteenth century, much of the press proudly and repeatedly denounced Mormonism as another false prophecy until the Mormon Church outlawed polygamy. In 1993 journalists unanimously branded David Koresh of Waco, Texas, as an extremely dangerous false prophet. Reporters sometimes label small, unpopular religions as "cults."

5. Various religions deserve acceptance as "normal" American faiths. After World War II reporters largely succeeded in prompting many readers, first, to accept Mormons as "normal," meritorious citizens and, second, to accept Jews as meritorious and worthy constituents of "Judeo-Christianity," a phrase that reporters popularized after 1945.

6. Claimed indications of the supernatural deserve press coverage. These include the reported discovery of Jesus' shroud and statements about visitations by the Virgin Mary.

7. Old-line "mainstream" Protestant churches are declining. In Silk's words, "Since the days of the Puritans, American religious leaders have rarely let slip the opportunity to lament the decline of religious devotion," especially dedication of the sort fostered by conventional Protestant denominations (1995, 135). Evangelical and fundamentalist Protestants, however, are gaining adherents, partly through commercial, media-savvy appeals and partly through enthusiasm and imagination that is lacking in "stodgy" churches.

We hold that journalists emplot their articles not only according to Silk's seven patterns but also following an eighth plotline: science conflicts with religion.[1] Journalists generally treat science and religion as diametrically opposed. Consider the media portrayal of the teaching of Darwinian evolution versus the teaching of religion. In 1999, evolution—a basic tenet of scientific thought—was dropped from the curricula standards for the state of Kansas. The coverage of this decision—and its later repeal in 2001—exemplifies the current mode of thought that religion and science are inherently contradictory. An even more contemporary example can be seen in the heated topics of cloning and biotechnology: more often than not, the headlines of such topics telegraph an alleged conflict between theology and the advancement of science. Also, reporters typically present prevailing astrophysical theory about the origin of the universe—the Big Bang—as clashing with religious explanations of creation. Even with the brief examples given, one can see that, while news media do not necessarily side with religion over science, the media often portray the two as incompatible.

Regarding these plotlines, we want to be clear that we wholeheartedly agree that helping the poor is meritorious, tolerance is desirable, and hypocrisy deserves opprobrium. But, as Silk argues, two problems arise from these often-repeated narrative threads. First, they reinforce unexamined paradoxes and contradictions. By some unreported, magical process—abracadabra presto!—dangerous movements led by false prophets suddenly become completely acceptable institutions. Allegedly bland "mainline" churches are touted as laudably tolerant, yet condemned as spiritually weak. Religious allegiance is forever declining, though a revival is always beginning to percolate. Signs of the supernatural deserve to be respected—for they might be true—even though the press is ostensibly secular.

A second problem is that the stereotypical narrative forms seriously oversimplify religion. By obscuring complications in favor of predictability, the plotlines, Silk maintains, wrap readers in "mental straitjackets" (1995, 149). Silk argues that the plotlines encourage passivity and discourage curiosity: "From reports on good works to exposés of 'cults,' a lot of religion news does not strike most consumers of news as reflecting any point of view, precisely because it is a point of view they share" (141). Reporters, he claims, fail to question and/or explore alternate explanations of various phenomena. For example, most Americans presume that "cults" are bad but never explore the ideology behind the "cults" that they deplore. Traditional plotlines use the term *cult* to demonize and ridicule any organization that warns of imminent Armageddon, yet the notion of a final judgment remains a principal tenet of socially accepted versions of Judeo-Christianity. While this example is a simplified comparison, it illustrates the passivity encouraged by the plotlines: curiosity and complex analysis are discouraged, perhaps in fear of uprooting the moral underpinnings of America and its long-standing tradition of conformity. As Silk incisively states, "coverage of religion based on a handful of *topoi* will necessarily fail to recognize other religious points of view" (147). A similar argument recently surfaced in regard to the phrase "under God" included in the Pledge of Allegiance. Given the religious makeup of the United States, the phrase "under God" fits the belief system of members of the dominant culture. However, as noted by many regarding a court decision in San Francisco, "under God" excludes atheists and those belonging to faiths with multiple deities, such as Hindus. The phrase "under God" also excludes those whose religious beliefs do not include a concept of God that fits the common conception of monotheistic religions, such as Judaism and Christianity. Silk observes that "We live in a country whose founding charters proclaim religious liberty, whose longest-standing *myth* is the right of all to worship according to the dictates of their consciences" (148, emphasis ours). By reinforcing the dominant culture, the use of the phrase "under God" and simplistic plotlines underwrite an idealized view of America as utopian in its religious tolerance.

For students to think critically about the complexity of religious issues, they must first understand the rhetorical situation and dynamics of the plotlines. Then students can explore the complexities of religious rhetoric through a series of assignments that invite them to analyze and rearrange the emplotments and then create their own newer and more complex frameworks and narratives. Students can fulfill the assignments through in-class workshops, in-class or out-of-class papers—either short or long—or some combination of oral and written, individual and collaborative analysis of religious issues in journalism—all of which will encourage them to think critically about the complex underpinnings of media portraits of religion. By identifying and analyzing unstated assumptions, students become better prepared to question and evaluate the relationship of beliefs and audiences.

Here are the writing tasks, with our comments on each.

ASSIGNMENT ONE: Choose a piece of religious journalism about some religion other than your own that conforms, or fails to conform, to Silk's plotline(s). Analyze its conformity or nonconformity to the plotline(s) and the usefulness and problematics of the plotline(s) for whatever is being reported.

This assignment encourages students to confront the problematics of the plot-lines, as one or more of them pertain to a specific instance. For example, a student named Lauren Savaglio (2003) analyzed journalist Alan Cooperman's "Is Terrorism Tied to Christian Sect?" As she explains, Cooperman raises the question of whether the press should label an extremist Christian group as "Christian terrorists," just as it often labels extremist Islamic groups as "Islamic terrorists." She concludes by stating that both phrases—"Christian terrorists" and "Islamic terrorists"—exemplify religious intolerance and should be dropped. Savaglio convincingly identifies this article as one that follows Silk's plotline about the importance of religious tolerance and argues for the value of that plotline. She also contends that American political leaders, reporters, and public too frequently stereotype and scapegoat Muslims and that "not one group is safe from intolerance as long as religion is used as a way to lower another group." (See Appendix A.)

Savaglio's essay succinctly demonstrates an understanding of one of Silk's plotlines and ably discusses its implications in a given scenario. In doing so, she effectively "focus[es] on a purpose" and "use[s] writing and reading for inquiry, learning, thinking, and communicating," both primary goals of the WPA Outcomes Statement. Her ability to effectively meet these goals within the parameters of the assignment illustrates the potential of analyzing religious plotlines in the composition classroom.

> ASSIGNMENT TWO: Write your own piece of religious journalism about some past, present, or imagined religious topic that fails to lend itself to any of Silk's plotlines. Be sure to write about some religion other than your own. While you are not analyzing examples of religious journalism, you may draw on public discourse (including journalism) to create and explore your topic.

Like the first assignment, this second task invites—but does not intrusively demand—that students spend time revising not only their writing but also, at least in a small measure, their common processes of conceptualizing religion, culture, and society.

For the second assignment, Lacey Jones (2003) reflected on current issues by reporting the claim by Raelians, who call themselves an "atheist, nonprofit, spiritual organization," to have cloned a baby girl. Unlike some journalists, Jones rejected Silk's plotline about dangerous prophecies and refused to label the Raelians a "cult" or to judge them. She also showed that the Raelians integrated their religion with science by enlisting the assistance of a group of scientists devoted to human cloning. By authoring a creative piece of semifictional journalism, Jones exemplifies the potential breadth of such an assignment. (See Appendix B.)

While the content of Jones' essay obviously speaks to her grasp of the critical thinking portion of the WPA Outcomes Statement, the structure and mechanics of her essay also convey her understanding of additional desired outcomes. Originally submitted in traditional, journalistic double-column style, Jones' essay demonstrates her understanding of rhetorical practices—another goal of the WPA Outcomes Statement, which contends that students should "use conventions of format and structure appropriate to the rhetorical situation; adopt appropriate voice, tone, and level of formality; learn common formats for different kinds of texts; and develop knowledge of genre conventions ranging from structure and paragraphing to tone and mechanics." Her double-columned essay mimics the format, structure, and tone of most newspaper articles and as such differs from the conventional notion of a scholarly essay. By making this leap from one rhetorical context to the next, she augments her understanding of different writing situations.

For our final assignment (below), we ask students to propose frames or plotlines that are richer, more complex, and more satisfactory than those that journalists ordinarily use. If they wish, teachers can make a comprehensive list of alternate plotlines from different groups of students, omitting any discriminatory or otherwise inappropriate suggestions. This process naturally invites a large-group discussion that addresses the advantages and disadvantages of possible new approaches. For teachers who wish to suggest possibilities to students, we provide six alternative plotlines—all of which we believe are more inclusive, more interesting, and more sophisticated than the plotlines normally employed by reporters. By discussing potential plotlines not explicitly championed by the media, students have the opportunity to see the breadth of potential in creating their own, new plotlines.

Our first alternative plotline argues this: *all people are equally religious.* John Dewey proposes that religion need not refer to the supernatural but should consist of the process of implementing ethical improvements. Paul Tillich provides an expansive account of religion. Challenging routine definitions, Tillich contends that a person's religion consists of her ultimate commitment: "Faith is the state of being ultimately concerned. The content matters infinitely for the life of the believer, but it does not matter for the formal definition of faith" ([1957] 2001, 4). A member of the clergy can commit herself to serving a religious body and her understanding of God. But a "national group," Tillich declares, can choose "the life and growth of the nation" as "its ultimate concern" (2). Assiduously climbing the ladder at work, some define their careers as their ultimate concern; social and economic success is, in Tillich's words, "the god of many people in the highly competitive Western culture" (4). When certain CEOs loot millions of dollars from their disintegrating companies, they evince an ultimate commitment to greed and wealth. For Tillich, ". . . secularism is never without an ultimate concern" (144). For that reason, Tillich holds that *any* ultimate commitment is religious, and every person is just as religious as everyone else. Reinhold Niebuhr makes a parallel observation, at least with respect to international conflict: ". . . all wars are religious wars, whether fought in the name of historic creeds or not." Soldiers, he explains, are "'religiously'" devoted to their causes; none of them will fight "until the cause seems to them the center of their universe of meaning. This is just as true in a supposedly secular age as in an avowedly religious one" (1935, 233–34).

Like Tillich and Niebuhr, Kenneth Burke blurs the distinction between religion and non-religion. Burke defines "secular prayer" as "the *coaching of an attitude* by the use of mimetic and verbal language"; he also defines prayer as "any mimetic act" ([1937] 1984, 321–22). He coins the phrase "God term," which, he explains, "designates the ultimate motivation" of a person. "Money," he notes, serves as a "God term" for some ([1945] 1969, 355–56). For Burke, God terms instantiate humans' overwhelming desire for perfection. Explicating Burke, David Tracy explains that, as wielders of symbols, we humans—including avowed secular thinkers like Freud—"are driven, wherever we begin, to god-terms" or "perfection-language" (2000, 187–88).[2]

The Tillich/Burke redefinition of religion undercuts a big problem that reporters characteristically fail to examine: their reinforcement of facile and unworkable binaries, especially conventional versus "deviant" religion and religious versus non-religious people. This redefinition also dismantles reporters' ready identification of religious devotion with formal membership in a recognized body or with intellectual adherence to well-established sets of denominational doctrines. Further, the new framework undermines journalists' binary of institutional religion versus make-up-your-own spirituality, which Robert Bellah and his co-authors term "Sheilaism" (quoted in Silk 1995, 146–47). Unlike the untenable, unexamined binaries that ballast Silk's seven (plus our eighth) standard plotlines, Tillich's redefinition accounts for religious complexity and ambiguity by including everyone.

Our second alternative plotline is this: *religion is a source of social reform.* Using arguments based heavily on the Bible and Christianity, Frederick Douglass, William Lloyd Garrison, Sojourner Truth, Harriet Beecher Stowe, Sarah Grimke, and many others assaulted slavery. In less than thirty years— between the founding of the American Anti-Slavery Society (1832) and the beginning of the Civil War (1861)—the abolitionist campaign reversed dominant attitudes in the North, making possible the eventual elimination of American slavery. In its overt appeals to the dominant religion, the American crusade mirrored British abolitionists' earlier, successful movement. Similarly, in the early 1950s and 1960s, Martin Luther King Jr., Fannie Lou Hamer, and many others made many, similar references to the Bible and Christianity as they sought to repeal legalized segregation. During the same period, Malcolm X appealed to Allah and Islam as his authority for denouncing white supremacy. Douglass, Garrison, Truth, Stowe, Grimke, King, Hamer, Malcolm X, and legions of other radicals and reformers theorized and harnessed religion as a source for extremely important social change.

Our third alternative plotline is this: *religion affirms tragic limits.* Despite the importance of reforms, no political or social system can eliminate tragedy. Niebuhr warned: "The highest achievements of social good will and human kindness can be guaranteed by no political system." He adds: "No system of justice established by the political, economic, and social coercion in the political order is perfect enough to dispense with . . . voluntary and uncoerced human kindness and tenderness between individuals. . . ." (1935, 201). He emphasizes that tragedies stemming from national conflicts are likely to continue because nations almost invariably act in a paradoxically impersonal, yet highly self-interested manner, rarely displaying the kindness and love that individuals sometimes manifest within smaller social units (1933).

Our fourth new plotline is as follows: *religion provides personal apprehension of the divine*. William James argues that specific private experiences form the cornerstone of religions, a basis from which "theologies, philosophies, and ecclesiastical organizations may secondarily grow" ([1902] 1982, 31). He maintains that "personal religion" of a religious founder is "the primordial thing" and that institutions are merely outgrowths of a founder's initial, private vision (30). In this view, to understand what is regarded as primary, mystical experience—not later thought or institutional formations—is to understand religion.

Our fifth new plotline claims this: *religion is inexorably communal*. Sociologist Émile Durkheim famously contended that religion, "an essentially social phenomenon," enables groups to cohere ([1893] 1968, 92–93). They range from a set of people engaged in a ritual to whole societies. One could say that Christianity helped Europe cohere while Buddhism and Taoism helped China cohere. One could also argue that anti-religious attitudes help certain secular groups cohere.

Our sixth new narrative form is: *religion and science intertwine*. Rather than conflicting, as popular thought and journalism suggest, religion and science have informed each other from the outset. In tracing the history of the two, Norbert M. Samuelson describes Egypt's dominance over scientific matters in *Judaism and the Doctrine of Creation*.[3] Egyptians developed and relied on geometry not only as a practical means to aid physical construction of buildings but also as insight into the nature of the universe and God. Thus, Pythagoreanism reduced the universe to numbers that represent shapes, a notion that impacted the development of the Western World. Babylonian astronomers, unequaled until the sixteenth century, used Egyptian math as a means to discern the proper time to pray.

Like Samuelson, Ian Barbour in *Religion and Science: Historical and Contemporary Issues* dismisses the notion of conflict between religion and science, instead postulating that religion and science are compatible ways of answering questions that provide order in life. Barbour highlights the parallels between religion and science while acknowledging the differences in emphasis: religion is tailored to answer the question "why," while science purports to answer the question "how." Both religion and science consist of rich theories. Likewise, both depend on paradigms and require reinterpretation of previous data when paradigms shift. While testing hypotheses derived from empirical data proves difficult in religious studies, maintaining the connection between religion and science is both possible and desirable since humanity exhibits a desire "to see patterns in wholes" (1997, 94). Both science and religion address this need to find order in life.

To reevaluate the relationship between religion and science is to recognize that each uses distinct narratives. All modes of human thought present stories; and, as Samuelson notes, religion and science are no exception. In *Reconstructing Nature: The Engagement of Science and Religion*, two prominent scientists, John Brooke and Geoffrey Cantor, note the importance of constructing stories to show various ways of explaining life, including geometric and genetic stories. However, each area of knowledge relies on perspective. Brooke and Cantor emphasize that "the absorbing question is why different individuals and social groups should be drawn to different interpretations and how far we may account for their predispositions" (2000, 22). Samuelson furthers this thought by proposing a combination of overlapping stories—those of religion and science—without dismissing the capability of each story to stand on its own. In other words, the stories contain meaning relevant within their own contexts as well as provide meaningful data to fill in gaps of other stories.

The full value of dialogue between science and religion has yet to be realized. Acknowledging and valuing similar aspects of religion and science would encourage a dialogue between the two and provide new plotlines that may help lift the limitations that journalism, academia, and popular culture now impose on discussions of religion.

After teachers and students have brainstormed new frames and plotlines, teachers can create their own assignments. We suggest the following:

ASSIGNMENT THREE: Write a paper applying newly generated plotline(s) to some phenomenon. Explain why your plotline is useful to expanding religious perceptions and portrayals. OR find one article that disobeys common plotlines; for example, find one that explains religion as devotion/commitment rather than formal adherence to religious doctrines or institutions. Analyze the plotline of that essay.

Student Jesus Davila created his own new plotline—people are individualizing religion—and explained how it pertains to the decentralization of churches (2003). He incorporated a philosophical perspective into his essay and wrote multiple drafts to achieve the interweaving of various perspectives, sources, and prewriting techniques to achieve the product. His essay exemplifies the possibilities of such a course by showing that "students' abilities not only diversify along disciplinary and professional lines but also move into whole new levels where expected outcomes expand, multiply, and diverge" (WPA Outcomes Statement). (See Appendix C.)

Lacey Jones (2003), on the other hand, analyzed an essay/interview authored by Kate Sullivan and appearing in *Spin* magazine that explores the Red Hot Chili Peppers, a rock/funk/punk band. Prefacing her essay with a reference to Jimi Hendrix's dictum, "Music is my religion," Jones analyzes the essay as an interpretation of the band as bent on an unorthodox religious quest through music and the bassist's 'epiphany' about the spiritual nature of rock music. In doing so, she demonstrates her ability to "integrate [her] own ideas with those of others" and to "understand a writing assignment as a series of tasks, including finding, evaluating, analyzing, and synthesizing appropriate primary and secondary sources" (WPA Outcomes Statement). Jones' essay demonstrates that students can understand religion as more than a choice of institutional affiliation while simultaneously expanding their understanding of writing. (See Appendix D.)

We hope that examining, unraveling, scrambling, deconstructing, and reconstructing religious plotlines might prompt students to investigate and reconceive not only religious plotlines but also other types of received plotlines and stereotypes in journalism and popular thought.

We unequivocally repudiate any pedagogical attempt to undermine students' convictions about religion, and we do not suppose that the course we propose would prompt students to volunteer to shift their convictions dramatically in one direction or another. We do claim, however, that composing essays about religious journalism can potentially enrich, vary, and complicate students' perspectives not only about writing and journalism but also about religion itself, in all its multifarious complexities. Composing and recomposing essays can mean taking steps toward composing and recomposing a culture—a goal with obvious assets to first-year composition.[4]

# Appendix A
# Religious Terrorists?
## Lauren Savaglio

"Is Terrorism Tied to Christian Sect?" by Alan Cooperman (located on A30 of *The Washington Post*, Monday June 2, 2003) was an unusual find. Where most religious journalism that I was able to come across supported the Christian religion, which most Americans consider themselves to be in association with, this article applied many stereotypes tied to other religions to Christianity. It questioned religious intolerance vigorously.

According to Cooperman, the arrest of Eric Robert Rudolph (the accused Olympic bomber) prompted many to make associations between his religious faith and his violent actions. This is more commonly practiced since the aftermath of September 11th. The reason why this is so notable in this situation is that Rudolph readily identifies himself a Christian. If one were to label him as other terrorists are in recent history, one would not only see him as a terrorist, but as a Christian terrorist. This has cause quite a stir among mainstream Christians in the United States who are uncomfortable with the word "terrorist" being associated with them. Idaho State University sociology professor James A. Aho feels that the phrase "Christian terrorist" is clearly an "oxymoron" and should be refrained from use (par 7). As the author points out only sentences later, Christians are beginning to feel what Muslims have been subjected to here in the United States (par 8). The term "Islamic terrorism" has become part of common vocabularies, especially since September 11th. Since many claim that Islam is inherently peaceful, the phrase "Islamic terrorism" would also be an oxymoron. However, few outside of Islam see any problem with this idiom. Many Muslims have felt the repercussions of correlating religion and violent actions. Many civil liberties have been revoked from Muslims and other Arabs in the United States and anti-Muslim sentiment has taken root in many. One may look around in the news and among one's community to see that often most who carry anti-Muslim sentiments seem to be Christians who want to fight, as President George W. Bush says, the evil-doers. According to President Bush's Axis of Evil, Arab countries happen to form the heart of evil-doers.

The underlying plotline, one could even say moral theme, is religious tolerance. While Cooperman makes one simple connection between the prejudice against Christians to Muslim discrimination, he shows that not one group is safe from intolerance as long as religion is used as a way to lower another group. One may see it as the golden rule, do unto others as you want done to yourself. Be careful, point a finger at any one religion as a breeder of terrorism or other "evil" and you may have a finger pointing right back at you. Using religion and all of its members as scapegoats for problems that plague everyday life will overlook the people who are to blame. Those individuals who commit such atrocities as September 11th and the bombings of the Atlanta Olympics typically do not follow the main teaching of religions, but rather the extreme version teachings. It is unjust to hold an entire religion, such as Christianity and Islam, responsible for the few people who take otherwise peaceful beliefs and practices to the extreme. This plotline is particularly beneficial since it educates readers in mass about the dangers and repercussions of intolerance.

# Appendix B
# Raelians Clone Baby Girl
## Lacey Jones

LAS VEGAS—Monday, May 25, 2003. Earlier today, representatives of the controversial company Clonaid announced that they had successfully cloned a baby girl. This news came as quite a shock to many, especially those in the scientific community and members of many religious groups. Immediately following the announcement a spokesman for the Archdiocese stated that the Church strongly denounces the cloning of human beings, stating that to even attempt such an endeavor was the "ultimate blasphemy" and "morally irresponsible." In response to the Church's statement Clonaid issued a response saying that "the pursuit of knowledge to achieve such marvelous miracles of science, medicine, and technology in order to improve the quality of life for all mankind is in no way 'morally irresponsible,' and that to imply such is to deny human nature." Members of the scientific community have speculated for years that this form of reproductive human cloning could have a tremendous impact on society, benefiting everyone from infertile and homosexual couples wishing to have children, to sufferers of the HIV and AIDS viruses.

Clonaid, the world's first human cloning company, was founded in February 1997 by Rael, a former French journalist and the leader of the Raelian Movement. The Raelian Movement is an international religious organization that claims that a human extraterrestrial race called the Elohim used DNA and genetic engineering to scientifically create all life on Earth. The Raelian Movement also claims that Jesus was resurrected using an advanced cloning technique performed by the Elohim.

Rael handed over the Clonaid project in 1999 to Dr. Brigitte Boisselier, a Raelian Bishop, who is now managing director of Clonaid. The main goal of Clonaid is to offer reproductive human cloning on a worldwide basis to infertile couples, homosexual couples, people infected with the HIV virus, and those who have lost a beloved family member, among others. Rael has said that, "Cloning will enable mankind to reach eternal life."

But even amidst the heated controversy surrounding the morality of cloning a human baby, officials for the Department of Health and Human Services as well as the Federal Bureau of Investigation have yet to confirm that the claims made by Clonaid and the Raelian Movement are true. For what Dr. Boisselier calls "obvious security reasons," the specific details of the project are being kept secret.

Despite the lack of certainty regarding the truth of Clonaid's announcement, religious groups worldwide are already voicing varied opinions. However, members of the Raelian Movement, which calls itself an "atheist, nonprofit, spiritual organization," have not been daunted by criticisms. They hold to their version of creation as firmly as most more well-established religious groups. Today the Raelian Movement claims more than 25,000 members worldwide and growing. In addition, Clonaid has projected an estimated one million customers interested in its services as well as several laboratories seeking partnership with it in this venture. Lila Morgan, a member of the Raelian Movement and a proponent of human cloning says, "We have as strong a sense of morality and the value and sacredness of life as anyone else. We simply don't shy away from using our minds and exploring our own potential and all of life's possibilities."

# Appendix C
## Postmodern Religion: a Brew of Beliefs
### Jesus Davila

Droves of people circle in line in the city of Mecca, the Wailing Wall commands piety from Jews, and a myriad of Catholics strive to catch an elusive glimpse of the Pope. But what does it all mean? Do these symbols of belief venerate the tenets of a religion? In order to believe, does humanity crave reassurance from the masses? Is religion held together by the shreds of that which is divine *and* tangible? I argue that one new plotline in religion is the individual quest for spirituality. This is a sojourn that the majority of individuals seek in our post-antiestablishment Western Society. With a melting pot of tolerance and a country with countless religious doctrines, every day more people are defining religion on their own terms. Religion is shifting from institutions of worship to an individual's own spiritual beliefs. The reason for this movement is that space between cultures is vanishing. People in Western Society experience a growing resentment and distrust of organized religion while simultaneously encouraging a respect for all theologies as valid.

This trend of decentralization of beliefs is pervasive in many areas of Western Culture, including the United States, Great Britain, and even New Zealand. In the late nineteenth century, almost 50 percent of the population of these predominately Christian countries attended church (*sPanz* 2002). Over the last seventy or so years, however, global influences ranging from the Vietnam War to immigration have caused Western culture to lose faith in institutions in general and to gain insight into the potential of the individual. This globalization has caused greater tolerance for cultures with different faiths, but it also has caused a drastic decline in church attendance. The result is a Western Culture that is becoming increasingly fragmented in faith because of loose individual and family beliefs that are relatively tolerant about other theological perspectives. This change was most drastically seen in the sixties and early seventies.

> In the 1960s the cultural shift returned in dramatic new forms; although intellectuals contributed to the shift, its chief carriers were the generation of young adults born during and after World War II. It was they who flouted traditional norms concerning sexuality, marriage, and personal appearance, who challenged "establishment" authority, and who stopped going to church. (Hoge, Johnson, and Luidens 1994)

The culture transformations from this generation caused a drastic drop in the importance of attending church, because many church annals went against new norms of society.

Spirituality differs, more than mildly, from religion. Religion is an organized system, an equation to get into heaven. Each denomination or sect feels that abiding by its principles is the true way to reach heaven, negating the validity of other theologies by ignoring them. Many people, however, are now finding that a more individual approach is just as viable a means to reach heaven, enlightenment, or any goal in life. For instance, the number of people attending church in 1871 in Great Britain to 1998 has gone from 40 percent to below 10 percent (Brierley 2000). One of the fears of humankind is to be alienated from a group, isolated and called eccentric, even crazy. However, with a mix of pervasive religious ideas in cities, suburbs, and quaint towns across all

of Western society, we are becoming more united and more open to other perceptions of life after death. People are beginning to accept the validity of other
views and to see the antiquated theory that God can only be reached in places
of designated sanction as hurting individuals more than helping them. The
baby boomers who started this revolution had a drastic change in moral value,
"A study by Roof on baby boomers indicates that they have changed from
denying themselves to self-fulfillment in order to 'find meaning,' 'to grow,' and
to find 'self-expression'" (Roof 1993, 165). The root of religion in the Western
World used to be the concern for what it could do for society. Now the individual is seeking out what religion can do for him or her. Theological philosophies are now congealed into a resource for individual gain, ". . . goals of personal advancement and success have displaced the collective purposes that
have traditionally under girded the organized church" (*sPanz* 2002). The idea
of looking for the religion with the greatest marginal benefit leads people to
not only accept the views of their neighbors but also to explore them. Another
key factor in the integration of religious beliefs is the juxtaposition of people
with near-antithetical views. Before the 1960s many neighborhoods and communities were built around moral tenets of religion, making it difficult for people to stray from their beliefs and the beliefs of their neighbors. Now, especially in suburbs, neighborhoods are rife with dissenting views and opposing
theologies, but instead of making suburban tribes and declaring war, America
not unlike the rest of Western Culture, has embraced diversity, seeing it not
only as politically correct but also as beneficial. The soul-searching that has
resulted from an increasingly diverse demographic has aided the overall
decline of organized religion, but transformed America into a more spiritually
diverse nation. "Religious life, like so many other features of post-industrial or
postmodern society, is not so much disappearing as mutating, for the sacred
undoubtedly persists and will continue to do so, but in forms that may be very
different from those which have gone before" (Davie 1994, 198).

The questions then come into light. Why did we ever need a base of people to stand on in order to reach divinity? And why are we ultimately separat-
ing ourselves from the social facet of religion that in the past seemed like such
a necessity? The most logical reason for this is the need to belong. This
changed after society began to embrace the individual's needs before the
masses wants. This does not mean that the belief in God is remiss in society.
On the contrary, according to American Demographics, "Amid crumbling
foundations of organized religion, the spiritual supermarket is on the rise.
Numerous surveys show that Americans are as religious as ever—perhaps
more than ever" (Climmo and Lattin 1999). People are still buying Bibles and
spiritual self-help books like, *Chicken Soup for the Soul*. For many this need
to belong that is no longer found in church is now satisfied in other aspects of
life, like the company they work for or where they live. Many indignant
churchgoers would regard the idea that they need a group to reassure them that
their beliefs in the divine are correct as insulting and preposterous, but it's

common in all walks of human life to cling on to each other as if we were in indigenous moral tribes. Why are some of us raised with biases to one religion or the other? This is the paradox that most commonly arises in a pluralistic society and is answered by tolerance and annexation of beliefs. The Massey ISSP Survey conducted in New Zealand perhaps says it best. They found that from 1991 to 1998 that 31 percent of people believed in God, an increase from 29 percent, a belief in the afterlife went up to 60 percent from 50 percent, and the people that prayed weekly was 30 percent compared to 22 percent in 1991 (International Social Survey Programme 1991, 1998). This increase occurred while overall church attendance declined.

When I used to attend church regularly I had the sense of robotic monotony, and although I enjoyed learning about God I questioned why my beliefs were more correct than my Muslim and Buddhist friends. On this subject I spoke to a friend of mine who is also Catholic and had asked a priest about the subject; he paraphrased the priest's response: "As long as you follow your beliefs, no matter your religion there is a place in heaven for you." To say the least I was shocked to hear a Catholic priest accept other religions as valid, but society is changing as we are all becoming more secularized. An increasing encouragement to become more politically correct and accepting has caused America to adopt a policy of, "if it doesn't hurt me it's ok." Gallup numbers indicate that in 1957 69 percent of Americans thought the Church was gaining influence while in 1970 only 14 percent thought that it was becoming stronger. Changes in tolerance and value shifts toward independence are seen as the causes of this increase in empty pews. Baby-boomer liberalism started this trend; as the authors of *Vanishing Boundaries* put it, "We did find that counterculture participants are more relativistic and more liberal regarding personal morality than other participants" (Hoge, Johnson, and Luidens 1994, 176). This growing tolerance from post Vietnam antiestablishment couldn't have come at a better time as more Hispanics moved into America, more West Indians moved into Britain, and more Pacific Islanders moved into New Zealand in the late 1960s (*sPanz* 2002). It's easier for someone to say, for example, that Hindus don't know what they're talking about when they are thousands of miles away, but when people start living and working with others of different cultures and they are productive, kind members of society, it's harder to disparage their beliefs.

Sociologists claim that as a society becomes more advanced then more and more specialization will occur. To some extent this is what we are doing with our beliefs. "The Presbyterian Church has historically been at the very center of American culture and society but with the culture itself disintegrating into increasingly hostile fragments, Moorhead fears—in the words of William Butler Yeats—that 'the center cannot hold'" (Hoge, Johnson, and Luidens 1994, 179). As individuals we have decided to take from religion what we need and break our culture into even more complex cliques down to the very individual. If most wars are in essence over ideals in religion then wouldn't a better understanding and a more eclectic belief system help the world in general? Perhaps America is doing the world a service without even knowing it.

## Appendix C
## Works Cited

Brierley, Peter W. 2000. *The Tide Is Running Out: What the English Church Attendance Survey Reveals*. London: Christian Research.

Climmo, R., and Lattin, D. 1999. "Choosing My Religion." *American Demographics*, April. www.demographics.com.

Davie, Grace. 1994. *Religion in Britain Since 1945: Believing Without Belonging*. Cambridge, MA: Blackwell.

Hoge, Dean R., Benton Johnson, and Donald A. Luidens. 1994. *Vanishing Boundaries: The Religion of Mainline Protestant Baby Boomers*. Louisville, KY: Westminster John Knox Press.

International Social Survey Programme. 1991, 1998. Department of Marketing, Massey University, New Zealand. http://masseynews.massey.ac.nz.

Roof, Wade Clark. 1993. "Toward the Year 2000: Reconstructions of Religious Space." *Religion in the Nineties: Annals of the American Academy of Political and Social Science* 527 (May): 155–70.

*sPanz*. 2002. Accessed at www.presbyterian.org.nz/spanz/feb2002/ward1.html.

## Appendix D
## The Religion of the Red Hot Chili Peppers
### Lacey Jones

We've all heard it before, the old line, "Music is my religion." Jimi Hendrix said it, Patti Smith said it, and countless lesser mortals have said it too. There are few who doubt the power of music. It touches our lives every day and helps to define us as humans and to distinguish us from our furry cousins in the animal kingdom. Yet, what exactly does it mean to say that music is one's religion? Is it a literal statement or just a way of expressing the importance of music in our life? Do people say that it all means the same thing? If it is literal, how is it practiced?

In order to answer these questions we have to consider what we mean by the word *religion*. Not everyone has the same conception of this often controversial and ultimately personal phenomenon. When most people think of religion, they probably visualize a traditional institution based on doctrines and teachings by a spiritual head or leader that dictate how one should live one's life. But is this the only way to conceptualize religion? There are many that would argue otherwise. Some say that all people are equally religious in that everyone has an ultimate commitment to some higher good, whether it be a formal deity, the pursuit of money, or the creation of music. I myself see religion as the embodiment of each person's own spirituality, their own inner core of peace and joy.

In August 2002 a biographical article/interview appeared in the popular magazine *SPIN*, featuring the band The Red Hot Chili Peppers (RHCP). The RHCP, an L.A.-based rock/funk/punk band that formed in the late seventies deeply rooted in jazz, early punk and grunge, proto rap, and funk, have been, as some might say, to hell and back. Over their twenty-odd-year career they have suffered heartache, loss, and failure. In the first years of the band, the original guitarist, Hillel Slovak, died tragically of a heroin overdose. Jack Irons, the original drummer, quit soon afterward. But the two remaining Chili Peppers, Anthoni Keidis and Michael Balzory (a.k.a. Flea) held it together and replaced their former band mates with Chad Smith (drums) and the boy guitar genius John Frusciante. But tragedy struck again when Frusciante, following in the footsteps of his predecessor, fell into heavy drug addiction in 1994 and disappeared from public sight for six years. Miraculously, the prodigal guitar genius cleaned up just in time to rejoin the band and appear on the 1999 smash hit *Californication*. But the author of the article in *SPIN*, Kate Sullivan, only glazes over this now well-known history of the Red Hots and focuses on something a little more interesting: the spirituality behind the music . . . or in front of it.

Within the article/interview, Sullivan talks to the two "weird" members of the band, musical soul mates as she puts it, Flea and John Frusciante. As she talks about and to the two unique musicians, a sense of their intense musical spirituality is readily apparent. In the first few paragraphs, Flea describes the experience he had one night listening to a favorite album: "One night I put on X's *Los Angeles* [1980 punk classic] *really loud*, and I just had a total epiphany about why I wanted to play rock music in the first place. I started jumping around and threw my plate against the wall! I was smashing shit! . . . I threw myself on the ground. I was on the verge of tears, but also of ecstasy" ("The Red Hot Chili Peppers" 2002, 62). As Flea continues to describe his feelings about making music, one cannot help but muse at how the religious side of music must be so much stronger for the people actually creating it, rather than those just listening to it.

Throughout the essay, all four members of the band talk of the different emotions and feelings that help to influence and create their unique sound.

> Frusciante's [reemergence] on *Californication* . . . has deepened the core of the band's music. "John's being back makes a huge difference," says producer Rick Rubin. "He's brimming with ideas and he lives and breathes music more than anyone I've ever seen in my life." Frusciante's songwriting has helped Flea and singer Anthony Keidis . . . capture a more complete vision of their L.A. "The soul of this city is a huge part of who we are," says Flea, "and I think the soul of this city is an old and beautiful thing." (62)

Rick Rubin, a legendary producer of bands such as Run D.M.C. and the Beastie Boys, could not have defined religion any better I think. To "live and breathe" for something is the essence of spirituality; it is having an "ultimate commitment." But there is more to religion than a commitment to something higher. There are benefits to a person's soul, to their well-being, that religion provides. Religion gives us comfort; it helps ease our pain. Religion also often offers us a leader, an idol, someone to whom we can look to for support and guidance.

Although Flea takes care of the funky bass lines for the RHCP, as a child he was thought to be a trumpet prodigy. He worshipped jazz legends and fancied himself to join their ranks someday. He describes how he was able to meet his idol, jazzman Dizzy Gillespie:

> "I snuck backstage, and there's Dizzy, holding his trumpet and talking to someone," Flea says excitedly. "I run up to him, and I'm like [looks up with wide eyes], 'Mr. Gillespie.' And I can't even talk. I'm in awe. And he just puts his arms around me and hugs me real tight, so my head's kind of in his armpit. He smiles and just holds me there for, like, five minutes while he talks. I'm just frozen in joy—oh my God, oh my God, oh my God." (62–64)

Later, Flea also talks about the violence of his childhood, his abusive stepfather and street life, and how he found solace only in his music; how it saved him. This can also be said of Frusciante and even of Keidis. The singer, referring to their music, stated that, "there's loss, but also joy and love and that little burst of euphoria when the whole world makes sense for about 30 seconds" (64).

Of all the damaged musicians in the band, Frusciante is probably the most damaged of all, according to Sullivan, but he also has the most intense spiritual life: "He speaks often of a Guardian Spirit and say that when he was closest to death during his heroin addiction, he was visited regularly by figures from the other side. 'I was so happy someone was visiting, I'd make food for them,' he says, 'when they were gone, I'd cry.'" (66). In the interview transcript, Sullivan asks Frusciante if he knew as a kid that he wanted to be a rock musician. He replies, "Well it was put to me by 'that guy' [guardian spirit] when I was, like, four" (66). Sullivan goes on to ask if he ever struggled as a beginning songwriter and he answers, "oh yeah. But I realized that there was a way to hold onto something that doesn't exist yet. That's what takes place when a song is written: You see something that isn't there. Then you use your instrument to find it" (66).

None of the RHCP ever actually say that old line about music being their religion. But if religion is simply the embodiment of a person's spirituality, then I cannot help but to conclude that making music is a religious experience, at least for this band. And whether or not it was Sullivan's intention to showcase the religious aspect of their music making is also unknown to me, but if it wasn't her intention then it becomes more significant because it stands out on its own. When William James argued that specific private experiences form the cornerstones of religions, I think he hit the mark. If music can be a religion for so many, then the experiences of musicians such as the RHCP must be the "primordial thing," the "primary mystical experience" from which all else grows. So Jimi Hendrix and Patti Smith were also probably very literal when they stated that, "Music is my religion."

# Appendix D
# Works Cited

"The Red Hot Chili Peppers." 2002. *Spin* (August): 42–66.

# Notes

1. Silk (1995) frames a discussion of the conflict between science and religion within the tolerance plotline. However, such a framing overlooks the important intricacies of the issue that could be elucidated with a clear topoi. In view of these intricacies, religion and science do not remain confined (nor do they neatly fit) within Silk's plotline of tolerance. See Appendix B, where a student essay addresses potential issues of religion and science via cloning.

2. Reflecting on the "perfection language" embedded in this alternate frame may lead to class discussions or student work on obsessive-compulsive behavior, such as alcoholism, gambling, drug abuse, or eating disorders, illustrating the additional breadth of possibilities associated with this type of course.

3. Samuelson's book does not deal explicitly with the history of religion and science but instead evaluates the relationship of God and creation; in doing so, Samuelson traces specific instances of the history of science and religion.

4. We thank Kelton Cobb, who initially suggested that we write this essay.

# Works Cited

Barbour, Ian G. 1997. *Religion and Science: Historical and Contemporary Issues*. San Francisco: Harper San Francisco.

Brooke, John, and Geoffrey Cantor. 2000. *Reconstructing Nature: The Engagement of Science and Religion*. New York: Oxford University Press.

Burke, Kenneth. [1945] 1969. *Grammar of Motives*. Berkeley: University of California Press.

———. [1937] 1984. *Attitudes Toward History*. Berkeley: University of California Press.

Dewey, John. 1934. *A Common Faith*. New Haven: Yale University Press.

Durkheim, Émile. [1893] 1968. *The Division of Labor in Society*. Translated by George Simpson. New York: Free Press.

James, William. [1902] 1982. *Varieties of Religious Experience*. Penguin: New York.

Niebuhr, Reinhold. 1935. *Interpretation of Christian Ethics*. New York: Harper.

———. 1933. *Moral Man and Immoral Society*. New York: London.

Samuelson, Norbert M. 2000. *Judaism and the Doctrine of Creation*. Cambridge: Cambridge University Press.

Silk, Mark. 1995. *Unsecular Media: Making News of Religion in America*. Urbana: University of Illinois Press.

Tillich, Paul. [1957] 2001. *Dynamics of Faith*. New York: Perennial Classics.

Tracy, David. 2000. "Prophetic Rhetoric, Mystical Rhetoric." In *Rhetorical Invention and Religious Inquiry: New Perspectives*, edited by Walter Jost and Wendy Olmsted, 182–95. New Haven: Yale University Press.

WPA Outcomes Statement for First-Year Composition. www.english.ilstu.edu/Hesse/outcomes.html.

# 7

# Religious Faith, Learning, and Writing
## *Challenges in the Classroom*

Mark Montesano and Duane Roen

> Tradition and custom, especially when emotionally charged, are
> a part of the habits that have become one with our very being.
> > —John Dewey,
> > *A Common Faith*

The two of us have worked together since 1996, when Mark was beginning his graduate studies at Arizona State University and I was serving as Director of Composition. As part of my responsibilities as director, I offered the formal support for first-year teaching assistants in the program. Although we do not work together daily as we did in 1996–1997, we still meet occasionally to discuss the joys and the challenges of teaching. One of those challenges is that students do not always find it easy to reconcile religious faith and academic skepticism.

Early in this chapter Mark describes how his experiences working with students of faith have challenged him to be more resourceful in the classroom—both in composition classes and in religious studies classes. I then reflect on Mark's experiences, using the lens of my own experiences as a teacher and a writing program administrator during the past three decades. I also offer some strategies for using writing to engage students in critical thinking about their own and other students' religious beliefs. Finally, Mark reflects on the discomfort that both students and teachers can encounter in a classroom in which religious beliefs become topics for discussion and/or writing. The dialogues in the following enactments are not direct quotes but rather a composite of several conversations, and provide a sense of the exchanges that spanned a semester.

# Mark's Story: The Challenges of Religious Faith in the Classroom

We, as teachers, live and work to prepare students to live in what Thomas B. Farrell calls a rhetorical culture. In such a culture rhetoric is "the only humane manner . . . to sustain public institutions that reflect on themselves, that learn, so to speak, from their own history" (1993, 213). As part of this culture, we must share our rhetorical awareness with others, and this sharing certainly applies to those with whom we have abiding differences in all manner of belief, including religion. Therefore, I would suggest that there are many important lessons for students as they learn to write in the context of our pluralistic culture and if they are to participate humanely and effectively in our culture—in academic, professional, civic, and personal realms. For the purposes of this essay, however, I focus on lessons related to religious faith.

In academic settings, students need to learn to ground their truth claims in bodies of knowledge that may be shared across belief systems. Students need to come into contact with knowledge that is constructed broadly, rather than narrowly, across religious and secular boundaries if they are to articulate their beliefs clearly, intelligently, and persuasively. By doing so, their beliefs become open for discussion. Students need to learn to listen respectfully though critically to people whose positions differ from their own. Members of each religion must willingly abdicate the goal of cultural domination. I believe that it is not only appropriate, but also important, that the college composition classroom accommodate the expression of religious belief as a model of "rhetorical culture."

The teaching of writing and rhetoric, if it is to serve our students in a variety of contexts, must recognize that students bring all of themselves to the rhetorical situation. This means not only that they use their religious beliefs in the public forum but that they also engage other beliefs in the process. If we do not provide opportunities for students to actively engage their belief systems in writing classrooms—where we encourage the use of critical lenses, then we implicitly tell students that religion should not be subjected to critical analysis. How does one do this without diluting one's own beliefs (religious or not)? With this in mind, I reflect on some experiences with my own students that have challenged my ability to provide a forum for the expression of religious belief in a pluralistic, rhetorical culture.

## Teaching in the Contact Zone

I am grateful for the opportunity to teach composition classes, not only for first-year composition students but for students enrolled in literacy (i.e., writing-intensive) classes within the Department of Religious Studies at

Arizona State University. In the first-year class in which I teach argument, Religion in the Modern World, my work with two particular students represents my pedagogy, which encourages students to express their beliefs. Both students made it clear from the beginning of the semester that their Christianity appreciably shaped their identity. Additionally, they expressed a concern that their college career would be designed to challenge, diminish, and, they hoped, modify their beliefs. Because I usually try to find ways to draw each individual student into a course, I made a point of engaging them in discussions about religious issues that concerned them, and I shared reading sources, both religious (e.g., Kierkegaard) and anti-religious (Nietzsche).

When we discussed examples of arguments on public issues in class, both students were hesitant at first to inject their religious perspectives. I encouraged them to participate in the discussion while insisting that their arguments be well reasoned, their assumptions and warrants examined and clearly owned, and their discourse generally respectful of peers with whom they might disagree. In this way I attempted to make it clear that religious language is rhetorical—that faith is not exempt from reason. Faith, beliefs, and assumptions underlie all discourse, religious or not. As theorists such as Richard Rorty, Thomas Kuhn, and Dell Hymes have noted, discourse is considered "normal" when faith, beliefs, and assumptions are shared among the users of language— among a discourse community. In such cases, language users understand one another with relatively few challenges. Across discourse communities, though, discourse can be considered "abnormal" because it does not fit the shared faith, beliefs, and assumptions of one of the communities.

Both students mentioned that they felt encouraged and somewhat exhilarated with the intersections of the religious and the rhetorical. When we reached that point in the semester where I asked students to write problem/solution essays, both students decided (they were in different classes in different semesters and didn't know each other) that they wanted to write an argument essentially promoting the ostensible solution to all human problems, the acceptance of Jesus Christ as Lord and Savior. This was a test for me. If I told them that there was no way that one could prove this to an audience of both believers and nonbelievers, what would this say about my earlier assertion that religious rhetoric was on par with secular rhetoric? I warned them that the only way one could be persuasive about such an claim—even if it was somewhat moderated—was to preach to the choir. However, if they were willing to make their assumptions clear to nonbelievers and to realize those limitations, then they could try it. I would judge their papers on the quality of how they argued from their assumptions and how they substantiated their assumptions through authority.

The first student (I will call her Kathy) made claims with no authority. She made many assumptions that she didn't state or examine and generally became tangled in the web of her own vague argument. The paper was full of my comments, most of them asking for clarification. Even though she understood that she had much revising to do, she was undaunted:

"It is important to me that I explore my faith whenever I can. I'm just not sure how to go about it; what writing I can use. I just know what I believe."

I agreed that her motivation was reason enough to attempt to articulate her beliefs. I believe strongly that the best topic for a student paper is one that reflects her passions. Her lack of intellectual background for her religious faith was a handicap. How does one make up for that deficiency in a semester of English?

"What is important, Kathy, is that you are able to learn to articulate and support your claims with clear arguments that relate directly to what your claims are. You also need to uncover the underlying assumptions of your claims. Consider this an opportunity to learn to do this. One thing you might do is read another Christian writer who does this well and outline his or her argument to see if you can understand what their assumptions are. Or you might just write out your beliefs/claims. I could help you organize them around some more specific arguments. Have you ever read C. S. Lewis? He has written some very popular arguments about why Christianity is true."

She brightened up, "I like the idea of reading someone who has already done a good job of what I want to do. Let me pick up some C. S. Lewis. I already admire his work. What books would you suggest?"

"*Mere Christianity* is his classic argument for Christianity. Why don't you start there?"

The results were remarkable. Although she might never be a theologian and may never persuade her fellow agnostic classmates, she did a fine job of articulating her own beliefs and was excited about her work.

"I feel that this paper actually has made my faith stronger. Now when I talk with people about what I believe, I am more confident and people seem to understand more easily where I'm coming from, whether they agree with me or not. I'm also excited that I am more at ease being religious in a public university. I couldn't afford to go to a private religious school and I had heard lots of stories about how you can go into public college a religious person and come out an atheist. I was afraid that would happen to me. I'm surprised and happy that it doesn't have to be that way!"

She came to understand that she could use writing as a tool for learning what she did and did not know about her own cherished beliefs. Further, she came to realize that by understanding her topic more fully she was preparing herself to write about that topic more publicly.

The second student (I'll call him Brett) handed in a first-draft rambling profession of his Christian faith. Overall, it seemed to be the halfhearted attempt of someone who realized early on that he had bitten off more than he could fit in his mouth, let alone chew. Instead of accepting that his writing suffered because of his lack of theological sophistication, he sought to place the blame on the public university, which he saw as hostile to religious faith and religious inquiry. He noticed that one of his classmates had earned a high grade for an essay on how to solve the disparity in players' payrolls in Major League Baseball. Brett was deeply offended:

"I am being penalized for wanting to explore ideas that are difficult. I guess the goal is to come up with the most superficial, nonthreatening subject for a paper. If that is what I have to do to be successful in this university, I'll do it," he complained to me, not without a healthy dose of self-pity.

I could understand his frustration, but I also realized that he did not see the extent to which the argument in the baseball paper was developed and supported. "The problem with your draft is that it isn't very carefully developed or argued. I admit that what you want to do is more difficult than writing about baseball, but in this class you are graded ultimately for the quality of your argument not the difficulty of your topic." I realized that, in a way, he was right. In a way my grading did discourage complexity. One could be sure of a good grade if one took on a pedestrian topic, so why strain yourself? That was Brett's logic.

For his final paper, then, he decided he would write about the exorbitant cost of education and how, perhaps, the cost was not worth what you got (an expression of his feelings about being at a public university). When I met with him for an individual conference, he hadn't done much research and was annoyed when I questioned his preparation.

"I've chosen a topic that everyone can relate to. Why do I have to back it up with lots of research? I can make my case from experience and interviewing students I know."

His sense of discouragement was palpable. I challenged his choice of topics:

"I think the lack of work you did on this draft is a reflection of your lack of interest in the subject. Why don't you try to find something that you are interested in? I will help you to develop an argument about whatever you like."

He replied, "Why bother? Anything I'm really interested in is discouraged in this school!"

I objected, "Brett, from the beginning I said you could write on whatever you wanted to, but you would have to do the work. You know I am willing to meet with you as much as is needed to help direct you to sources and help you shape your argument, so don't blame the school. I am telling you to do what you want. Will you? The low grade on your last paper had less to do with the subject than with a lack of effort. In spite of offering myself as a resource you really haven't taken advantage of that offer, until now. I want you to meet with me after our next class period to discuss a religious theme that you want to write about. But you have to think it through more carefully than you have."

He had calmed down and was actually smiling. In retrospect, I think that I had not communicated very well the possibilities of what he could do. In our next meeting, he showed enthusiasm but wasn't sure about what he wanted to do.

"I've thought about it, but haven't been able to narrow it down."

"What particular issues in religious thought interests you?" I asked.

"I am curious about the many different definitions of 'faith.'"

Knowing he had a philosophical mind, I suggested—somewhat reck-lessly, I thought—that he find Søren Kierkegaard's rather dense essay on faith, *Fear and Trembling*, as a place to begin. To my surprise, he came to class the next day toting a copy of *Fear and Trembling* with a big grin on his face.

It spoke to him, he said. "Continue," I urged.

At our next meeting, he not only showed a remarkable understanding of Kierkegaard's essay but claimed to see both the strengths and weaknesses in Kierkegaard's argument. He was nearly ecstatic that he had read and under-stood such a challenging text and that it was having an influence on the way he thought about his own religious faith. I suggested that he outline Kierkegaard's basic argument and give a brief accounting of the ideas to which he objected. His final paper was way beyond my expectations. His under-standing of the issues involved was sophisticated and his objections insightful and well argued. Most important, he expressed his faith in a clear and rhetor-ical way and brought it into his public education in a way that legitimated both. In fact, he later dropped out of Arizona State and entered a religious university with the intent of becoming a minister.

Both Kathy and Brett might well be honors students with a philosophical bent. But all students can be directed toward more specific research literature to guide the development of their discourse. The importance is the message that this exploration is important and well within the parameters of public school education. I believe that students can be encouraged to bring religion into the classroom as long as they are striving to follow rhetorical principles as the primary goal.

I happen to have a broad familiarity with religious literature. What about teachers who are not so familiar with such literature? It seems likely that there are resources in college and university (religious studies departments, local clergy, etc.) from which students can seek help with sophisticated and rep-utable sources.

## More Teaching in the Contact Zone

One of the classes that I teach for the Department of Religious Studies is called Religion in the Modern World. I designed it so that it begins by show-ing students how to do a simple rhetorical analysis of different perspectives on religion, ranging from Jerry Falwell, Joseph Smith, and Martin Buber to Freud, Nietzsche, and Marx. We also study films, poetry, and editorials that take positions on contemporary issues. Through these readings we discuss issues such as pluralism and religion, homosexuality, and abortion. I encour-age them also to engage these rhetorics in regular journal writings and in-class discussion with the goal of being clear about differences and similarities. The

first two essays are essentially analyses. The final project is more elaborate
and includes visiting a religious community with which they are not familiar.
They also read about the religion, talk to community members, experience a
service if possible and try to make sense of this community in terms of their
values, their worldview, their ethos, and so forth. In other words, they look at
the community's behavior rhetorically. In the paper they must also give a
personal narrative about their preconceptions/prejudices and how their experience affected them. Most students find that this exercise stretches their
intellectual muscles.

One semester, however, I encountered two distinctly different reactions to
the assignment. Both young men were avowed strong Christians and made that
clear in class. Both were especially concerned about what they saw as the
breakdown of morals in the modern world. Charles was particularly vocifer-
ous in stating that our society was in danger. One evening as we discussed
parts of Nietzsche's *Thus Spoke Zarathustra*, Charles was noticeably uncomfortable—understandably, because in these passages Nietzsche berates the
religious for being sleepy and unthinking. Charles raised his hand. He went on
to dismiss Nietzsche as an elitist who appeals only to intellectuals and who has
nothing to do with real life. "Okay," I answered. "Explain more."

"Nietzsche wants us all to be animals, follow our instincts, and do whatever we want. This can only be destructive."

"Where does it say this in our text?"

"It doesn't say it here, but I have read a lot of Nietzsche, and that is his
basic position."

"There are many, myself included, who would disagree, but we can't
argue that point now because that's not what Nietzsche is saying here. Let's try
to stick to the reading before us."

"But that's implied in everything he says!"

"Again, that's your opinion and unless you can show us what in our reading says this, we can't really debate this tonight."

Reluctantly, Charles stopped. "I guess I should keep my opinions to
myself."

"No, Charles, I value your opinions. You're the only religious person who
always has the guts to speak out, and I think your contribution is stimulating
and enriches the class. But if we are going to have an intelligent discussion,
it's important that we stick to the text. Does that make sense?"

Charles seemed satisfied. During the break, I approached him to see how
he felt about what had happened. "I hope you don't stop speaking out in class."

He gave me a friendly, tentative smile and assured me that he wouldn't.
Then his expression turned serious. It was like he was confiding in me when
he leaned toward me and said in an almost hushed tone, "Reading Nietzsche
is dangerous. Many of these people in class don't understand this and think
that it's harmless, but it may influence them to think that it's all right to be so
godless."

"I believe that any faith worth keeping should be able to stand up to critical scrutiny. People need to learn to encounter all kinds of opinions in faith. To hide from them is to have a sheltered and shallow faith."

He said that he understood but didn't agree. He also said it was an interesting class, though he felt that it didn't necessarily follow the course description in the catalogue ("Introduces the nature and role of religious beliefs and practices in shaping the lives of individuals and societies, with particular attention to the modern world"). Charles continued to speak out until we read a letter from a gay Christian man speaking about the abuse he suffered through the hands of the church and other Christian figures in his life. Somewhere during our discussion, Charles walked out. Because he never formally withdrew, he ultimately failed the class. I never saw him again.

James was also forthright in expressing opinions about the various readings that we studied. He was always clear about what his values were. He tended to speak and write against such things as abortion and premarital sex. But if we discussed a Christian writer with whom he didn't agree, he would tell us exactly why. For his final project, he decided to visit a gay Christian community, initially because one of his best friends came out as gay and he wanted to better understand why someone would do that. In James' final report, he was very critical of how the church seemed to adapt what he characterized as a "new-agey" theology rather than the biblical theology to which he was accustomed. He believed that this community was selectively reading the Bible and substituting "psychobabble" to help give the group a feel-good atmosphere. Although he didn't object to the existence of such a group, he argued in his paper that this group may have been dishonest in calling itself Christian. He supported his argument with specific examples and made clear his assumptions about what it meant to be Christian. He objected strongly to this community's approach; yet, he did so in a respectful and reasonable way. He never took the position that non-Christians were "bad" or "wrong." They were certainly not right for him, and that was all he needed to say. Where he became forceful was in his defense of what he believed it meant to be a Christian. The "point" of being Christian, for James, was to maintain a distinctly Christian moral center in the midst of ever-changing and sometime destructive practices of the "host" culture. Much like the Hebrews of the Old Testament and the early Christians, the test for modern-day Christians is to "be in the world, not of it." That is, one must not confuse the fads and fashions of current culture for the "will of God." It was this belief that led him to be so impatient with Christians who seemed to capitulate to "non-Christian" positions such as the use of "self-help" strategies to supplement the Bible and acceptance of sexual behaviors traditionally considered deviant by some Christians. At the same time, this does not give Christians the license to be disdainful of others: love and compassion for those who are different, however misguided, is at the center of Christian practice. By clearly asserting this complex position, James, I believe, achieved a level of engagement—in contrast with Charles—in a secular university that might serve as a model for other students of deep faith.

### Reflecting on Teaching in the Contact Zone

As I ponder the two types of courses that I teach, first-year composition courses and writing-intensive courses in religious studies, I realize how challenging these courses are for students who hold strong religious perspectives. In the first-year composition courses, I ask them to engage both the rhetorical and the religious. Although I know that there is at least a 2,000-year history of such syntheses, for my students it is a new and demanding task. In my writing-intensive religious studies classes, the task may be even more daunting because I ask students to read difficult texts—difficult because they bring critical lenses to bear on religion. At the same time that I ask students to express their religious beliefs, I am asking them to focus intensely on the difficult texts I assign.

Because I want to continuously enhance my work with students in writing and religious studies courses, I frequently engage my colleagues in conversations about their teaching and mine. Such conversations help me develop multiple perspectives on effective teaching and its effects on learning. My colleagues, including Duane, tell me that they also find other perspectives invaluable as they strive to enhance their teaching and their students' learning.

## Duane's Suggestions for Teaching in the Contact Zone

Mark's interaction with Charles during the discussion of Nietzsche's *Zarathustra* probably resonates with many readers. It is the kind of interaction that Louise Rosenblatt has addressed throughout her career and most pointedly in *Literature as Exploration* (1983) and *The Reader, the Text, the Poem* (1978). Rosenblatt argues that emotional responses to texts can serve as powerful tools for engaging with those texts. In many university classes such as Mark's, though, faculty expect students to engage with texts at a more critical level. As I have noted elsewhere (Roen 1992), engaging students in reflective informal writing about texts before engaging them in classroom discussions can prepare students for more critical conversations. For example, a teacher might ask a student like Charles to respond to a text in writing from several perspectives. The task might be to do any of the following:

> Before class next Tuesday, write about *Zarathustra* in your course learning log. In the first entry, describe some of your initial emotional responses to the text. In the second entry, take on the persona of St. Augustine, whose work we read earlier in the course, as you explore the text. As did Augustine, list (a bulleted list is sufficient) where you find specific points of agreement and disagreement with Nietzsche. In the third entry, list some examples (at least six) of the appeals (ethos, pathos, logos) that Nietzsche uses on pages 31–44. Be

prepared to read an entry in class on Tuesday. We will use some of the entries as the basis for a large-group discussion. Also, in small groups of three, I'll ask members of each to compare/contrast what they wrote in each entry.

These informal writing tasks can accomplish several goals. First, they can provide students opportunities to emote before coming to class, which can help to reduce the quantity of in-class emoting. To reinforce this point about emoting in class, we discuss the nature of pathos in persuasion. We address some fairly standard questions: When does pathos work most effectively? When does it work least effectively? When do ethos and logos work more effectively than pathos? Second, these informal writing tasks can engage students in some critical thinking before class so that they are prepared to do more of that kind of thinking in small- and large-group discussions. Third, such writing can help to ensure that more students are more prepared to engage in any kind of discussion about assigned texts. Fourth, these kinds of writing tasks can help students feel more confident that they are prepared to contribute to a discussion. (See John Bean's *Engaging Ideas* (1996) for further suggestions.) Because some students can complain that all this preparation constitutes a kind of coercion, we need to talk with them about the nature of learning and the strategies that they can use if they are to develop a full range of knowledge and skill sets that will serve them well not only in the academic realm of life but also the professional, civic, and personal realms. Further, my responsibility as their teacher is not to help them get good grades but to help them learn. Of course, if they do learn, good grades will probably follow.

Over the past two decades I have come to realize that argument is very challenging (pun intended) for many first-year composition students. They seem fairly accustomed to discussing topics—even controversial ones—with friends and close acquaintances, but less experienced at discussing controversial topics with those who hold views that differ substantially from theirs. Given this observation, I try to provide in-class and online opportunities for students to put their own perspectives—the Bakhtinian *svoj,* "one's own word, one's own world view"—in dialogue with other views—the Bakhtinian *cuzoj,* "the world view of another" (Bakhtin 1981, 427).

To encourage this kind of dialogue, I ask students to come to class with their ideas committed to paper (or disk or website) so that their peers can readily see—if not understand—what they are thinking. The ground rules for the discussions are basically Rogerian, as described in Nathaniel Teich's book *Rogerian Perspectives: Collaborative Rhetoric for Oral and Written Communication* (1992)—peers need to listen/read so that they can understand what the writer's position is, and their primary purpose in the conversation is to help the writer construct a piece of rhetoric that will resonate with readers who hold diverse views.

Of course, this listening for understanding is not an easy task, especially when emotional responses are bubbling just below the surface. For some students the task of understanding is, as Clifford Geertz observes, nothing short of the interpretation of another culture with a particular kind of lens, a particular perspective. And as Geertz emphasizes, the religious perspective contrasts markedly from scientific, commonsensical, or aesthetic perspectives. In contrast to the scientific perspective, in particular, "Rather than detachment, its watchword is commitment; rather than analysis, encounter" (1972, 112). Further, as Geertz suggests, the stakes seem high to the participants because, "Religion is never merely metaphysics. For all peoples the forms, vehicles, and the objects of worship are suffused with an aura of deep moral serious-ness" (1973, 126). With a plethora of such strong commitments in any class-room, finding common ground can be a challenge.

To encourage students to listen for understanding in discussions about religion (as well as other controversial topics), teachers in Mark's situation can draw on the logic that Anatol Rapoport offers in *Fights, Games, and Debates*: If we listen to understand those who disagree with us, they are more likely to listen to understand us (1961, 288).

Directions for a small-group discussion might, for example, encourage peers to pose the following kinds of questions to the writer:

How have you altered your position on this topic since you began investi-gating it?

What would it take for you to reverse your position on this topic?

What kinds of research do you need to do to learn about other positions on this issue?

What has brought you to your current position on this topic?

What do you need to do to strengthen your ethos as you argue for your position?

What would it take for you to abandon or reverse your position?

What kinds of emotions (pathos) does this topic evoke in people?

Responses to these questions can be limited, but when students compare their responses with those of other students, they encounter the Bakhtinian "other voice" that at least opens the door to other perspectives.

To help the writer engage as fully as possible in alternative points of view, I also encourage peers to brainstorm counterarguments for the writer to address. Peers can also help the writer generate strategies for addressing those counterar-guments—simply acknowledging some of them, conceding some, and refuting others. Of course, composition teachers need to model these kinds of interactions for the whole class before expecting small groups to engage in them effectively.

When I model these kinds of interactions, I bring to class a paragraph or two that articulates some emerging arguments on a topic. I then ask students to work individually to list as many counterarguments as possible. After that, I randomly call on students to utter one counterargument at a time, while I list them on the board. Once we have generated a list of ten or fifteen counterarguments, we rank order them in terms of their importance to the most students in the class—students who generally come from diverse backgrounds and locations. We then talk about how I as a writer might address each of counterarguments: "Which ones do you think I should concede?" "Which ones should I refute?" "How do you think I should refute them?" "Which ones should I simply acknowledge, without concession or refutation?"

One of the principles of Mark's instruction described earlier in this essay is that it acknowledges and engages the whole learner, an approach that John Dewey consistently advocated. That is, Mark recognizes that students in his class have full lives—lives that include not only the academic realm but also the professional, personal (including religious), and civic. Too often we focus so much on the academic realm of life that we fail to help students develop knowledge and skills that will serve them in the professional, personal, and civic realms. Mark is also helping students make connections among those realms rather than keeping them separate and distinct. This approach is useful because the realms of life tend to interact dynamically for most of us—even for those of us who try mightily to separate them.

Finally, Mark might ask students to read Chapter 7, "Judeo-Christian Rhetoric," in George Kennedy's *Classical Rhetoric and Its Christian and Secular Tradition from Ancient to Modern Times* (1980). Kennedy clearly distinguishes the ways in which rhetoric functions in a variety of contexts—in the Old Testament, in the New Testament, in the early church, in preaching, as well as for a range of specific theologians. Reading Kennedy's respectful analyses of these various forms of religious rhetoric helps students to see that even those who are deeply committed to their religious beliefs understand the importance of diverse rhetorical principles and practices. Such readings can help students see that there are many rhetorical situations for discussions of religion, and that those discussions have a rich history.

## Mark's Response to Duane's Suggestions for Teaching in the Contact Zone

Although Duane's suggestions seem compelling, the sensitive nature of personal religious faith keeps me from feeling comfortable about encouraging open, and potentially adversarial discussion about religion in my classes—even though I am quite comfortable discussing such topics with individual students. I tend to be afraid that someone will be offended—or that some student may consider the classroom a hostile place. In spite of this, I would like to be able to have the larger class participate in some way with personal exploration of religious positions.

In one of my religion classes, I divide the class into small groups and assign each one an essay that explores a religious topic (such as works by Mircea Eliade or Clifford Geertz). Then I pair them off with another group examining a different theorist. I then give them a religious artifact, like a myth about an African god. Their assignment is to convince the larger class that their theory would provide the best method to study this artifact. They have to include this within a mock proposal that is consistent with their theorist's methods. This exercise engages them in an argument about what religion "is" and encourages them to be critical of another theory. This certainly works to get them thinking in terms of argument and religion, but it still falls short of engaging more personal issues of personal religious faith. I believe that setting up a "debate" about religious belief can be both instructive in showing the rhetorical element of faith (see Burke 1970; Kinneavy 1987) but also risks alienating both the religious and non-religious students if and when stronger emotions emerge that could be taken personally. Yet to keep discussions of faith limited to talks between the teacher and individual student doesn't really allow faith to be a part of education.

Duane's suggestion that teachers can diffuse the emotional element by having students write in journals before class time holds much potential. Also, there are many possible topics for such debates. One of them, for example, might be something like this: Half of the class takes the position of president-elect Thomas Jefferson, who has just written a letter to the Danbury Baptists on January 1, 1802, to argue for the separation of church and state (www.loc.gov/loc/lcib/9806 /danpre.html). The other half of class opposes the separation. However, students do not choose which side they are on; rather, they are randomly assigned to one side or the other—in the same manner that debaters in U.S. high schools today are randomly assigned "affirmative" and "negative" roles.

I also see the potential of asking students of faith to argue from multiple perspectives—the classical tradition of *dissoi logoi* that the Sophists used in their teaching. Yet, although it would be difficult for some, this has the potential to strengthen students' understanding of their own subject positions within the larger culture. In Paulo Freire's vision of education, such work can help students to problematize the world: "To present this human world as a problem for human beings is to propose that they 'enter into' it critically, taking the operation as a whole, their action, and that of others on it" (1973, 154–55).

I am now more committed to asking students to write in preparation for each class meeting and for individual conferences. In the past I tended to "suggest" that they prepare something but would not insist on it by grading their preparation. Consequently, most students came to class with vague positions, discouraging most of them from participating. Duane's suggestion that students be ready to share what they have written is key because it encourages them to record their perspectives and to share them with classmates. I also think that, as in the case of Brett, I could have provided more guidance, sooner, when I understood how strongly he wanted to write about religion. In the future, I would like to be clearer about possibilities that students like Brett might explore and expect them to follow through.

If I had another chance with Charles, I might have invited him to bring in passages from Nietzsche that backed up his objections. Perhaps I would ask him to follow through in some other way, such as giving a presentation to the class, or allow another student to debate him instead of him having to debate me (the classroom "authority"). If there had been more journal writing before class it might have been easier to enlist other students either to Charles' side or against it.

In spite of all the situations cited and the advice offered, I still feel uneasy when personal faith is raised in class because I understand the challenges for students. Such encounters ask students to mix religious perspectives with rhetorical, philosophical, intellectual, literary, sociological, psychological, and historical perspectives. Further, at times, during their reports on religious community, a student may say something that could be seen as insensitive. Perhaps the greatest challenge is to fulfill my desire to foster a classroom climate in which students freely state their perspectives and readily listen to others.

# Works Cited

Bakhtin, Mikhail. 1981. *The Dialogic Imagination: Four Essays by M. M. Bakhtin.* Edited by Michael Holquist and translated by Caryl Emerson and Michael Holquist. Austin: University of Texas Press.

Bean, John C. 1996. *Engaging Ideas: The Professor's Guide to Integrating Writing, Critical Thinking, and Active Learning in the Classroom.* San Francisco: Jossey-Bass.

Buber, Martin. 1958. *I and Thou.* Translated by Ronald Gregor Smith. New York: Charles Scribner's Sons.

Burke, Kenneth. 1970. *The Rhetoric of Religion: Studies in Logology.* Berkeley: University of California Press.

Dewey, John. 1934. *A Common Faith.* New Haven: Yale University Press.

Eliade, Mircea. 1959. *The Sacred and the Profane: The Nature of Religion.* New York: Harper and Row.

Falwell, Jerry. 1981. "Future-Word: An Agenda for the Eighties." In *The Fundamentalist Phenomenon: The Resurgence of Conservative Christianity,* edited by Jerry Falwell, Ed Dobson, and Ed Hinson. Garden City, NY: Doubleday.

Farrell, Thomas B. 1993. *Norms of Rhetorical Culture.* New Haven: Yale University Press.

Freire, Paulo. 1973. *Education for Critical Consciousness.* New York: Seabury.

Freud, Sigmund. 1961. *The Future of an Illusion.* Translated and edited by James Strachey. New York: W. W. Norton.

Glassick, Charles, Mary Huber, and Gene Maeroff. 1997. *Scholarship Assessed: Evaluation of the Professoriate.* San Francisco: Jossey-Bass.

Geertz, Clifford. 1972. "Religion as a Cultural System." In *The Interpretation of Cultures: Selected Essays,* 87–125. New York: Basic Books.

———. 1973. "Ethos, World View, and the Analysis of Sacred Symbols." In *The Interpretation of Cultures: Selected Essays,* 126–41. New York: Basic Books.

Hymes, Dell. 1972. "Models of Interaction of Language and Social Life." In *Directions in Sociolinguistics: The Ethnography of Communication*, edited by John J. Gumperz and Dell Hymes, 35–71. New York: Holt.

Kennedy, George A. 1980. *Classical Rhetoric and Its Christian and Secular Tradition from Ancient to Modern Times*. Chapel Hill: The University of North Carolina Press.

Kierkegaard, Søren. 1983. *Fear and Trembling/Repetition: Kierkegaard's Writings, VI*. Edited and translated by Howard V. Hong and Edna H. Hong. Princeton, NJ: Princeton University Press.

Kinneavy, James L. 1987. *Greek Rhetorical Origins of Christian Faith: An Inquiry*. New York: Oxford University Press.

Kuhn, Thomas. 1970. *The Structure of Scientific Revolutions*. 2d ed., enlarged. Chicago: University of Chicago.

Lewis, C. S. 1943. *Mere Christianity*. New York: Macmillan.

Marx, Karl, and Friedrich Engels. 1957. *On Religion*. New York: Shocken Books.

Nietzsche, Friedrich. 1976. *The Portable Nietzsche*. Edited and translated by Walter Kaufmann. New York: The Viking Press.

Perelman, Chaim, and Olbrechts-Tyteca. 1958. *The New Rhetoric: A Treatise on Argumentation*. Translated by John Wilkinson and Purcell Weaver. South Bend, IN: Notre Dame University Press.

Rapoport, Anatol. 1961. *Fights, Games, and Debates*. Ann Arbor: The University of Michigan Press.

Roen, Duane H. 1992. "A Writing-to-Learn/Reader-Response Approach to Teaching Antigone." In *Reader Response in the Classroom: Evoking and Interpreting Meaning in Literature*, edited by Nicholas J. Karolides, 176–84. New York: Longman.

Rorty, Richard. 1979. *Philosophy and the Mirror of Nature*. Princeton, NJ: Princeton University.

Rosenblatt, Louise M. 1988. "Writing and Reading: The Transactional Theory." Technical Report No. 13. Berkeley and Pittsburgh: Center for the Study of Writing.

———. 1983. *Literature as Exploration*. New York: MLA.

———. 1978. *The Reader, the Text, the Poem: The Transactional Theory of the Literary Work*. Carbondale: Southern Illinois University Press.

Teich, Nathaniel, ed. 1992. *Rogerian Perspectives: Collaborative Rhetoric for Oral and Written Communication*. Norwood, NJ: Ablex.

# Part III

# Negotiating Cultural Divides

# 8

# Cultural Contexts for Religious Faith, Religious Contexts for Cultural Practice
## *Introductory Comments*

### Elizabeth Vander Lei

While religious faith may be held by an individual, scholars of the sociology of religion such as Robert Bellah and Peter Berger have explored how religion acts as a cultural force, shaping the cultural assumptions and civic practice of believers and non-believers alike. And, in turn, culture shapes religious faith and practice. As Berger puts it, "My point is that the assumption that we live in a secularized world is false. The world today, with some exceptions . . . is as furiously religious as it ever was, and in some places more so than ever" (1999, 2). David Herbert reports on surveys that correlate "church-going" with participation in volunteer civic organizations, concluding that because religious values often correspond to civic values, "all but the most inward-looking of religious groups can contribute to the development of a civil society" (2003, 91). Those of us who grew up in environments woven of religious belief and distinctive cultural practice know that untangling these threads is tricky business indeed; the effect of each is subtle and pervasive, and they are often mutually supporting.

Raised in the small farming community of Byron Center, Michigan, I grew up presuming that most Caucasians were of Dutch ancestry—after all, nearly everyone I knew (and I knew only Caucasians) had a Dutch surname: DeVries, Steenwyk, Vanden Heuvel, Kerkstra, the names rolled off my tongue with ease. These were neighbors and schoolmates and friends from church. Of course I had friends at school who did not attend my church, but that was only because they were part of a different congregation of the same denomination. In the seventies, the township of Byron Center (population 7,500) was home to seventeen churches, all of them Christian, three from the same small Protestant

101

denomination; these three churches were distinguished neither by doctrine nor by worship style but by slight nuances in membership: one church seemed to attract more farmers and blue-collar workers (my parents' church); another, shopkeepers and teachers; and the third, professionals—those for whom Byron Center was a bedroom community for Grand Rapids, Michigan. Most of these congregants were of Dutch descent; most (although not all) sent their children to the parochial school in town—often at great financial sacrifice—because they believed that children learn best when they learn in the context of their religious faith. Now undoubtedly, Catholic parents in Byron Center took their religious faith seriously; undoubtedly their religious faith shaped their parenting practices, too. But the Catholic kids attended the public school. I suppose if there had been a Catholic school, many of Catholic parents would have chosen it instead. What explains the educational choices that Byron Center parents made for their kids? To what extent were Byron Center parents motivated by religious faith? To what extent by cultural practice? It's impossible to say: theology shapes cultural practice, and cultural practice invites theological justification. They are weft and warp of a single cloth.

While religion and culture still interweave today as much as they did in Byron Center thirty years ago, the texture of the religious thread is changing. Berger notes, "On the international religious scene, it is conservative or orthodox or traditionalist movements that are on the rise everywhere . . . Conversely, religious movements and institutions that have made great efforts to conform to a perceived modernity are almost everywhere on the decline" (1999, 6). The big winners in this resurgent interest in traditional religions are, according to Berger, Islam and Christian Evangelicalism (7). These are the religious traditions that Bronwyn Williams and Brad Peters take up in this section, considering the writing practices of a Middle-Eastern Muslim student and an African American Christian student. For both students, culture and religious faith are thoroughly entangled. In the writing of these students, both Williams and Peters discover strong assertions of authorial presence, assertions rooted in and nourished by cultures starved for political capital. Raised in marginalized cultures and religious faiths, these students assert themselves by writing out of the rich rhetorical traditions that are so often fostered in the parched soil of political or social oppression. Berger describes how religion often serves as the fuel for expressing an ostracized cultural identity:

> We have then, in sum, a situation in which the revitalization of religion is a way of asserting a particular (group) identity, which in turn is a prime method of competing for power and influence in the global system; but this to a large extent is because religion has an affinity for particularistic identities and because it, like so many groups in our world, has become marginalized as a consequence of globalization. (4)

The question that these strong, disenfranchised student authors present to writing teachers is a familiar one: How do we respect the writer's rhetorical commitments (both cultural and religious) while simultaneously preparing her to meet the expectations of an academic audience?

Such work is difficult when the teacher is steeped in the tradition of the student as I am in my teaching at Calvin College, an institution owned and operated by the same small denomination I was raised in. The work is even more difficult when teachers are outside the tradition; and more than likely the teacher *will* be an outsider: the multiplicity of religious faiths ensures that. So what's a writing teacher to do? Williams and Peters offer two models for how to do this work well. Modeling a humble, interested openness to the students' writing and the religious and cultural experience that shapes it, Williams demonstrates that by interrogating his own religious experience he gains insight into the subtle religious and cultural forces shaping his interactions with Mohammed. Peters, in his careful research and patient exploration of possibilities, offers hope that through scholarly attention to the social forces that shape our teaching we can serve as a mediating force between the religious and cultural experience of the student and the expectations of readers and institutions, expectations that may have been shaped by different cultural or religious experiences.

Bronwyn Williams describes his work with Mohammed, a Muslim student from Oman, to demonstrate how our insistence on quarantining the secular can frustrate our desire to encourage civil discourse. Describing the scope of religion in Muslim society, Mohammed frames the relationship between his faith and his academic work in terms that would sound familiar to the Dutch farmers of Byron Center: "To Muslims, religion is not just a part of life. It is, in fact, that life is part of religion." In Mohammed's view, to secularize his writing is to marginalize it and the culture that produced it as well. And to secularize Mohammed's writing is to misapprehend its claim for power.

Williams offers us Mohammed's insights as a rare opportunity—little in composition studies has been written by or about Muslim thought or rhetorical practice. The same, thankfully, is no longer true of African American rhetorical practice. In his essay, Brad Peters surveys the impressive research done in recent years on the cultural and religious influences on the rhetoric of African American writers in an attempt to understand what went wrong in a failed tutoring session between an African American student and a white tutor. Peters focuses our attention on the concept of "a rhetoric of conscience," a rhetoric that encourages writers to acknowledge their subjectivity relative to both their audience and their cultural and religious heritages. Recognizing the influence of culture and religion, students may better understand the convictions they bring to their writing, and they may better use all the means of persuasion available to them.

Perhaps more important than anything in this section is the faithfulness that Williams and Peters model in their work with these two students, faithfulness to education as a potentially transformative act for teachers, students, and cultures. By trusting their students to bring their faith to their writing in ways that enhance the writing, Williams and Peters model the kind of trust teachers must offer students if we hope to shape an open, civil society.

# Works Cited

Berger, Peter L. 1999. "The Desecularization of the World: A Global Overview." In *The Desecularization of the World: Resurgent Religion and World Politics*, edited by Peter L. Berger, 1–18. Grand Rapids, MI: Eerdmans.

Beyer, Peter. 1994. *Religion and Globalization*. Thousand Oaks, CA: Sage.

Goff, Phillip Kevin. 2004. "Cultural Shifts: The Sacred and the Secular." *The Chronicle of Higher Education* (October 22): B11–12.

Herbert, David. 2003. *Religion and Civil Society: Rethinking Public Religion in the Contemporary World*. Hampshire, England: Ashgate.

# 9

# The Book and the Truth
## *Faith, Rhetoric, and Cross-Cultural Communication*

Bronwyn T. Williams

Pick up most multicultural composition readers and you can find sections such as Growing Up, Education, Families, Places We Call Home, Ways by Which We Learn, The Imaging of Ignorance, Our Sameness Our Difference, Women and Men, Popular Culture and Media Messages, Individuals and Institutions, Turning Points, and so on (Knepler, Knepler, and Knepler 2002; Divakaruni 1997; Stanford 2001; Verburg 1997). Few of these anthologies, however, explicitly address matters of faith. Even as multiculturalism has become a well-accepted part of Rhetoric and Composition during the last fifteen years, it has often avoided any direct engagement with matters of faith or the tenets of a religion that structure that faith. Yet religion is not only an essential element of culture, it is often the hottest button one can push, one that will elicit the strongest emotional and often defensive response, even from people who may not consider themselves deeply religious.

If Rhetoric and Composition has been reluctant to address issues of faith in rhetoric and pedagogy in the Judeo-Christian tradition in the United States, it has been even more reticent toward issues of faith in multicultural settings and pedagogies. In this chapter I both reflect on the reasons for this reluctance as well as discuss the challenges presented when religion is recognized as a factor in a cross-cultural[1] classroom. I will draw on postcolonial theory and cross-cultural rhetoric as well as my experiences with international students to illustrate how, when a teacher faces a conflict of faith in a cross-cultural classroom, any response is complicated by issues of power, history, and politics. Finally, I will discuss how writing teachers, by interrogating their own backgrounds and assumptions of faith, rhetoric, and truth, can engage with students in a reflective, critical, and constructive manner, the goal of which is not conflict-free multicultural pluralism, but instead simply continuing an engaged cross-cultural dialogue.

## In Search of "Common Ground"

In the late '80s and early'90s I taught international students at the English campus of an American college. I had arrived on campus a devoted adherent to a multicultural[2] pedagogy grounded in a liberal, humanist ideology that foregrounded the importance of individual agency and universal human traits over cultural and social structures. Like many teachers and scholars of the time (for example, Wurzel, Lynch, or Banks), I believed that by reading writers from other cultures, writing about our own cultures, and discussing the differences and similarities we could work toward a pluralistic common ground that would lessen conflict and promote understanding. At a small, liberal arts college with students from twenty-three countries it seemed particularly important to employ such an approach.

The possibilities and tensions of a multicultural society were also very much in the news at that time. It had not yet been a year since Salman Rushdie had published *The Satanic Verses* and then gone into hiding after having a death sentence pronounced on him by Iran's Ayatollah Khomeni. Though the public book burnings in such British cities as Bradford, which has a large Muslim population, had passed, the controversy was still very much alive. Rushdie had just published a lengthy essay in *The Times* attempting once again to explain his position, and there continued to be periodic and strident protests on both sides of the issue.

In the spring of 1990, during my second-semester College Writing course, I assigned a persuasive essay. As we discussed the rhetorical conventions of argument I urged students to write on an issue they felt strongly about. Before I asked for a completed draft, I asked for a one-page brief that would sketch out their position. Mohammed, as he often did, produced more than was required and turned in a completed draft. Mohammed was from Oman and was one of the brightest students on campus. He had chosen to take College Writing II again, in the last semester of his senior year, to improve his already strong writing skills.

His draft was titled, "Why *The Satanic Verses* Is an Outrage and Should Be Banned."

My initial response was surprise. Though I knew that Mohammed was an observant Muslim, in my somewhat youthful naiveté I had not expected this issue to confront me so directly on our sleepy little campus in the rolling hills of Sussex.

At the same time I had a deep emotional reaction against his position. The son of an American history teacher, I was taught to regard the Bill of Rights as the essential and preeminent civil and moral document. Its secular, liberal, humanist values of individual freedoms and civil tolerance were nothing less than the essential values of humanity. And during my previous professional life as a journalist I had come to believe that the First Amendment was the most vital of these rights. Nothing was more important than the rights of people to express themselves fully and freely. Nothing.

Yet as is clearer to me now than it was at the time, my struggle with Mohammed's paper grew not only from my secular values, but also from my religious faith. I was raised a Quaker, a denomination born in dissent from proscribed religious truths and dogma that still prides itself on the perpetuation of that tradition. Quakers search for truth in contemplation and consensus. Ultimate religious authority resides in the individual seeking the light, not in a clergy or any book. It is a tradition that is easily adaptable to the Western academic life of inquiry and reflection. Yet in Islam, ultimate religious authority is invested in the Koran, in the Book. Mohammed and I were two men of faith, both seeking truth and justice in two seemingly incompatible places.

The aversion of many writing teachers and scholars to issues of religion or strong student pronouncements of faith has been addressed by several scholars (Chris Anderson 1989; Beth Daniell 1994; Rhonda Dively 1997; Lizabeth Rand 2001; Juanita Smart, this volume, Chapter 2) in the context of Christian students in U.S. classrooms. The roots of this aversion include an unease with religious authority, a postmodern belief in the social construction of "truth" and the slipperiness of language, a belief in the separation of church and state, and a Western, positivist conviction that knowledge is progressive, rational, and evolutionary. The cross-cultural classroom raises additional concerns for writing teachers, especially those from Western cultures adopting multicultural pedagogies that emphasize individual human rights, tolerance and respect for all beliefs and practices, and resolution of conflict through negotiation and compromise.

Religion, however, is specifically often *not* available to rational negotiation and compromise. Though faith very often reflects our deepest-held and least-negotiable values, its very nature makes it among the most difficult elements of culture to communicate to others. As Chris Anderson notes, "Faith is a matter of intuiting the inexplicable and of making a leap that cannot be justified to anyone who hasn't made that leap" (1989, 13). Faith is never completely persuasive until the nonbeliever gives herself over, without reservation, to the belief in what cannot be proved or seen or explained in words. Indeed, rather than operating as an instrument of compromise for finding common ground, religion often acts as a means of helping people identify themselves as specifically different than others around them.

If religious faith can create difficulties when teachers and students share a culture with a common religious tradition, in a cross-cultural classroom, trying to understand, often across language barriers, the meaning of faith to an individual and his relationship to the unspeakable, undefinable, and unprovable becomes all the more frustrating and ripe for misunderstandings. And the core values of religious faith are also often the foundation for other manifestations of culture, such as gender relations, family structures, art, justice and morality, and certainly language and rhetoric.

In addition, the emphasis in multicultural pedagogies on tolerating the religious practices of marginalized or nondominant groups leads some teachers to fear commenting on students' religious statements or writing lest their comments be considered intolerant and risk silencing the students and destroying the sense of community in the classroom. The anxiety of appearing intolerant, particularly for a teacher from the dominant culture, carries with it implicit identifications of the teacher as racist or imperialist. Such a perceived failure of tolerance toward others becomes a perceived moral failing, not just a professional one.

These anxieties, when combined with the implicit values of a secular, individualist civil society, can place the teacher at the center of an uncomfortable conflict. Yet eliding religion and relying on an atmosphere of tolerance can create a situation in which the teacher and students are all the less prepared to deal with questions of faith when they do arise.

## Life Is Part of Religion

Certainly I felt blindsided by religion when I read Mohammed's draft. I knew that he was an observant Muslim, as were many of my students from the Middle East. Still, in my multicultural pedagogy I had not explicitly addressed religion, and I assumed students would understand that the focus and the discourse of the class would be secular.

Even as I felt startled by Mohammed's essay and resistant to his argument, I knew that I needed to respond to him. When confronted by students who write about religious topics or use religious rhetoric, some writing teachers advocate avoiding a response to the writing by raising the concept of audience. They tell their students that the academy is not the appropriate context for their work and ask how the students might reframe the issue for a secular, academic audience (Anderson 1989). Though I support raising students' awareness of audience, relying on this strategy to avoid responding to writing that is clearly of profound importance to students is unethical. If we encourage students to write about what matters to them, to put their thoughts and ideas on the page, we have an ethical obligation to let them know that they have been heard (Elbow 2000, 31). This is particularly true if they have the courage to address issues that risk alienating their teacher (Payne 2000, 120). If we tell students the academy values the free exchange of ideas, we cannot refuse to respond to their ideas.

At the time, however, I had no idea how best to respond to Mohammed. It helped me that he had framed his argument with care. He made clear that he was not going to address the ongoing debate about Rushdie's fate, but instead wanted to explain to a Western audience why the book outraged adherents to

Islam and should, as a consequence, be banned and recalled from stores. And though some of my Arab students displayed more characteristically general traits of Arabic rhetoric—such as a more poetic emphasis on metaphor, rhythm, and repetition (Lisle and Mano 1997), Mohammed had taken a detached, linear approach to this, having learned well how to construct an argument in the Western tradition. An admirer of Plato and Cicero, Mohammed had also demonstrated an Aristotelian sense of *ethos* by displaying "good sense, good moral character, and goodwill" (*Rhetoric* 2.1.10–11). It is worth noting that I refer to secular rhetoricians, for my audience of secular rhetoricians, to describe Mohammed's presentation of *ethos*. Mohammed, though I did not have the insight at the time to ask him to do so, would more likely have turned to passages from the Koran to explain the nature and source of the same qualities because Mohammed believed that all life flowed from his faith.

Mohammed's essay became more difficult for me on the second page where he said he had not read *The Satanic Verses*, which he called a "dense and tortuous book," but explained that he did not have to in order to reach his judgment.

> The very idea of using the prophet Mohammed as a character in a novel is painful to many Muslims. The entire Islamic system consists of the so-called "Hodud" or limits beyond which one should simply not venture. Islam does not recognize unlimited freedom of expression. Call them taboos, if you like, but Islam considers a wide variety of topics as permanently closed. Most Muslims are prepared to be broad-minded about most things but never about anything that even remotely touches on their faith. "Better that I be dead than see Islam injured," said an Islamic leader in the last century. An Arab proverb says: "Kill me. But do not mock my faith."

On the one hand, I respected the deep moral foundation on which he built his argument. I also recognized that writing this essay was an act of some courage in a Western educational institution and culture that did not necessarily recognize the authority of that tradition.[3] Mohammed tried to define the fundamental distinction he saw between Western culture and Islamic culture: "To Muslims, religion is not just a part of life. It is, in fact, life that is a part of religion."

Obviously my background as a secular, Western academic had instilled in me exactly the opposite view of religion and culture. Like Mohammed I hoped to display "good sense, good moral character, and goodwill" and live a life that was kind, honest, compassionate, and intellectually curious. We both saw ourselves as seekers of knowledge; the difference was that his touchstone for that knowledge was not my Western belief in "rational" secular discussion, but the word of Allah.

And it is the *word* of Allah, specifically the printed word, that is the source of great authority in Islam. Like Judaism and Christianity, Islam is constructed on a tradition of authority in the printed word of sacred texts that function as repositories of divine truth and generate solidarity and orthodoxy among

believers through literate practices (Kapitzke 1999, 115–16). As Cushla
Kapitzke notes, "because written religion is textualized and abstracted, it is eth-
ically universalistic: that is, believers are subject to the same generalized,
impersonal behavior standards" (115). It is the Book, the Koran, that in Islam
serves not only as the guide for Allah's expectations of human morality and
behavior, but also as the primary symbol of Islam that binds the faithful and
provides a common focus. That the central symbol of Islam is a *book*, great portions of which are memorized by many Muslim men from the time they can first
read, invests literacy with sacred powers and duties. Indeed, though I regarded
Mohammed's essay as a secular text in a secular classroom, he may very well
have regarded it more as a sacred use of literacy to defend his faith. In the West,
literacy, though rooted in religious foundations, is in contemporary culture portrayed more as a necessity for maintaining secular civil societies. In Islam literacy is always, at some level, sacred. For the Muslim writer, "the power of
words (lies) not in their ability to reflect human experience, but in their ability
to transcend it, to reach toward . . . the divine" (Anderson 1991, 98).

That ultimate authority resides in the words of the Koran, the definitive
symbol of Islam, means that words, which always serve some sacred function, must be used with care so as not to create blasphemy in print. Books,
and the words they contain, have a special power and special responsibility
not to challenge the authority of *the* Book. Mohammed argued that this
importance of the Koran and the sacred nature of the printed word was in part
what was so troubling about Rushdie's novel. The author had committed his
blasphemy—satirizing the writing of the Koran—in print, the same medium
as the sacred book. Mohammed wrote:

> Islam is the religion of the Book. Few cultures hold the written and printed
> word in so much respectful awe as Muslims, even though the vast majority
> are illiterate. When a Muslim wants to clinch an argument he says, "It is writ-
> ten." What is written and printed must, ideally, confirm the teaching of the
> Koran or at least conform within them. Christians, Jews, and Zoroastrians are
> accepted as believers because they, too, have holy books and are people of
> the book (*Ahl Al-Ketab*). Any attempt to use a book to demolish or even cast
> doubt on the authenticity of even a small part of what is The Book is intoler-
> able to most Muslims.

## Different Ways to the "Truth"

As a Quaker I had been raised with a quite different conception of the nature
of sacred texts and their importance to the individual's spiritual being and
growth. In a well-known Quaker hymn, the denomination's founder, George
Fox, refuses to swear on the Bible, replying in defiance that "the truth is more
holy than the Book to me." In the Quaker tradition the Bible is viewed as a
valuable book that offers important teachings. Yet the Bible is not the source

of ultimate spiritual authority. "Compiled from the inspiration of many ancient writers, the Bible has been for Friends not a blueprint or final authority but a source of knowledge of God's ways with us" (New England Yearly Meeting 1986, 77–78). That knowledge, along with experience and contemplation, guides each believer in an individual search for the light within. The Bible, like other texts created by humans, is a book open for interpretation and discussion. (The other religious tradition in my upbringing, my mother's Presbyterianism, places a similar value on the human interpretation of the Bible, if for somewhat different theological ends.)

Quakerism also privileges human discussion and consensus as a way of reaching decisions and solving conflicts. There are no ministers in most Friends' meetings, no official hierarchy to interpret the Bible or doctrine. Instead it is the individual, in contact with equal individuals, who comes to an interpretation. And it is the collection of individuals in Meeting that decides matters of policy and doctrine, including often how to respond to issues of social justice in the secular world. In many ways, with its emphasis on contemplation, interpretation, and group consensus, a Friends' Meeting is not unlike an academic department (with, perhaps, more consensus and less argument). Also, the emphasis on individual enlightenment and negotiated social truths makes it relatively easy to be a Quaker and accept a postmodern worldview. Consequently, while my religious background, such as my commitment to pacifism, often puts me at odds with prevailing national politics, my faith rarely puts me in a fundamental, irresolvable conflict with my professional life or the secular world in which I live.

Though our perspectives on free expression and the centrality of religion in society differed, with my multicultural goals of tolerance and compromise intact I hoped Mohammed and I could find a way to reach a mediated meeting of minds. Here was an opportunity for two reasonable people to engage in Habermas' "ideal discourse"; we could prove that the divisive and emotional name-calling and histrionics that had marked and marred this issue could be avoided and a settlement satisfactory to both sides could be reached.

In long, quiet, respectful conversations during the weeks to follow we discussed Mohammed's essay and the arguments supporting our conflicting positions. As he considered my counterarguments his draft became stronger, and I learned much about Islam I had not known. But his argument never wavered; nor did mine. We walked away from the project friends, and he walked away with an "A" paper. On many levels this was a pedagogical success story. His writing skills and grasp of Western rhetorical concepts improved. On those terms, and they are not unimportant, I could be satisfied that I had reached a student and helped him learn. I could also be satisfied that we had learned a great deal from each other, and when this happens I know that I am doing my job.

Yet in retrospect I realize that I was not engaged in honest negotiations with Mohammed, but was instead trying to find ways to convince him of the value of secular rights to freedom of expression. I did not talk to him about the religious nature of his argument, but instead tried to make him see how such an argument was viewed in the secular West. Such an approach helped him understand the culture in which he was living. Mohammed, like many of the non-Western students at the college, was there explicitly to receive a Western education that would help him succeed in the worlds of international business and politics.[4] Yet my response was incomplete in a way that was ultimately unsatisfying to both of us because, even as I thought I respected his position, I kept hoping I could change his mind. At the time I did not fully recognize the reasons, both secular and religious, for my resistance to his essay. Even had I recognized the reasons, I'm not sure that, as the young teacher I was then, I would have found a way to own up to how they were affecting my work, let alone to let Mohammed know how they were influencing my responses. I also did not see past the content of his essay to consider how other issues of rhetoric and culture were influencing this moment of cross-cultural conflict.

## Religion, Power, and Politics

An important rhetorical issue I did not consider at the time was the influence of cultural differences on our conceptions of epistemology and education. These differences were both connected to and separate from our different religious backgrounds. For example, in some Asian and Middle-Eastern cultures, the goal of education is to appreciate knowledge, to grasp it as a whole and to find wisdom in what is ancient. In a Western school this puts students at odds with a system that values the critique of information and sources and the creation of new ideas.[5]

This deference to established wisdom and authority is often found in non-Western students toward both texts and their professors. Many cultures maintain a veneration and respect for wisdom and authority that we, in the West, have long since ceased to privilege and have replaced with a respect for the creation of new ideas and empirical data that challenge the old concepts. No Nobel Prizes for the sciences are awarded for work that reinforces the essential truths in a field. When we read research we examine the "timeliness" of the references and raise questions about the work if the sources are too "old." Many writing teachers and writing texts (Hacker 1999, 68; Connors and Lunsford 1996, 566; Buscemi, Nicolai, and Strugala 1997, 94) pass these lessons along to students. As a culture we are enamored with the new, with innovation, with the perception of knowledge contributing to "progress." By contrast, as Helen Fox notes, "For many world majority students, knowing your place in the hierarchy and deferring to those of greater knowledge and to timeless, 'original' wisdom have been part of life since childhood" (1994, 51).

For Mohammed and many Muslims, the Koran offers a timeless, authoritative source of original wisdom. Anything he might learn in my class or any other would be filtered through and subordinate to the truths he knew from his religion. It is impossible to overstate the importance of Mohammed's statement, "To Muslims, religion is not just a part of life. It is, in fact, life that is a part of religion." Not only is life a part of religion, so are knowledge, education, and rhetoric. For many believers in Islam, as in other religions, religion transcends political, economic, and social boundaries, holding stronger claims on their behaviors and allegiances. Although Mohammed, who several times in his essay invoked the support of "Muslims all over the world," stopped short of calling for Rushdie's death because the novelist was living in a non-Islamic state, he also said that recognizing the national boundaries and distinctions of civil law was something he could do in his head, but not deep in his heart. There was no meaningful response I could have made to Mohammed's writing from a purely secular tradition when his words and his rhetoric were so completely a matter of faith for him.

Just as important to our impasse was my inability to articulate how issues of power, politics, history, and hybridity shaped the controversy in general and both of our responses in particular. Although many would try to separate religion and politics, literacy practices are inherently connected to systems and displays of power, and therefore religions that find some authority in print inevitably connect spiritual literacy events with power and politics (Kapitzke 1999, 117). The nature of power invested in priesthoods has often been based on who gets to write, read, and interpret religious texts. Discourse is indeed power, and those who control the discourse of religion in a deeply religious culture can control political and social power. In the Christian tradition, for example, such authority in the power of priests and ministers to interpret the Bible has often supported the political status quo or, in the case of the U.S. civil rights movement or the Solidarity movement in Poland, created a moral basis for resistance to civil authority. Islamic clerics performed a similar function of resistance in the Iranian revolution of the 1970s. In the case of *The Satanic Verses*, the religious power and authority of the Ayatollah Khomeni to interpret and define the work for millions of Muslims as blasphemous was also a political act with both domestic and international implications. My conflict with Mohammed stemmed in part from his qualified acceptance of, and my objection to, the political consequences of the religious interpretation.

Certainly the controversy about *The Satanic Verses* was as much about power, politics, and the legacy of colonialism as it was about religious doctrine. My reading of the controversial parts of the novel was as a critique of how extreme political forces had used religion to repress millions of people. The debate about the book sped across national borders on the airwaves and pages of global media and ranged from questions of freedom of expression to the role of religion in society to the politics of reading and literacy. Although nation-states were involved, the issue focused on the conflict between a Western secular worldview and an Islamic religious worldview. Postcolonial theorist Arjun Appadurai, in writing about the fluid and often conflicting nature of global cultural forces, says the affair was about a "text-in-motion" that moved beyond its origins in Western cultural concepts of artistic freedom and into the realm of religious scholars and theological debates about "blasphemy" (1996, 9)—a term which itself seems antique to the Western academic ear. Yet if it was about a text-in-motion it was also about writers- and readers-in-motion and even faith-in-motion that brought the divergent ideas into direct contact. Appadurai notes that the global movement of texts and readers "create[s] implosive events that fold global pressures into small, already politicized arenas, producing locality in new globalized ways" (9). Mohammed and I were inside one such politicized arena, trying to talk to each other under the weight of global political, cultural, and economic forces we could only understand incompletely.

Although Mohammed's essay was written by one student for one instructor, it situated us in historical forces and contemporary power relationships that we could not fully recognize or articulate. Mohammed understood that the Rushdie controversy was about more than the blasphemous material in a single book. In describing how he believed the majority of Muslims approved of the death sentence against Rushdie, he wrote:

> The mass of the Muslim poor, who feel their religion and culture have been humiliated by the West for too long, are unlikely to consider the complex issues involved in this very complex case. Most of them live in conditions of misery unimaginable in the West and feel that all they have in this world is their religious faith. Today they are being told by the Mullahs that even this is being threatened by the West and its allies.

In this controversy, in Mohammed's essay, in my responses to his work and my teaching approaches in the classroom, there was a history of Western political and cultural imperialism that remained a powerfully disturbing force. Clearly I was in a position of power in relationship to these students, not just because I was their teacher, but also because I was a member of the Western secular culture in which they felt estranged; in which they had to try to adapt their behaviors; in which they could only write about their concerns and complaints in the language of the culture that had, and continued to, humiliate and threaten them. As a member of a wealthy Omani family who was in England getting a degree in International Business from a Western institution, Mohammed was hardly a member of the "mass of the Muslim poor." There was nothing politically radical about him. And yet the lines from his essay about the humiliations suffered by Muslims at the hands of West—humiliations in which he identifies himself with Muslims who live in deep poverty—contain a clear-eyed anger and frustration that transcend lines of class and nationality and cannot be ignored. Though Mohammed was a soft-spoken, gentle person, it is also worth pondering that the majority of hijackers in the September 11 attacks were well-educated young men from middle- and upper-class families who felt the sting of Western humiliations in ways similar to those Mohammed had described so many years before.

In my discussions with Mohammed issues of religious authority and freedom of expression dominated our conversations. Not only don't I recall talking about the excerpt I quoted above, I didn't remember it being in the essay until I reread it several years later. In retrospect I think I found the passage and the ideas intimidating, not from some imagined threat, but from a lack of confidence that I could enter a conversation on the subject and not somehow make it worse. Multicultural pedagogy, as focused as it is on individual behavior and beliefs, is not always effective at dealing with structural power inequities. I'm sure I understood and sympathized with Mohammed's statements and feelings, but at the time could have done little better than offer a weak individual apology that would have been beside the point and expressed primarily to absolve myself of responsibilities for my continuing position of privilege. So I sidestepped the issue.

In the years since that class I have become more able to recognize how my position of power and privilege in regard to those students resulted from the cultural structure I inhabited, reproduced, and benefited from. Homi Bhabha criticizes the attempts of multiculturalists to seek a happy Disney-like pluralism as not recognizing the "disjunctive, 'borderline' temporalities of partial, minority cultures" (1996, 56). The multicultural approach with its emphasis on individual agency and tolerance does not recognize the "construction of cultural authority within conditions of political antagonism or inequity" (58). Had such thoughts been available to me in my discussions with Mohammed I would have been better able to see the intersections and articulations of how global religion, politics, and power played out in our local interactions. In later classes with international students I worked differently, often using postcolonial theory to engage such issues, with varying levels of success.[6]

## Keeping the Conversation Going

Aside from employing concepts of postcolonial theory, what could I have done differently with Mohammed? I believed in free expression and the defense of unpopular ideas. I saw the limits on the free exchange of ideas as a fundamental denial of human rights and a significant problem in many cultures. He believed in "Hodud," in rules that govern what can and cannot be discussed as a way of maintaining a just and moral culture. He wrote, "Muslims cannot understand a concept that has no rules, no limits. The Western belief in human rights, which seems to lack limits, is alien to Islamic traditions." Indeed in our discussions he saw this lack of limits as the source of many of the problems in the United States and Europe such as crime, divorce, and substance abuse. It also reflected how Islam can be used, in the same way Christianity often is, as a response to what is perceived as a postmodern culture spinning out of control.

For all of my professed defense of "freedom of expression," however, I know that such an ideal has many economic, political, and cultural constraints in the West. My individual tolerance in a multicultural setting is limited not simply by my personal tastes, but by the systemic power considerations of the dominant culture. The paradox of what I would accept or reject from students in a class where I asked them to "write about issues important to them," is not simply a matter of personal beliefs, but stems from the collision between the professed values of a culture and the real, but often unarticulated, constraints of the structures of power. Indeed, had Mohammed's essay advocated the killing of Salman Rushdie, my dedication to free expression would have ended at that moment, and I would have told him that I could not accept an essay that advocated murder. In the end, however, I was not going to force him to recant his beliefs or risk the punishment of a bad grade. Forcing his assimilation into the cultural views of the dominant culture would be only perpetuate the kind of imperialist humiliation that he was speaking out against.

It is tempting to say that we should have just "agreed to disagree"; such cultural relativism is one logical endpoint of multiculturalism. It is the fundamental problem with the concept of teaching "tolerance" as individual responses to individual actions, and has been justifiably criticized by scholars both on the right and the left. Although we cannot simply shake our heads and see our cultural differences as absolutely insurmountable, a complete cultural relativism is also an undesirable impossibility.

I could have adopted a third approach and encouraged Mohammed to produce hybrid texts that drew on both cultural traditions. Such a strategy can produce dynamic, creative works that help to erase some of the boundaries that exist within contact zones (Pratt 1991). Here there is a risk as well. Hybrid texts on religious issues could trigger collisions of values and discourses that would obscure the meaning of the texts for members of both cultures. Just as Pratt maintained that cross-cultural contact zones could produce new forms and voices to energize a society, such spaces can also result in "miscomprehension, incomprehension, dead letters, unread masterpieces, (and) absolute heterogeneity of meaning" (Pratt 1991, 37). There are moments when the stakes are too high to risk such misunderstandings, situations where the clear communication of positions are too important to gamble with hybrid forms of writing that may not be comprehensible to those on either side of the contact zone.

Because the stakes in cross-cultural communication are so high, we as teachers need to learn how to examine and interrogate rhetorical situations in contact zones, not in the expectation of persuasion, but with a goal of continuing dialogue and increasing understanding on all sides. Rather than begin with agonistic argument, we should adapt the work of Chaim Perelman and first engage students in a dialogue about the underlying values and assumptions that structure our positions. Such conversations help both sides understand more about each other's cultures and create possibilities for finding mutual areas of agreement. Only after engaging in such a dialogue should we proceed to discussions of what divides us.

Mohammed and I could have examined my assumptions about the value of free speech. What kinds of constraints—political, economic, and social— do we place on free expression in the West? Why do I regard those as acceptable but not religious constraints? Is acting from reason and rationality always preferable? How are cross-cultural issues of religious faith inextricable from issues of power and political and cultural domination? To what extent can I expect students from other cultures to question religious beliefs that order their way of experiencing the world? For Mohammed it could have meant asking questions about the intersections of politics and religion, such as the ones he was already touching on in his essay, and how such intersections influence how religion is perceived and practiced. It would have meant asking questions about how cross-cultural conflicts could be resolved, about the nature of individual rights, about interactions as a person of faith finding himself inhabiting a secular dominant culture.

Discussing these questions we would have clarified the nature and sources of our values as well as the often inherent contradictions. We might also have recognized the values we shared: a hope for a peaceful society, a reverence for learning and books, the need for religious expression, the desire for self-determination. Could he have persuaded me to call for the banning of *The Satanic Verses*? Could I have persuaded him to read the novel from a secular, Western point of view? Both possibilities strike me as unlikely. Yet perhaps those are the wrong questions. The more useful question might be whether we could we have used the tools of rhetoric to maintain a civil dialogue to open the possibility for greater understanding and possibly more genuine, pragmatic negotiation.

There are no simple solutions to cross-cultural conflicts involving faith and rhetoric. Yet it is folly to imagine that they are not already in the classroom with us. We must bring religion into open discussion—including our own backgrounds and feelings—so that we can engage in thoughtful conversations about its influence on how we write and read. This is not easy for me to advocate, because I still believe at a fundamental level that the classroom is a secular, humanist environment. If we don't address these issues directly, however, they will still emerge, but in ways that anger and frustrate both teacher and students. Had I discussed religion and its influences more openly with my students, I would have been better able to respond not only to Mohammed's essay but also to the writing of other students, be they Buddhists, Hindus, Jews, or Christians.

I kept Mohammed's essay for a number of years, long before I ever considered writing about it, because our interaction and the issues involved continued to intrigue and trouble me. As I have reread it over the years, and read other works about cross-cultural rhetoric and postcolonial theory, I have come to a better understanding of Mohammed's position and culture. I have a better sense of the religious reverence for books in Islamic culture that is different from the secular way I read, and of how a scholar can reconcile a literal interpretation of the Koran with intellectual curiosity.

A clear sense of principles, and a willingness to define and defend them, is important for the creation of a moral identity and a moral society. Yet the consequences of what happens when deeply held principles collide in the public space is no longer simply an academic question. It was easy, at one time, in the United States to imagine that religious conflicts happened in faraway places such as Northern Ireland, or India and Pakistan, or Israel and Palestine.

Yet recently we in the United States have had a tragic reminder of how religion has become the focus and means of expression for the humiliation and anger that Mohammed described more than a decade ago. As a teacher and as a Quaker I cannot believe that the ultimate answer to this anger and violence is more anger and violence. Though the recent rhetoric on all sides may be focused on hatred and retribution, I believe that in the end the only way to find peace and inhabit the same world is through continued dialogue.

It is true that Mohammed and I did not change our positions on the conflict of secular free expression versus sacred respect for religion. Yet we continued to talk. We continued to learn. Any rhetorical situation in which conversation and learning continues has to be considered successful. We cannot expect we will always persuade those who disagree with us, or even reach a complete compromise. Still, now more than ever, we must keep the conversation going.

## Notes

1. I prefer the term *cross-cultural* to *multicultural* to refer to the contact of individuals from different cultures because it emphasizes how each culture in such a setting must cross boundaries to come into contact with others, rather than implying that there is a dominant culture that tolerates an undifferentiated margin of multiple cultures.

2. In this essay I use the terms *multiculturalism* and *multicultural* to refer to philosophies and pedagogies based on a foundation of liberal humanist principles.

3. It is worth considering that it was a multiculturalist emphasis on tolerance and, by extension, my overt willingness expressed to the class to read essays "on any subject you feel is important for you to write about" that allowed Mohammed to feel he could bring such an honest essay to me and that I would not reject it out of hand. The paradox of secular tolerance and openness, of course, is that it is often tested by ideas we find unpalatable or distasteful. And, as I mentioned above, religion can be the source or justification for such ideas in ways that threaten our most deeply held values.

4. For a more detailed discussion of the complex issues confronting writing pedagogy in such a cross-cultural setting, see Williams, Bronwyn T. 2003. "Speak for Yourself? Power and Hybridity in the Cross-Cultural Classroom." *College Composition and Communication* 54 (4): 586–609.

5. As Juanita Smart notes in Chapter 2, this is also a source of conflict for teachers and fundamentalist or evangelical students in the United States.

6. See Williams, Bronwyn T. 2003. "Speak for Yourself? Power and Hybridity in the Cross-Cultural Classroom." *College Composition and Communication* 54 (4): 586–609.

## Works Cited

Anderson, Chris. 1989. "The Description of an Embarrassment: When Students Write About Religion." *ADE Bulletin* 94: 12–15.

Anderson, Janice Walker. 1991. "A Comparison of Arab and American Conceptions of 'Effective' Persuasion." In *Intercultural Communication*, edited by Larry A. Samovar and Richard E. Porter, 96–106. 6th ed. Belmont, CA: Wadsworth.

Appadurai, Arjun. 1996. *Modernity at Large: Cultural Dimensions of Globalization.* Minneapolis: University of Minnesota Press.

Aristotle. 1984. *Rhetoric.* New York: McGraw-Hill.

Bhabha, Homi. 1996. "Culture's In-Between." In *Questions of Cultural Identity*, edited by Stuart Hall and Paul du Gay, 53–60. London: Sage.

Buscemi, Santi, Albert Nicolai, and Richard Strugala. 1997. *The Basics: A Rhetoric and Handbook.* 2d ed. New York: McGraw-Hill.

Connors, Robert, and Andrea Lunsford. 1996. *The St. Martin's Handbook.* 3rd ed. New York: St. Martin's Press.

Daniell, Beth. 1994. "Composing (as) Power." *College Composition and Communication* 45 (2): 238–46.

Divakaruni, Chitra B., Ed. 1997. *Multitude: Cross-Cultural Readings for Writers.* 2d ed. New York: McGraw-Hill.

Dively, Rhonda Leathers. 1997. "Censoring Religious Rhetoric in the Composition Classroom: What We and Our Students May Be Missing." *Composition Studies* 25 (1): 55–66.

Elbow, Peter. 2000. *Everyone Can Write: Essays Toward a Hopeful Theory of Writing and Teaching Writing.* Oxford: Oxford University Press.

Fox, Helen. 1994. *Listening to the World: Cultural Issues in Academic Writing.* Urbana, IL: NCTE.

Hacker, Diana. 1999. *A Writer's Reference.* 4th ed. Boston: Bedford/St. Martin's.

Kapitzke, Cushla. 1999. "Literacy and Religion: The Word, the Holy Word, and the World." In *Literacy: An International Handbook*, edited by Daniel A. Wagner, Richard L. Venezky, and Brian V. Street, 113–18. Boulder, CO: Westview Press.

Knepler, Myrna, Annie Knepler, and Elinor Knepler. 2002. *Crossing Cultures: Readings for Composition.* 6th ed. Boston: Allyn and Bacon.

Lisle, Bonnie, and Sandra Mano. 1997. "Embracing a Multicultural Rhetoric" In *Writing in Multicultural Settings*, edited by Carol Severino, Juan C. Guerra, and Johnnella E. Butler, 12–26. New York: MLA.

New England Yearly Meeting of Friends. 1986. *Faith and Practice of New England Yearly Meeting of Friends.* Worcester, MA: New England Yearly Meeting of Friends.

Payne, Michelle. 2000. *Bodily Discourses: When Students Write About Abuse and Eating Disorders.* Portsmouth, NH: Boynton/Cook.

Perelman, Chaim. 1997. "The New Rhetoric: A Theory of Practical Reasoning." In *The Rhetoric of Western Thought*, edited by James L. Golden, Goodwin F. Berquist, and William E. Coleman, 234–52. 6th ed. Dubuque, IA: Kendall/Hunt.

Pratt, Mary Louise. 1991. "Arts of the Contact Zone." In *Profession 91*, 33–40. New York: MLA.

Rand, Lizabeth A. 2001. "Enacting Faith: Evangelical Discourse and the Discipline of Composition Studies." *College Composition and Communication* 52 (3): 349–67.

Stanford, Judith. 2001. *Connections: Reading and Writing in Cultural Contexts.* 3rd ed. New York: McGraw-Hill.

Negotiating Cultural Divides

Verburg, Carol J., ed. 1997 *Making Contact: Readings from Home and Abroad*. Boston: Bedford/St. Martin's.

Wurzel, Jaime S. 1988. "Multiculturalism and the Human Condition." In *Toward Multiculturalism*, edited by Jaime S. Wurzel, 1–14. Yarmouth, ME: Intercultural Press.

# 10

# African American Students of Faith in the Writing Center
## *Facilitating a Rhetoric of Conscience*

### Brad Peters

## Academic Exorcisms

In 1994, a groundbreaking interchange among Ann Berthoff, Beth Daniell, JoAnn Campbell, Jan Swearingen, and James Moffett on "Spiritual Sites of Composing" in *College Composition and Communication* (*CCC*) opened areas of inquiry that many scholars and instructors in rhetoric-composition might have considered beyond the scope of the writing classroom. As a result—and as this volume substantively argues—scholars in our discipline are just beginning to explore how to work effectively with students of various religious faiths who bring their faith into their writing. Why? As two of the 1994 interchange participants asserted, "public education sometimes alienates rather than enlightens" precisely because "it fails to take seriously the spiritual and religious values of students . . . " (Daniell, paraphrasing Moffett 1994, 239).

Meanwhile, composition studies have yielded a body of critical research that illuminates the literacies of African American students of the Christian faith[1] whose academic writing is especially influenced by faith-based literacy events in church such as memorizing Bible verses, reading scripture aloud, interpreting hymns, and participating in sermons as a community text (e.g., Smitherman 1977; Balester 1993; Moss 1994, 2001, 2002; Gilyard and Richardson 2001; Richardson 2003).[2] We have not sufficiently tapped this resource, perhaps because many of us believe we do not have adequate cultural or linguistic knowledge to help—let alone instruct—African American students of faith so they can, as Holmes puts it, *write black*, "neither in terms of protest against nor in reverent imitation of mainstream discourse," but from a distinct, African American worldview (1999, 56). Nonetheless, Holmes finds that such "neither/nor" writing can become an outgrowth of "mutual influencing," "a melding together of a new American culture" (55).

I was reminded of Holmes' assertions and the claims that the *CCC* interchange posed when an African American student brought a research paper on capital punishment to the Writing Center I direct. Our Center serves a Midwestern research university with 24,000 students from urban and rural areas alike. Although this African American student's instructor had not provided an assignment sheet, the student's draft clearly showed that the assignment emphasized classical arrangement: introduction, statement of fact (or problem), thesis, preview of analytical method, support of thesis, refutation, and conclusion.

In her essay, the student had conflated her introduction and statement of fact, referring to the U.S. Constitutional and Bill of Rights' guarantee that all people have a right to life. In her thesis, she claimed that capital punishment as practiced in the United States contradicts those guarantees, because the courts "play God" with human life. In her analytical preview, she said she would summarize a three-part series on capital punishment from the *Chicago Tribune*, and then she would elaborate on how capital punishment went contrary to God's will. Her summary of thesis support—the most detailed, lengthy part of her draft—detailed how courts admit (1) unreliable witnesses, (2) confessions obtained from police torture, (3) questionable evidence, and (4) incompetent legal defense to adjudicate the death penalty for too many innocent people. Her refutation implied that even the most indisputably guilty criminals might repent their crimes and get right with God, if the death penalty didn't foreclose that possibility and violate a spiritual law—the sixth of the Ten Commandments: "Thou shalt not kill" (Exodus 20:1–17). If the United States defined itself as a Christian nation, she argued, this situation was not acceptable. Her concluding appeal to conscience was that the United States should abolish capital punishment.

Because her draft was still a work in progress, the student had some revising to do. But from the "traditional" academic perspective, the student demonstrated a keen understanding of the assignment and had already addressed it successfully in terms of arrangement. Moreover, she seemed to have a reasonable instinct for what strategies might move public conscience. Why, then, had her instructor written on her draft: "Hopeless paper. Go to the Writing Center"?

One of our most capable tutors began working with the student. The tutor focused first on what Beverly Moss also tells her African American students: "[I]n an academic essay, citing the Bible as the ultimate authority is not always the most appropriate strategy" (2001, 201). From there, the session went badly. The student did not respond, even though the tutor noted many things the student had accomplished in her draft and tried to move on to other concerns that they could address together. When the student left, I suspected we'd never see her again—and I was right.

Afterward, I asked the tutor why she'd immediately taken aim at the religious features of the essay instead of letting the student set the agenda (as this consultant usually did). The tutor replied that in our first-year composition program: "Some T.A.s won't even accept a paper when students quote the Bible or mention God."

The tutor and I talked about alternative ways to conduct such a session. Much that we discussed resonates with Nancy Grimm's suggestion that while the student's African American sermonic discourse contrasted sharply with academic discourse, "the academic view is not necessarily more 'right'" (1999, 23). We even saw how the student could have used an academic view to defend her appeal to conscience, with slightly different strategies of reasoning, e.g., noting an alliance of views between African American and Roman Catholic churches, the latter of which has helped sway other nations' laws regarding capital punishment. Such an approach could have helped the student see how a religious content could support an academic goal (see Grimm 1999, 25).

Yet the tutor and I failed to discuss the uniquely African American strategies that the student could have built on to make her faith-based appeal to public conscience more effective. We assumed that the student needed to exorcise not only God, but also African American features from her draft, even if these were the places where her writing most powerfully showed her commitment to her topic, her opportunity to influence a wider readership, and her ability to meld culturally different discourses.

Since this incident, I've been rethinking how we can encourage African American students of faith to draw on the discursive features of African American Vernacular English (AAVE) to improve their writing.[3] What, for example, might have become of the student's draft had she been encouraged to state outright in her essay that she intended to provide an expressly African American, religious perspective on capital punishment and explained the importance of this perspective? Would a more cogent sense of audience have emerged if she had been advised to write *with soul* to an academy that doesn't really know what to do with one? And how might this young woman (categorized as "at risk" by the university placement system as well as by her writing instructor) have been better guided to invent her academic ethos, using the discourse patterns she'd probably heard repeatedly in church?

In her scholarly examination of faith-based writing in the Writing Center, Grimm begins to address such questions by suggesting that tutors must tell students of faith up front that they are among the marginalized ones who "will have to work harder and smarter than most ['mainstream'] students to be successful," since public, state-funded universities (along with many private ones) were "not designed with them in mind" (1999, 104). Moreover, Grimm's Writing Center experience confirms that tutoring and writing instruction "either ignore religious identification or provide primarily negative representations of religiosity" (116; see also Penti 1992). Yet Grimm believes that if we recognize the literacies of students of faith, we will "learn more about [their] literacies and cultural worldviews," even while we help them access and develop the (possibly melded) discourses that can serve them best in formal academic settings (24). Then we'd avoid the egregious blindness that prevents us from recognizing when such students—particularly African American students of faith—are making successful transitions from their own literacies to the literacies that the academy prizes.

But better—if, as Daniell and Moffett urge, Writing Center tutors and writing instructors *do* decide to "take seriously the spiritual and religious values of students," I believe we need to deploy what I call a "rhetoric of conscience." In the pages that follow, I suggest how a historical perspective of a rhetoric of conscience illuminates and reinforces scholarship that has explored ethical questions about faith-based writing, specifically from an African American perspective. Then, by deliberating on AAVE *techne* that African American students of faith might effectively deploy in a rhetoric of conscience, I provide an analogue to the failed Writing Center session I've recounted.

## Conscience as a Topos

Similar to our discipline's limited but important scholarship on the right of African American students of faith to their own language, a rhetoric of conscience showcases the negative effects of foundational thinking on all students of faith. The following discussion will trace how both a rhetoric of conscience and our discipline's ethical perspectives on AAVE encourage a more egalitarian stance that eschews the notion of one dogmatic Truth, one standard for language, and an insistence on consensus by majority.

Walter Jost, a scholar of religious rhetoric, observes that the nineteenth-century English prelate and theologian John Henry Newman identifies two contradictory views about religious belief: (1) "that faith in God and religious truths were objectively provable—or refutable—by 'enlightened' (which is to say, secular) reason"; and (2) that "they were a matter of romantic feelings, private intuitions, or will" (Jost 2000, 102). Newman attempts to ameliorate the problem by positioning Christian belief and action within his notion of the human conscience. Defining conscience as a dynamic topos of rhetorical invention that stands—as science itself—"on antecedent first principles that are unprovable in any scientific way," Newman demonstrates that these principles derive from a *sensus communis* of "experiences, beliefs, opinions, judgments, actions that are not reducible to empirical fact, to logical or statistical calculation, or to epistemological or ontological determinacies" (108, 103). Noteworthy for its socially constructed nature, Newman's definition of conscience connects with a "Someone" who is superior and external to individuals, i.e., God, who has created human conscience as the "rule" (or measure) for determining what is "real" (see 106). Individuals thus tolerate others' spiritual experiences to the extent, and under the conviction, that conscience compels in each a personal, prudent judgment that keeps her critical consciousness in line with God's judgment and mercy (104). Accordingly, Newman identifies conscience as the universal foundation that persuades disparate members of Christendom, each with different spiritual experiences, to seek unity in faith while working toward a greater common good.

Scholars in rhetoric-composition may see that Newman's position resembles a kind of foundational reasoning that avers that students should know and accept certain tenets about writing—the practice of classical rhetoric, for instance—so as to contribute more effectively to responsible civic action (see Stotsky 1992). Sheryl Fontaine and Susan Hunter note that here "the goal is to . . . control or guide behavior in students' writing, in the classroom, in the office, in our departments and programs, at professional meetings, and so forth" (1998, 2). From the start, unfortunately, this foundational approach leaves students whose rhetorical skills draw from AAVE, as it is practiced in African American churches, at a disadvantage. Richardson explains that "Students want to learn standardized American English conventions, and to become skilled rhetors, but these are often presented as neutral practices, isolated from the history of power relations and the politics of literacy" (2003, 2). Writing Center tutoring and classroom instruction, so informed, advises such students to relinquish the language of their local community for that of the dominant one, often erasing an African American student's meaning in her faith-based writing (2).

To compensate for this kind of ethical failure, Jost updates Newman's doctrine with Michael Novak's concept of "intelligent subjectivity" and Stanley Cavell's notions of the "criteria" and "acknowledgements" that mark human conscience (Novak 1994; Cavell 1972). Novak suggests that in developing intelligent subjectivity, a person of faith enables her "human ongoing drive to understand" by engaging "in civil conversation" with community voices that differ from hers, to help her shape her "spiritual awareness, insight, and judgment" (Jost 2000, 110–11). Civil conversation with others helps the person of faith discern analogically what makes sense, so she can align "God-talk" and her own intelligent subjectivity as she works toward "a meaningful order that can survive criticism" of the community (113, 1l0–11). Therefore, for Novak, conscience becomes an inexorable impulse rather than a rule, and the stabilizing arbitrator of knowledge of the self-in-the-world, even as that knowledge—shaped by community—continues to change and, in turn, effects change upon the self.

Novak's position on conscience resembles the pluralistic approach that scholars in rhetoric-composition have taken in theorizing the ethics of community. In such instances, Fontaine and Hunter note that we try to create communities of students and scholars who aim for consensus by negotiating "contradictions and conflicts," because such negotiation always raises ethical sensibility

(1998, 3). But these kinds of "consensual discussions" can still seem (or indeed become) coercive to some participants, who infer that negotiation really means the victory of the majority, even when—or especially when—pervasive and ongoing social wrongs have clearly shaped the minority's personal values, and the majority does not acknowledge or sense its role in sustaining those wrongs. Too often, this is the case with African American students.

Such implicit coercion not only works against the development of intelligent subjectivity, but can also incite an African American student of faith to respond with scriptural recitation, religious catchphrases, indignation, or anger to challenges to her beliefs (e.g., when an African American student of faith feels that her own authority has been publicly disrespected). Why? Because, as Moss observes:

> Helping [African American] students understand that the academy resists the view that ultimate authority rests in any one text [or person, or group], even the Bible [or Jesus, or a pastor], often means asking students to think in a manner that differs significantly from the ways they've been taught to think in their home community. (2001, 201)

Tutoring or classroom instruction, so conducted, may therefore send the message that a consensus on matters such as spiritual awareness, insight, and judgment (the same as Standard American English) is the possession of one group—and as Richardson says, African American students of faith may infer that strong, socially conscious black people are not included in that group (2003, 3).

Jost is alert to such problems and remedies them by adapting Cavell's concept of "criteria" (that which we use to justify our own belief and action) and "acknowledgment" (how we measure others and the world itself) (2000, 113). The Christian concept of confession illustrates how Cavell's notion of criteria functions: in confession, conscience prompts a believer to evaluate her moral character, realign it with Christ's, and alter her active life in the world. In a related sense, Cavell's notion of acknowledgment expands on conscience as a force that "calls us back to our practical interest in the world" (see Jost 2000, 116). For Cavell, this call to conscience does not function uncritically, but compels a person of faith "to identify the world and identify with it," while prompting her to try "to change those identifications when [she] encounter[s] aporias, contradictions, and the like" (119). In other words, Cavell's definition of conscience comes from claims that other human beings put on a person of faith as she confronts an imperfect society that needs her personal spiritual insights, compassionate awareness, and worldly involvement (117). In this way, a person of faith will not succumb to the implicit assumption that Novak fails to anticipate; i.e., that the majority has a right to silence the minority— which indeed, African American scholars have recognized as a problem all along. Rather, she will learn to use her intelligent subjectivity to assert that consensus becomes the means by which the majority agrees to do the hard work of listening closely to a minority's personal experiences, of examining itself critically, and of ceasing its participation (passive as well as active) in the social wrongs that keep the majority and the minority from actualizing common aims.

This final approach provides neither a particular ethical code nor restricts itself to consensus, but instead adopts a dynamic of critical ethical awareness that is at once profoundly socially oriented and subjective. Fontaine and Hunter, in the spirit of Jost, view this third approach as one that requires us constantly to heed such alternative discourses as those which African American students of faith may reproduce, to take stock of our values and obligations in all of our changing disciplinary situations, where simple or partial answers to perplexing social issues, old and new, must not prevail or shut down the need for persistent inquiry and consequent action (1998, 4–5).

This final faith-ethics connection opens the way for African American students to exploit the discursive features of AAVE that will most effectively help them develop intelligent subjectivity and ethical awareness. Through AAVE they can thus develop an academic *ethos* that bears witness "to the efficacy, truth, and power of some experience in which all blacks have shared" (Smitherman 1977, 58). At the same time, this final faith-ethics connection informs Writing Center tutors and classroom instructors that when a faith-based rhetoric of conscience appears in African American students' academic writing, that rhetoric most often marks the writer's intent to get her readers to do the right thing—because arguably, this is the rhetoric by which the African American community participates in self-transformation, consensus-making, social reform, and unified action (see Balester 1993, 43–45). Tutors and instructors need to ask how such discourse can represent—and/or be shaped into—the writer's best available means of persuasion.

Jost's historical tracing and assessment of a rhetoric of conscience significantly elucidates the work that rhetoric-composition has already done to resist such concepts as one standard of English, which represents what Ann Berthoff denounces as "positivism . . . a variant of context-free ideology" (1994, 238). Equally important, Jost validates all spiritual literacies as the speculative instruments of writing for students of faith. So theorized, a rhetoric of conscience can guide students toward imagining how they might change cultural practices; it can show writing tutors and instructors how to teach more inclusively; it can indicate how we all might become more equitable human beings, while avoiding "utopian vagueness or partisan passion" (Berthoff 1994, 238).

But "how?" is the key question. How do we apply such a faith-ethics connection to a pedagogy that does not alienate African American students of faith from their spiritual literacies? Only if we prompt them to access and work effectively with the *techne* that those spiritual literacies deploy can we anticipate and forestall remarks such as "Hopeless paper. Go to the Writing Center."

# Responding to Faith-Based Writing

Scholars of AAVE have established that for many Christian (and indeed, non-Christian) African Americans, sermonic discourse has a pervasive influence on all other levels of AAVE discourse (Balester 1993, 82, 93; Smitherman 1977, 55–56). Although formal genres such as sermons and prayers follow an established arrangement (e.g., biblical text, "thematic bridges" to secular experience, call-and-response, and peroration—usually a petition for divine guidance), sermonic discourse also demonstrates the informal, unstructured, and conversational features of a tradition that challenges a more systematic rhetoric (Moss 2001, 202–207; Balester 1993, 43–44). Why? Moss says that if African American sermonic discourse were too prescribed, it would foreclose the congregation's participation—or what Moss calls the congregational text—which provides evidence that the persuasive act is infusing both speaker and listener with the Holy Spirit (2001, 203). It follows that when African American students of faith write sermonic discourse, they might well expect response and write with response in mind. For tutors and instructors, the crucial part is knowing African American sermonic discourse strategies well enough to shape our response appropriately.

To do so, it helps to know from the start that African American sermonic discourse serves as what Jost would call a *rhetorica utens* in its basic task of finding first principles and organizing religious growth (2000, 98). Tutors and instructors can thus look not only for first principles in African American students' sermonic discourse, but also notice how those principles are arranged. This approach yields useful insights for the writer as well as the tutor or instructor. For example, in the draft that I summarized at the beginning of this essay, the student opened her argument against capital punishment with a secular first principle: the constitutionally guaranteed right to life. She offered her faith-based first principle only in her refutation, when she claimed that all human life comes from God and can be redeemed by God. She felt this *logos* should serve as a foundation for the U.S. justice system. It seems she intended to guide her readers first by the secular evidence that she had gathered—to align them with the constitutional principle—and then to introduce the idea that this constitutional principle derived from the sacred one.

This kind of analysis gives tutors and instructors several points of entry to ask questions that don't require a student of faith to justify her beliefs so much as to clarify them. It also affirms the logic of her beliefs. Indeed, a student who is developing such a *logos* would revise better, should a tutor or instructor ask questions that give the student the opportunity (1) to explain her strategy for developing the beginning of her draft from the constitutional first principle and (2) to discuss her strategy for arguing—in her refutation—from the faith-based principle that informs the constitutional one. Tutors and instructors could ask the student what audience would be most persuaded by such a logic of arrangement. What does the student assume about the moral and the spiritual beliefs of this audience, if she reasons that they will examine their own motives, once they are subjected to a *logos* that essentially challenges them not to judge if they do not want to be judged? How and why might she want to reveal that her argument reflects a commonly held value in the African American Christian community?

Equally important, tutors and instructors should recognize that African American sermonic discourse serves as what Jost would call a *rhetorica docens*. A *rhetorica docens* provides a writer with a *techne* that helps her avoid "the figure of the self alone with itself and its God," positioning her instead as an active participant in a well-defined community and in the wider world, where she must acknowledge and be acknowledged by others (Jost 2000, 120–21). Accordingly, this *techne* can help African American writers avoid the problems we associate with uses of the personal that Suzanne Clark tactfully calls "excess not easily retrofitted to the norm" (1998, 98). Furthermore, understanding this *techne*, tutors and instructors can respond more knowledgeably to students of faith who are its heirs. I will, therefore, list some discourse features that belong to the *techne* and then suggest how the knowledge of them might lead to a more successful Writing Center session than the one I recounted.

I limit this *techne* of African American sermonic discourse features to the ones that the student specifically used, because a comprehensive list remains contested. The student's repertoire includes:

- Expressions of deeply felt, faith-inspired emotions

- Expressions of affirmation and reaffirmation of belief

- Dialogue-like structures that resemble call-and-response

- Rhythmic or rhyming language (musicality)

- Proverbial sayings and paraphrased or quoted scripture

- Storytelling to implicitly emphasize a point (narrative sequencing)

- Field dependency (personalization of broader social events, phenomena, and situations)

- "Double-voicedness" (addressing two audiences—one is usually black, the other white—who, as intended, get two different meanings)

- Associated serial segments implicitly linked to a topic

- Signifying (an often witty, indirect critique aimed at someone present— possibly even a reader of a writer's text—that ritually draws on the full repertoire of other African American discourse features)[4]

The drafted essay on capital punishment that I have so far referenced draws richly from the discourse features above. For example, the student's secular thesis support is, in effect, a narrative sequence of the unreliable witnesses, coerced confessions, questionable evidence, and incompetent legal defense that have led to unjust death sentences. The student structures this narrative sequence as a call and response: she tells a story first, as if it were a "call" (e.g., a story about a well-known "snitch" who offered testimony against alleged malefactors in exchange for lighter sentencing for his own crimes), and then responds by describing the problem (e.g., she reconfirmed the snitch's motives for serving as a witness, and explained why this was faulty evidence). Her tutor could have helped the student take her critique beyond a field-dependent, reiterative affirmation of the story's point by asking her who a reliable witness might be and what kind of evidence such a witness might present. The tutor could also have noted that the student rightly attributed the story and quotations to her sources in the *Chicago Tribune*, but that she needed to document that attribution in an accepted academic format. The tutor could then have modeled a citation and asked the student where she should do more of the same, prompting her to practice citation. Both of these initial tutorial responses build academically on the African American discourse features in the draft, yet do not precipitate a clash with the discourse or the values of faith it represents.

The student's narrative sequence also seems to have been written in a double voice that possibly, at one point, signifies to African American readers on the racialized nature of the U.S. justice system's flaws. She summarizes a *Tribune* story of how one death sentence was based on the evidence of two hairs found on a victim's body that could have belonged to the accused murderer. Yet she elaborates that hair analysis has proved faulty in too many cases, and she reinforces this information with rhyming language: "Death by a hair leads to death by the chair of the innocent men whose life cannot be shared."[5] Here, the tutor might ask if the student thought capital punishment was an example of racial profiling (the student did not mention race at all in the draft, only alluded to it). Such a question could open a discussion of racial profiling. Then the tutor could ask the student to reexamine her sources for evidence of this problem. Again, this kind of response *works with* discourse features that indicate an African American critique, while encouraging the student more fully to meld that critique with academic expectations.

Working on such issues would let the student know that even if she needs to make revisions, much of her thesis support rests on solid conceptual ground. Then the tutor could turn to the sermonic discourse in the student's refutation.

The student's refutation consisted of associated segments that linked indirectly with the topic of innocent people receiving the death sentence. She started by citing and explicating the Sixth Commandment ("Thou shalt not kill"). Once she explained her deeply felt, emotional conviction that God was the only rightful judge of life and death, she alluded to a scriptural commonplace that humanity is created in God's image, and then she quoted John 3:16 ("For God so loved the world that he gave his only begotten Son"). After that, the student noted that society might judge notorious killers such as Hitler and Jeffrey Daumer as worthy of death. But she reasoned that in God's eyes, no sin was greater than another, so no man should judge another.

In response to this faith-writing, the tutor might suggest that this idea would help form a topic sentence for her refutation: even abominable, guilty criminals deserved the chance to live and repent according to God's judgment. Then the tutor might ask which other associated segments in the student's refutation directly supported that idea. Thus, the student might consider which indirectly supportive—or unrelated—segments she could eliminate. Perhaps then, the tutor could ask the student how the main point of her refutation related to the constitutional principle that she'd stated in her introduction: a person's right to life. How could she make that relationship clearer; for example, to what extent did the constitutional principle seem to support what scripture revealed as God's principle? The most important concern, it seems, is that the student's refutation suffers from lack of explicit, logical sequencing, not from recourse to faith-based rant. Would this reordering and refining of the student's logic provide her the opportunity to build on her perspective as an African American student of faith? It might be appropriate to do so, because such a development of ethical awareness in this refutation does not exclude intelligent subjectivity.

Although this sketch of a tutoring protocol does not promise that such a Writing Center session would undo the negative impact of the instructor's labeling a student's draft "hopeless," it does indicate the possibility of providing an African American student of faith with the means to develop her critical powers without attempting to erase or repress her faith. In closing, I turn to Grimm's concern that the teaching of writing—as practiced by tutors and instructors alike—is indeed a frequent attempt to

> regulate not only white middle-class identity but also a coherent and unconflicted identity. The modernist evaluation criteria of clarity, coherence, and focus do not readily encourage students to explore the slippage between the identity their assignments call for and the identities formed by their lived experiences. (1999, 55)

For an African American student of faith, such an attempt to regulate creates a double bind that not only belittles her cultural discourse practices but also disregards the high value her spiritual literacies have taught her to place on textual interpretation and production. This discussion has been an attempt to imagine what might happen if, as a profession, we chose to consider how a student of faith's spiritual literacies—and the language with which she has acquired those literacies—could yield up a melding of discourse practices by which such a student might acquire academic literacy.

Not only students of faith, but *all* students need more opportunities to recognize and develop this skill in melding. Such opportunities urge them to examine how their beliefs could make an impact upon social practices outside the classroom—an impact that just might urge them as well to try to improve the world in which they live.

# Notes

1. By using this term—and later abbreviating it to "African American students of faith"—I mean to limit this essay to one specific group, even though, of course, I recognize that not all African American students practice Christianity or are churchgoing Christians.

2. Along with Moss, I borrow Heath's definition of *literacy event*—"Any activity involving one or more persons surrounding the comprehension of and/or production of print" (1982, 92).

3. Existing research indicates that African American students so encouraged demonstrate more improvement in writing courses than students who aren't (Smitherman 1994; Gilyard and Richardson 2001; Richardson 2003).

4. The above list is only partial but useful shorthand for an introductory understanding of a complex rhetoric that has formed in reaction to an unremitting history of social and economic inequity (see Smitherman 1977; Ball 1992; Gilyard and Richardson 2001; Richardson 2003).

5. Students in our Writing Center sign feedback forms to indicate that they give permission for us to cite very brief examples such as the one above for use in assessment, research, and tutor training. The student under discussion signed such a form. To protect confidentiality, we never identify names.

# Works Cited

Balester, Valerie. 1993. *Cultural Divide: A Study of African-American College-Level Writers*. Portsmouth, NH: Heinemann Boynton/Cook.

Ball, Arnetha. 1992. "Cultural Preference and the Expository Writing of African American Adolescents." *Written Communication* 9 (4): 501–32.

Berthoff, Ann. 1994. Introductory Remarks. In "Spiritual Sites of Composing." *College Composition and Communication* 45 (2): 237–38.

Campbell, JoAnn. 1994. "Writing to Heal: Using Meditation in the Writing Process." In "Interchanges: Spiritual Sites of Composing." *College Composition and Communication* 45 (2): 246–51.

Cavell, Stanley. 1972. *The Senses of Walden*. Chicago: University of Chicago Press.

———. 1979. *The Claim of Reason*. Oxford: Clarendon.

Clark, Suzanne. 1998. "Argument and Composition." In *Feminism and Composition Studies: In Other Words*, edited by Susan Jarratt and Lynn Worsham, 94–99. New York: Modern Language Association.

Daniell, Beth. 1994. "Composing (as) Power." In "Interchanges: Spiritual Sites of Composing." *College Composition and Communication* 45 (2): 238–46.

Fontaine, Sheryl, and Susan Hunter. 1998. "Ethical Awareness: A Process of Inquiry." In *Foregrounding Ethical Awareness in Composition and English Studies*, edited by Sheryl Fontaine and Susan Hunter, 1–11. Portsmouth, NH: Heinemann Boynton/Cook.

Gilyard, Keith, and Elaine Richardson. 2001. "Students' Right to Possibility: Basic Writing and African American Rhetoric." In *Insurrections: Approaches to Resistance in Composition Studies*, edited by Andrea Greenbaum, 37–51. Albany: State University of New York Press.

Grimm, Nancy. 1999. *Good Intentions: Writing Center Work for Postmodern Times.* Portsmouth, NH: Heinemann Boynton/Cook.

Heath, Shirley Brice. 1982. "Protean Shapes in Literacy Events: Evershifting Oral and Literate Traditions." In *Spoken and Written Language: Exploring Orality and Literacy*, edited by Deborah Tannen, 91–117. Norwood, NJ: Ablex.

Holmes, David. 1999. "Fighting Back by *Writing* Black: Beyond Racially Reductive Composition Theory." In *Race, Rhetoric, and Composition*, edited by Keith Gilyard, 53–66. Portsmouth, NH: Heinemann Boynton/Cook.

Jost, Walter. 2000. "Rhetoric, Conscience, and the Claim of Religion." In *Rhetorical Invention and Religious Inquiry: New Perspectives*, edited by Walter Jost and Wendy Olmsted, 97–129. New Haven: Yale University Press.

Moffett, James. 1994. "Responses." In "Interchanges: Spiritual Sites of Composing." *College Composition and Communication* 45 (2): 258–61.

Moss, Beverly. 1994. "Creating a Community: Literacy Events in African American Churches." In *Literacy Across Communities*, edited by Beverly Moss, 147–78. Cresskill, NJ: Hampton.

———. 2001. "From the Pews to the Classrooms: Influences of the African American Church on Academic Literacy." In *Literacy in African American Communities*, edited by Joyce Harris, Alan Kamhi, and Karen Pollock, 195–211. Mahwah, NJ: Lawrence Erlbaum Associates.

———. 2002. *A Community Text Arises: A Literate Text and a Literacy Tradition in African-American Churches (Language and Social Processes).* Cresskill, NJ: Hampton Press.

Newman, John. 1970. *Newman's University Sermons: Fifteen Sermons Preached Before the University of Oxford, 1826–1843.* London: S.P.C.K.

Novak, Michael. 1994. *Belief and Unbelief: A Philosophy of Self-Knowledge.* 3rd ed. New Brunswick, NJ: Transaction.

Penti, Marsha Elizabeth. 1992. "Religious Identities in Student Writing: Understanding Students of Difference." Ph.D. diss., Michigan Technological University.

Richardson, Elaine. 2003. *African American Literacies.* New York: Routledge.

Selfe, Cynthia, and Richard Selfe. 1994. "The Politics of Interface: Power and Its Exercise in Electronic Contact Zones." *College Composition and Communication* 45 (4): 480–504.

Smitherman, Geneva. 1977. *Talkin' and Testifyin': The Language of Black America.* Detroit: Wayne State University Press.

———. 1994. "'The Blacker the Berry, the Sweeter the Juice': African American Student Writers." In *The Need for Story: Cultural Diversity in Classroom and Community*, edited by Anne Haas Dyson and Celia Genishi, 80–101. Urbana, IL: National Council of Teachers of English.

Stotsky, Sandra. 1992. "Writing as Moral and Civic Thinking." *College English* 54 (7): 794–809.

Swearingen, Jan. 1994. "Women's Ways of Writing, or, Images, Self-Images, and Graven Images." In "Interchanges: Spiritual Sites of Composing." *College Composition and Communication* 45 (2): 251–58.

# Part IV

# Negotiating Institutional Spaces

# 11

# Religious Faith in Context—Institutions, Histories, Identities, Bodies
## *Introductory Comments*

bonnie lenore kyburz

> The notion that religion tunes human actions to an envisaged
> cosmic order and projects images of cosmic order onto the plane
> of human experience is hardly novel.
>
> —Clifford Geertz,
> *The Interpretation of Cultures*

As Elizabeth says in the introduction to this collection, "While it may be more or less affiliated with theology or a religious community, religious faith is inherently personal and spiritual. It is how people live out theology or religion, whether they're embracing it, fleeing from it, or only suspecting that it shapes their lives." It is not difficult to agree with this statement in some form or another, and it emboldens me to suggest that we must think about how students and teachers negotiate faith-based and academic ways of knowing (and to inquire of their differences). Our project wants this work to matter beyond the personal, however, for it is through various forms of negotiation—self and world, writer and reader, doubt and faith, teacher and student, believer and nonbeliever—that we discover possibilities for teaching and learning within classrooms at least partially shaped by faith.

Theorizing the roles of institutional context as we negotiate faith in the writing classroom may function as a sort of social science, given the seem-ingly vast differences between the "societies" of (any) Faith and the society (ostensibly singular) of the Academy. Pierre Bourdieu is interested in exploring the complexities of any "official language" that suppress nuanced alternative discourses (Thompson 1991, 6). His work speaks to the academic assumption that students of faith must subordinate their discourse to the ostensibly superior "official language" of an academic rationality. It seems to me that these arguments (regarding audience) often limit our sense of the sociohistorical and identity-saturated nature of text production/reception, as though asking students to attenuate "their" discourse to "ours" is a simply matter of flicking a cognitive switch. When we make these arguments, we often assume that audience consideration is a simple matter requiring full cooperation on the part of the writer, and we fail both to consider and to honor the infinite negotiations writers experience. In particular, we too often neglect matters of personal faith—which are in so many ways matters of identity—and persist in privileging an oversimplified audience concept that devalues the (in this case, faith-based) sense of exigence, identity, and sociohistoric context from which a writer's work emerges.

Speaking to similar concerns regarding dominant and subordinate discourses, Bourdieu imagines the evolution of official languages (I am imagining "academic discourse" as just such an "official language"). His analysis seems relevant for thinking about the rational objectivity of academic discourse in contradistinction to articulations of subjectivity that attend writing shaped by alternative ways of knowing (i.e., faith). For Bourdieu, "official language" operates as a kind of myth in its seeming uniformity; nevertheless, it is available for nuanced analysis that may speak to/of culture.

Lauren Fitzgerald, Rebecca Nowacek, and Jeff Cain recognize a kind of official language, a sort of linguistic hegemony as a powerful myth that they feel compelled to examine within their respective institutional contexts. Each seeks insight into their cultures of teaching and learning; each works in a faith-based institution of higher education, where the sense of a linguistic hegemony is profound, a sense of community unavailable for dispute.

As a way of suggesting ongoing questions, I want to argue that while the authors in this section find notions of linguistic hegemony and community available for analysis, we must also read against such notions. Recognizing its importance and at the same time identifying it as illusion, Joseph Harris has complicated "community" as a familiar myth that operates within Composition Studies, arguing that "communities"

> are all quite literally utopias—nowheres, meta-communities—tied to no particular time or place, and thus oddly free of many of the tensions, discontinuities, and conflicts in the sorts of talk and writing that go on everyday in classrooms and departments of an actual university. (1997, 100)

Having complicated the "community" myth that ostensibly moves us and our students toward something better, Harris suggests that "rather than framing our work in terms of helping students move from one community of discourse into another" we might instead "view our task as adding to or complicating their uses of language" (103). Negotiating.

Speaking more broadly of a "community" myth, of sorts, James Thompson explains Bourdieu's contention regarding the illusion of an official language: "the completely homogenous language or speech community does not exist in reality; it is an idealization of a particular set of linguistic practices which have emerged historically and have certain social conditions of existence" (1991, 5). In other words, any discourse claiming superiority by virtue of widespread use—excluding consideration of additional factors—is operating at the level of illusion. When we accept the illusion as reality, we engage in acts of discursive disambiguation (think of the discourses of "good" and "evil" that want to limit discussions on the war in Iraq and elsewhere). To unproblematically accept the illusion of (Good) "official language," we implicitly if often unwittingly endorse oppression. Such a realization, Harris seems to argue, calls for negotiation. We agree, as do the authors in this section, as they seek to understand and negotiate the social, moral, economic, and—here's the complicated addition—doctrinaire/faith-based/religious/ spiritual conditions that shape institutional contexts for writing and the teaching of writing.

My worry here is that for the sake of community we may often exclude students' expressions of faith and the linguistic habits/discourses that attend these expressions. As do the authors in this section, we might consider how this powerful audience concept operates as a form of *context*, thereby possibly limiting—in damaging, distressing, even oppressive ways—a writer's sense of what may be said and written. We struggle to attend to context in ways that we imagine as helpful, and we believe that we are making various "transitions" easier for students to experience (I dare say that we imagine the transitions as unproblematically necessary, which should be alarming). Rarely do we consider our work on/in audience as harmful; more often we think of it in terms of "rites of passage." Instead, I would ask us to imagine, analyze, and critique the audience concept as a tool we use to inculcate students, to encourage in them dispositions that Bourdieu sees as "structured in the sense that they unavoidably reflect the social conditions within which they were acquired" (Thompson 1991, 12). Bourdieu argues that such moves operate as "rites of passage," and are somewhat distressingly—although commensurate with discussions of religious faith—reclassified as "rites of consecration or rites of legitimation or, quite simply, *rites of institution*" (117).

Bourdieu's sociological reading of the kinds of negotiations that take place between discourses (and ways of being) may underscore aspects of the audience/context concepts that can help us to think more critically, more frequently about the roles of institutional context that shape our work in the classroom. The authors in this section move us in this direction; Lauren Fitzgerald, Rebecca Nowacek, and Jeff Cain theorize institutional context and its formative (sustaining? oppressive?) power. Thus, they begin to imagine context in ways that gesture toward negotiations that may ultimately value students' ways of talking, writing, and knowing as forms of communication that struggle (or not) to respond appropriately to (adopt? resist?) the official language of the institution.

Fitzgerald, Nowacek, and Cain inspire us to reflect upon the institutional contexts in which we work—particularly if we work in religiously affiliated institutions—as a way of manifesting increasingly critical, thoughtful, and effective pedagogies. That institutional context *matters* may seem plain and obvious, as Clifford Geertz maintains, but we hope that the range of approaches to theorizing institutional context represented here will suggest the expansive complexity of this work, the comprehensive and necessary nature of these sorts of negotiations. We hope also that such work will become increasingly sensitive to the ways in which we often subordinate students' ways of knowing, speaking, and being when we operate with a narrowly defined and uncritically examined version of audience/context. And we want to think about how institutional contexts delimit this audience concept in both problematic and potentially promising ways.

I hope that these essays resonate as forms of Cultural Studies, or maybe they read more usefully through the lens of Sociology, or Cultural Anthropology. Perhaps—as with the history of Composition—our work will operate in multimodal/cross-discplinary fashion, for as Bourdieu's work suggests, we might theorize our work mindful of the ways in which the privileging of a discourse operates as oppression. My hope is that theorizing various student, teacher, administrative, (Church) official, and (sacred) textual dispositions motivates negotiations that make teaching and learning increasingly meaningful and nonoppressive as we work in and across the distances we find between us.

# Works Cited

Bourdieu, Pierre. 1991. *Language and Symbolic Power*. Cambridge, MA: Harvard University Press.

Geertz, Clifford. 1993. *The Interpretation of Cultures*: *Selected Essays*. New York: Basic.

Harris, Joseph. 1997. *A Teaching Subject: Composition Since 1966*. Upper Saddle River, NJ: Prentice-Hall.

Thompson, James B. 1991. Introduction to *Language and Symbolic Power*. Cambridge, MA: Harvard University Press.

# 12

## Torah U' Madda Institutional "Mission" and Composition Instruction

Lauren Fitzgerald

Those of us teaching writing and running writing programs at religiously affiliated colleges and universities often find little relevant advice in the professional literature. Recent discussions of students of faith in the composition classroom can help, as can recommendations that we attend to institutional context. The best advice I received, however, urged me to consider individuals' beliefs and institutional characteristics not as separate entities but intertwined in a kind of *institutional* "faith." Soon after I began as a faculty member and writing program administrator at Yeshiva University, the first and largest American institution of higher education under Jewish auspices, Muriel Harris advised me "to start with some sort of ethnography" to investigate the implications of this context for the writing center I direct (1999b). Though I did not end up mounting an ethnographic study, Harris' recommendation prodded me to try to better understand this institution and my place in it, particularly as an outsider (a status you might have guessed from my Irish- [and Catholic-] sounding last name). As Harris writes in her contribution to *The Writing Program Administrator as Researcher*, "writing center directors, like other writing program administrators, must necessarily deal with the particulars of their institution" (1999a, 1). She lines up the usual suspects—local policies, populations, and resources—but the advice she gave me indicates that religious affiliation is equally worth examining.

Whether secular or religious, whatever the degree or kind, institutional context necessarily affects teacher-student relationships because student and teacher beliefs are not articulated in a vacuum but are mediated by policies, practices, and histories. For example, each year at Yeshiva College (YC)

(Yeshiva University's undergraduate college for men and where I teach), first-year composition students write essays about their recent, usually religious, experiences in Israel. Knowing about the meaning of Israel for Jews certainly helps faculty respond appropriately to this writing, yet it will not reveal the whole story since there are institutional factors at work as well. YC students write about Israel not only because it holds crucial religious importance for them (not to mention cultural and political significance in post-9/11 New York) but also because of its curricular relevance. The typical incoming YC student spends at least a year after high school at an Israeli yeshiva, a religious academy dedicated to the study of Talmud and other sacred texts. YC officially recognizes this study by awarding it credit.

My argument, then, is that at least as important as the faith and religious backgrounds of individual students or teachers is this institutional mission. By "mission" I mean something more than what the term implies in business, and even educational, settings (in mission statements) and something less than what it signifies in some Christian contexts (with missionary work). With the phrase "institutional mission," I want to play on both secular and religious (though not necessarily Christian) meanings to suggest ways that the particular identity of a religiously affiliated college or university is enacted by its members and through its culture. In many ways, YC, where the University's identification with Orthodox Judaism is particularly pronounced, is ideal for considering the implications of such missions for composition instruction. YC's origins as a late-nineteenth-century yeshiva, and the relevance of these origins even now in its dual secular and religious curriculum, make it unique among other American institutions of higher education and as a result help to foreground what might seem "natural" and commonplace elsewhere.

Identifying an institutional mission can be difficult, especially for newcomers. Rather than speaking with one voice (if "voice" is even the right metaphor), institutions "express" themselves through the multiple, sometimes contradictory, partial (in both senses) voices of various situated and self-interested parties (including faculty, students, administration, and alumni). This is no less true at YC, where the dialogue between the religious and secular resists monolithic (and even monolingual) articulation. Such dialogic resistance is best exemplified by the University's motto, *Torah U'Madda*, Hebrew for "Bible and"—variously— "knowledge," "wisdom," or "Western learning."

The *U* in *Torah U'Madda*—that deceptively simple conjunction "and"— might seem to imply that this dialogue is complementary. Instead, as my colleague Shalom Carmy writes, it is the site of debate between those who see the concept of *Torah U'Madda* "as a means to reconcile the tensions between traditional Judaism and mainstream American society, and those who believe that a genuine engagement with the liberal arts is as likely to sharpen the inevitable conflicts between the service of God and the values of man as to smooth them over" (2001, 33–34). This debate is similarly embodied by YC's unique combination of yeshiva—the religious education that gives the institution its special identity—and college—the accredited, liberal arts curriculum that links the institution to the mission of higher education at secular institutions around the country. By employing this metaphor of debate, I do not want to suggest that YC can be reduced to an opposition between the secular and religious. Indeed, they often interact in fascinating ways. For instance, though all YC students are Jewish and nearly all of them religiously observant, YC faculty, by contrast, include Gentiles and non-observant Jews who teach courses that are resolutely secular.

I examine the interaction of this institutionalized (false) binary through three increasingly complex (and roughly chronological) episodes from my history as a writing program administrator (WPA) and writing teacher at YC. I begin with the YC Writing Center. In many ways this writing center is like many others, founded in the mid-1980s, and staffed largely by undergraduate peer tutors who work primarily with other undergraduates. But here's the crucial difference: this center is housed in the men's college of an Orthodox Jewish institution. As a result, all of its peer tutors are Jewish men, most of whom have received a specific kind of collaborative, religious education during their yeshiva training. This religious training more than other factors (gender, for instance) seems to have a distinguishable influence on their writing center work (though this training is itself a condition of their being Orthodox Jewish men). There is, one could say, a little yeshiva in the Yeshiva College Writing Center, a point of confluence between the religious and secular aspects of the institution.

## The Writing Center in the Religiously Affiliated College (or Vice Versa)

To support her claim that writing center directors should be sensitive to their institutional contexts, Harris cites Dave Healy's attention to "the particular" in writing center scholarship, Stephen North's famous "*idea* of a writing center" notwithstanding (Harris 1999a, 1, my emphasis). Healy argues that we would better understand these particulars if, instead of "labs," or "clinics," or "birthing rooms," or any of a host of metaphors, we were to think of writing centers as "churches." Doing so, he maintains, would illuminate both their "range of beliefs and practices" and "some common resonance" (Healy 1995, 12–13). Healy's extended comparison offers useful insights, not least because houses of worship are also defined by institutional settings and purposes. But what he does not consider is what happens when "church" is more than simply a metaphor for the writing center, and institutional context is not church-*like* but truly religious. At the YC Writing Center, the point of intersection between tutors' religious lives and their work operates specifically by way of a form of collaboration in Orthodox Judaism called *havruta*, the collaborative study of Talmud.

I first began studying tutoring sessions at the YC Writing Center to persuade my colleagues that my relationship with the undergraduate peer tutors was not (just) that of boss and workers but rather teacher and learners. It was therefore important to make the general, if unoriginal, claim that tutors learned transferable skills from their jobs. Assuming (wrongly, it turned out) that the tutors would need help seeing that they, too, can learn from writing center work, I brought in copies of Ken Bruffee's early article on the relevance of collaborative learning to tutoring, "Peer Tutoring and the 'Conversation of Mankind.'" For good measure, I'd underlined Bruffee's statement "peer tutoring made learning a two-way street" (2001, 207). Late in our meeting, after I had gone over Bruffee's "groundbreaking" theory, one tutor said—politely, even shyly, as if he were pointing out something obvious that I had simply forgotten—"You know that we already do that, right?" Another tutor agreed. A third cited a saying from the Talmud that "we learn most not from our rabbis or even our peers but our students." They all talked about their extensive histories with collaborative learning, with *havruta*. In other words, Bruffee and I were not telling them anything new.

If the yeshiva is the oldest organized educational institution in the world (Helmreich 1982, xviii), then *havruta*, the central mode of learning in the yeshiva curriculum, is the oldest institutionalized collaborative pedagogy. With roots in the group study that emerged after the destruction of the Second Temple in 70 CE and the compilation of the Oral Torah a century or so later (Goldman 1975, 31; Goldenberg 1984, 131), *havruta* as a pedagogical method seems to have been formalized in the eighteenth and early nineteenth centuries, to become the "optimal" way of studying Talmud (Tedmon 1993, 98; Helmreich 1982, 110–11). More complex than simply reading (Holtz 1984, 18), *havruta* is a process of working through the difficult, elusive, multilingual text of the Talmud. Partners take turns reading passages aloud, translating them, and, if advanced enough, trying to make meaning out of the text, challenging each other's interpretations to weed out inaccuracies and refine their understandings (Schwarcz 1987, 66; Helmreich 1982, 110). *Havruta* partners work together for months and even years, sometimes for hours at a stretch, often many days a week.

It was several years, many conversations, and quite a few trips to the Judaica library later before I learned even this much about *havruta*. Prompted by Harris' advice, I realized that the tutors who had compared *havruta* to their tutoring had made an exciting connection. I've since learned that Susan Tedmon, in an ethnographic study of high school–level *havruta* partners, also links this process to secular theories of collaborative learning. More remarkable, a YC graduate, Charles Persky, who cofounded the Hunter College Writing Center, in the City University of New York, told me that his own extensive background with *havruta* informed his thinking about peer tutoring. When he first heard about collaborative learning in the 1970s, he recalled saying to himself, "Why is that being considered new?" (see Fitzgerald 2005).

The YC tutors gave me new ways to understand the Writing Center. I have since noticed, for example, that several pairs of tutors and writers will sit together at a single table, even if room is available elsewhere, and that, unlike the quiet murmurs of many centers, ours is often loud. I've been told that something similar happens in the study halls of the yeshiva where *havruta* learning most often takes place, and where there is a "constant, incessant din" (Holtz 1984, 18). Some students even call their tutors their "*havrutas.*" *Havruta* functions as a key mode of learning elsewhere at YC as well. Students, faculty, rabbis, and alumni have told me that students commonly study together for secular subjects, indicating an openness to and perhaps preference for collaboration that seems to have been shaped by their experience with *havruta.*

Even with such an obvious example of the confluence of religious and secular practice—the collaboration of yeshiva and college, *Torah* and *Madda*—the comparison should not be taken too far. Considering the implications of *havruta* for secular education, Tedmon suggests that there are "dangers" in "the temptation" to see it as easily transported from its yeshiva context (1993, 177). The "relationships—among texts, students, and teachers" necessary for the *havruta* partnership to work, she holds,

> function as aspects of a particular environment. They interact with, affecting and being affected by, other aspects of the learning context. These relationships, the contexts in which they occur, are interdependent: They cannot be removed from the context (although something faintly resembling the original relationship might be), nor can the context exist without them. (1993, 185)

In the final analysis, writing center tutoring is not a form of religious practice, student writing is not divine, and the Yeshiva College Writing Center is not a yeshiva. But the YC Writing Center's unique institutional context, which combines, if not always comfortably, yeshiva and college, makes possible not so much a pale imitation of *havruta* as a collaborative practice with its own, institutionally specific identity.

## What Is (the Religiously Affiliated) College For?

Shortly after I began at YC, I asked my first-semester composition students to read and respond to an excerpt from Allan Bloom's *The Closing of the American Mind*, reprinted as "The Student and the University," in Lunsford and Ruszkiewicz's *The Presence of Others*. I had chosen this anthology assuming that its more conservative selections would appeal to my students. In most cases, this assumption paid off, but liberal that I am, I had neglected to distinguish between various *kinds* of conservatism. Bloom's nostalgia for the old-fashioned liberal arts curriculum missed its mark entirely. When he throws up his hands in despair and declares that it is "Better to give up on

liberal education and get on with a specialty in which there is at least a prescribed curriculum and prospective career" (1997, 54), nearly every student
agreed, failing to hear his irony or his real point, that college has a higher
calling. For these students, college was, and could only be, intended to help
them get a job: "What else *could* it be for?" one asked.

My students might have disagreed with Bloom for a number of reasons.
They could have been reacting to his elitist tone; new to college, they might
have been too inexperienced to imagine what could be gained from a liberal
arts curriculum; or they might have been thinking about college as many
Americans do, as a means of professional preparation and eventual gainful
employment. When my partner taught the same excerpt in a required first-year
writing course at a secular university, his students rejected Bloom's argument
as well. The crucial difference between these two discussions, however, was
context: the idea of the liberal arts curriculum, indeed "college" more generally, is continuously contested on religious grounds at YC. In many ways, my
students' argument about the purpose of college was only the most recent in a
long history of debates.

According to Jeffrey Gurock's *The Men and Women of Yeshiva*, the history of the institution is punctuated by questions about whether it serves primarily a religious or secular purpose. To offer but one revealing example, the
proposal for founding YC initially met with resistance from strictly Orthodox
Jews who worried that the dual curriculum would imply that "Gentile learning" was "not only compatible but comparable to Jewish teaching" (Gurock
1988, 112). As a result, Yeshiva University's synthetic *Torah U'Madda*
approach led one strictly Orthodox rabbi to say, years later, "When they put
the word 'University' in, they spoiled everything" (Helmreich 1982, 234).
Ultimately, secular education was (and still is) considered to be problematic
because it is said to lead "to *kephirah* (unbelief)" (Gurock 1988, 254). Such
concerns might seem easily dismissed—after all, secular education should by
definition be religiously neutral—but the history of American education shows
otherwise.

James Turner's and George Marsden's research into the "sacralization" of
the liberal arts curriculum in the increasingly secular American universities of
the late nineteenth and early twentieth centuries reveals that the study of Western Civilization was seen "as the bearer of the Christian heritage, broadly conceived" and invested "with the vestigial spirit, if not the substance, of the religious heritage" (Marsden 1994, 365). (In fact, Harvard declared in 1945 that
"education in great books can be looked at as a secular continuum of the spirit
of Protestantism" [Marsden 1992, 23].) Interestingly, Bloom seems to have
had something similar in mind for his great books curriculum. By linking liberal education to "a unified view of nature and man's [*sic*] place in it" (1997,
61), he calls up the "unifying principle" of the liberal arts curriculum that
Turner holds was "to replace the divine order" lost through secularization
(Turner 1992, 80).

My students probably had little or no idea of the history of American education that seems to have informed, on the one hand, Bloom's devotion to the liberal arts and, on the other, Orthodox Jewry's ambivalence about it. But their argument with Bloom nonetheless contributes to the history of debates about the mission of YC. I hasten to add that this involvement does not suggest that these students were one with and able to speak for this institutional history, especially since I have no evidence that they were cognizant of it. YC students, like students at other institutions, have plenty of reasons for rejecting Bloom.

What this history can influence, however, is how I, as their teacher, might interpret and respond to their arguments—and avoid being backed into the awkward corner of supporting Bloom when I have my own reasons for disagreeing with him. For instance, the history of YC's contested mission offers a way to contextualize Bloom's pronouncements and, more generally, the question of the purpose of college. Though I stopped using Bloom in this course, I have continued to address the problem he presents by asking students to consider YC's yearlong writing requirement: Putting aside their own feelings about it, why do they believe the College's founders thought it was a good idea? What might the founders have hoped students would gain? Do these outcomes support the institutional mission? What *is* this mission anyway? How is it similar to or different from that of other schools? I find this discussion helps to complicate from the onset the fairly typical assumption that composition courses serve only English Department (or secular) ends. I hope too that my appeal to religious authority, in the figures of YC's founders, redirects at least some of the frustration students continue to feel about the requirement.

However they are put, questions regarding the purpose of college can lead in many directions: to inquiries into a particular institution's history; to investigations into the history of American higher education; and to speculations about how these histories might inform or negate each other in a particular institution's mission. Composition classes—first year, required, small—may be the only and most appropriate context for students and teachers alike to wrestle with the implications of what college is for, at religiously affiliated institutions and elsewhere.

## "The Kingdom of Heaven Is Like unto a Treasure Hid in a Field" (Matt. 13:44)

Not to be ignored in exploring the ways institutional mission can affect composition instruction at a religiously affiliated college are the discipline-specific assumptions embodied by textbooks, curricula, pedagogies, and teachers. Curiously, many of the same forces that led to the secularization of the American university contributed to the development of composition as a college requirement and an academic field (Brereton 1995; Connors 1997). It is therefore tempting to speculate that the "vestigial spirit" of Protestantism is hidden within the field of composition studies, a hypothesis that my experiences of teaching writing at Yeshiva College support.

These Christian assumptions are sometimes articulated through the conversion narrative, which Priscilla Perkins calls "an almost classic genre in composition studies" that continues "to grip our imaginations" (2001, 585). The late Wendy Bishop, for example, portrayed her own and others' entrance into the field in such terms. In her Chair's Address for the 2000 Conference on College Composition and Communication, she described her "conversion into composition and rhetoric" (2001, 325). In *Something Old, Something New*, graduate students in a writing pedagogy seminar shared their "powerful change process" by way of similar "religious metaphors": as Bishop writes, "they 'confessed'"; "they marveled at their leaps of faith, and they announced that they were converted" (1990, 129). Conversion narratives are influential ways of thinking about and enacting important change in our field.

Yet these narratives are not always positive. Nancy Welch finds that "metaphors of testimony, confession, baptism, and conversion" in a graduate training program can also function as coercion, leading her to prefer the "critical consciousness . . . that arise[s] from resisting, not embracing, a faith" (1993, 388). Along these lines, Lizabeth Rand and Perkins point to moments when teachers attempt to save the saved, as it were, to "convert" Christian fundamentalist students from their apparently narrow ways of thinking; as they remind us, critical consciousness can be its own kind of missionary work, another way of embracing faith (Rand 2001, 355, 359; Perkins 2001, 588, 589). This speculation can help to explain why student testimonials of Christian conversion, such as the one Juanita Smart so sympathetically portrays in Chapter 2, can be irritating for some of us: students might seem to be reflecting what we are trying to do to them.

Why is the conversion narrative such a compelling genre for composition studies? One possible culprit is Romanticism. Sherrie Gradin, in *Romancing Rhetorics*, draws a line of influence from the British Romantic poets, particularly William Wordsworth and Samuel Taylor Coleridge, to twentieth-century expressivists such as Elbow, Murray, and Berthoff. Gradin, like other composition scholars, uses M. H. Abrams' tidy taxonomy from *The Mirror and the Lamp* to outline Romantic notions of imagination (Gradin 1995, 2; Faigley 1986, 529; Fulkerson 2000, 3). More helpful for my purposes is Abrams' later book, *Natural Supernaturalism*, which presents Romanticism as a secularization of Judeo-Christian, though mostly Christian, culture. According to Abrams, the conversion narrative represents change as "right angled": "the key events are abrupt, cataclysmic, and make a drastic, even absolute difference" (1971, 47). Abrams' discussion also suggests a historical and generic link between conversion and literacy narratives. Certainly, other traditions have contributed to more recent incarnations, as evidenced by Mike Rose's *Lives on the Boundary* and Richard Rodriguez's *Hunger of Memory*. But they all share a right-angled, fundamental change, what Mary Soliday calls "those moments when the self is on the threshold of possible intellectual, social, and emotional development," making the genre itself a "site of self-translation" (1994, 511).

One of the most famous literacy-as-conversion narratives appears in *The Narrative of the Life of Frederick Douglass*. Drawing on the language of election and divine prophecy, Douglass recounts his response to Mr. Auld's remark that literacy "would forever unfit him to be a slave":

> These words sank deep into my heart, stirred up sentiments within that lay slumbering, and called into existence an entirely new train of thought. It was a new and special revelation, explaining dark and mysterious things. . . . I now understood what had been to me a most perplexing difficulty—to wit, the white man's power to enslave the black man. (1986, 78)

Douglass' "new and special revelation" draws on the notion of Scripture, for most Protestants the only kind of divine revelation available in modern times (Berkhof 1938, 14, 15). Equally significant is Douglass' reference to being "called," which in Protestant traditions signifies seeking a sign of election through the unmediated call of God. This calling also invokes the spiritual autobiography, a radical Protestant version of the conversion narrative that informs the *Narrative* (Baker 1980, 28). Rather than a complete turn away from one's former beliefs or sinful nature, the Protestant spiritual autobiography recounts a discovery of what is already present, such as one's election or Douglass' own knowledge of "the white man's power to enslave the black man."

This episode from Douglass' *Narrative* can be found in a number of composition textbooks, including one that is intriguingly, and I think not coincidentally, titled *The Call to Write*. John Trimbur employs "calling" as the book's operative metaphor in order to foreground the complex rhetorical relations of writer and audience, internal motivations and outside forces. Even Trimbur's publisher has taken advantage of the power of this metaphor, asking instructors in an advertisement for the second edition, "Have you answered The Call?"

One might well imagine that using *The Call to Write*, with its "vestigial spirit" of Christian traditions, would present difficulties in a composition course at an Orthodox Jewish college. At the time that I ordered it, however, I was unaware of this religious underpinning. Though my students seemed to like the book, their lack of familiarity with the particularly Protestant resonances of a literacy narrative assignment framed in part by Douglass' *Narrative* caused a few complications. Especially complicated was the response of a student I'm calling "Daniel."

In the face of Trimbur's call to "Select a particular moment or episode in your experience that involves writing" (1999, 35), Daniel wrote about his reaction to the assignment itself and its sample literacy narratives, including Douglass'. In response to the part of the assignment that asked him to "explain what [this literacy event] reveals about the meaning and use of writing" (35), he suggested that the literacy narrative genre was not complex enough to merit the term "writing," arguing instead for a different genre, poetry. Though Daniel made interesting claims, it seemed to me he had purposefully avoided the assignment. As a result, our conference on how he might revise his literacy narrative was uncomfortable. I tried to persuade him to make his piece more explicitly narrative; he argued that he didn't want to write something that obvious. Then came what I took to be the moment of "revelation."

"Do you know what I'm doing?" Daniel asked. My memory of what he said is a little sketchy; luckily, he wrote about it in the cover letter for his final portfolio:

> After two years of learning the different structure found in the Bible, I was listening to you tell me the [literacy narrative] I had done, with biblical analysis, wasn't applicable to writing in this class. You told me that there was a different style of writing. The goal of this approach was clarity.
>
> I started to argue with you about the pro's and con's of each approach. . . . It wasn't that I felt hurt religiously, I just couldn't understand what would motivate someone to follow your approach. The biblical or poetic style made sense. Readers should fight to understand the significance of every word. The reader would appreciate the unique form embedded in the authors work.

At the time, Daniel's revelation about this interest in "biblical analysis" seemed to explain almost everything I had not been able to follow in his literacy narrative.

Daniel obviously valued at least one kind of writing, Biblical poetry. This preference suggested to me that the following passage from his literacy narrative was not merely a comparison between poetry and prose but the religious and secular:

> These [types of poetry] can't be fully understood unless one sits and thinks about the way they were put together: the order, the refrains, the different structures whether they be chiasmus, parallel, or the like. . . . Because of the difference in styles between a poem and a literacy narrative, a poet has to think in a more structured and organized fashion. . . . If one were simply to read a poem off to an audience, the level at which its understood isn't the same as if someone sat down and studied it.

His own apparent ambition, to achieve a complexity and depth in his writing of seemingly biblical proportions, is played out in the last paragraph of his literacy narrative:

> I could write a literacy narrative with an underlying structure that would enhance and emphasize the point I was trying to make. Which would enable the reader to understand the work on two levels: if s/he *just* reads it they are doomed not to fully appreciate the full meaning of the story.

All of the pieces seemed to fall into place: Daniel's desire to emulate the Bible in his own writing; his yeshiva training that taught him to value difficult readings; and, perhaps most significant, his rejection of a form that implicitly mimicked stories of Christian conversion. I realized that Daniel's literacy narrative—or rather his resistance to it—was informed by his religious practice, and specifically the yeshiva practices of working with challenging texts. Like that untutored reader he had described, I had been "doomed not to fully appreciate the full meaning of the story." Now, armed with the truth, I saw the light.

But if one expression of Daniel's religious practice was the purposeful rejection of the conversion narrative form, how do I explain his final essay, which, with its detailed review of the errors of his earlier ways, enacts the classic conversion of composition studies, complete with a turning point and testimony? According to Daniel:

> It was only after I had reviewed someone else's work that I started to understand the importance of clarity. When I studied in Yeshiva [in Israel], I had the time to zero in on every word and sometimes every letter. You helped me realize that there is a world out there that communicates. People not only have to, but should speak to each other, and that type of communication demands clarity.
>
> After a while, this idea sunk into my head, and I think that my writing is a testimony to that.

Daniel has learned to follow the pattern that Perkins maps out as "the development of individual first-year college writers as they shed their inexperience, resistance, and narrow-mindedness and don garments of (relative) enlightenment and grace" (2001, 585). Clearly, his final essay should not be read as a conversion to a genre-bound, vestigial form of Christianity, but it does suggest the power of such right-angled narratives of change.

I offer this story not simply as another example of a teacher's misreading student writing (though it is that). Nor only as a teacher's version of the conversion narrative of composition studies (though it's probably that, too). I hope instead that it serves as testimony to the significance of institutional mission—and beliefs about this mission—for a teacher's act of interpretation. Had Daniel been my student at a secular college or university, would he have written this literacy narrative? Even if he had, would I have understood it as an expression of religious belief and practice? I don't think so. For one thing, I wouldn't have known what little I do about the Orthodox community. What might not have changed, however, was my desire that he learn to write and value a literacy narrative that followed the right-angled, redemptive turn of conversion. Institutionalized yet also extra-institutional, this genre has traveled with me from context to context. Teaching at YC only made visible to me its "vestigial spirit."

## Conclusion: Institution(al) Matters

Like learning about the values of our students of faith, researching the practices and history of the religiously affiliated college or university can be what Perkins calls "a sanity saver," especially for faculty new to such institutions and with backgrounds different from those of their students and colleagues (2001, 587). Knowing even a few of the particulars of our contexts can explain apparent mysteries and provide coping strategies for completing day-to-day business. For instance, what is elsewhere the ordinary task of planning a course syllabus and scheduling assignments is at YC exceptionally complicated. As Sabbath observers, YC students do not write or complete other forms of work on Saturdays, and as participants in a dual curriculum, many are in class eight or more hours per day, four days a week, some engaging in evening sessions with their *havrutas*. Moreover, there are two calendars in operation— the Gregorian calendar used by the Western (Christian) world and the Jewish calendar that follows a lunar cycle and is composed of holidays unfamiliar to many outside of the Orthodox community. Since the academic calendar changes drastically from year to year, faculty must also start from scratch nearly every semester. The seemingly simple matter of time, which can elsewhere be taken for granted, turns out to be a culturally constructed, religious matter.

The religiously affiliated college and university can make visible what is otherwise transparent, and investigating such institutions' missions can transform mundane aspects of our work into intellectual pursuits. Serving as WPA and a composition teacher at Yeshiva College has opened up avenues of research for me that I could never have predicted. Likewise, the research into religiously affiliated institutions represented in this collection can produce knowledge about often overlooked sites of composition instruction. By analyzing the missions of these institutions, we reveal the vestigial spirit and religious practices of not only sites of writing instruction and the field of composition studies but also the religious roots of American higher education as a whole.

For their knowledge, insights, and advice, I want to thank the undergraduate peer tutors of the Yeshiva College Writing Center as well as my YC colleagues Joanne Jacobson and Gillian Steinberg. I would also like to thank the editors of this collection, Elizabeth Vander Lei and bonnie kyburz, for further inspiring me to consider my institutional context; my friend Rita Malenczyk for responding to several earlier versions of this chapter; and Brian Culver, my partner, for generously sharing his wisdom in matters institutional and religious.

# Works Cited

Abrams, M. H. 1971. *Natural Supernaturalism: Tradition and Revolution in Romantic Literature*. New York and London: W. W. Norton.

Baker, Houston A., Jr. 1980. *The Journey Back: Issues in Black Literature and Criticism*. Chicago: Chicago University Press.

Berkhof, Louis. 1938. *Summary of Christian Doctrine*. Grand Rapids, MI: Erdmans.

Bishop, Wendy. 1990. *Something Old, Something New: College Writing Teachers and Classroom Change.* Carbondale: Southern Illinois University Press.

———. 2001. "Against the Odds in Composition and Rhetoric." *College Composition and Communication* 53: 322–35.

Bloom, Allan. [1987] 1997. "The Student and the University." In *The Presence of Others: Voices That Call for Response*, edited by Andrea A. Lunsford and John J. Ruszkiewicz, 52–61. 2d ed. Reprint. New York: St. Martin's Press.

Brereton, John C., ed. 1995. *The Origins of Composition Studies in the American College, 1875–1925.* Pittsburgh: University of Pittsburgh Press.

Bruffee, Kenneth. [1984] 2001. "Peer Tutoring and the 'Conversation of Mankind.'" In *The Allyn and Bacon Guide to Writing Center Theory and Practice*, edited by Robert W. Barnett and Jacob S. Blumner, 206–18. Reprint. Boston: Allyn and Bacon.

Carmy, Shalom. 2001. "Orthodox Judaism and the Liberal Arts." *Academe* 87: 32–37.

Connors, Robert J. 1997. *Composition-Rhetoric: Backgrounds, Theory, and Pedagogy.* Pittsburgh: University of Pittsburgh Press.

Douglass, Frederick. 1986. *Narrative of the Life of Frederick Douglass, an American Slave.* Edited by Houston A. Baker, Jr. New York: Penguin.

Faigley, Lester. 1986. "Competing Theories of Process: A Critique and a Proposal." *College English* 48: 527–32.

Fitzgerald, Lauren. 2005. "'Torah Is Not Learned but in a Group': Talmud Study and Collaborative Learning." In *Judaic Perspectives on Literacy: Contexts for Rhetoric and Composition*, edited by Andrea Greenbaum and Deborah H. Holdstein. Cresskill, NJ: Hampton.

Fulkerson, Richard. [1979] 2000. "Four Philosophies of Composition." In *The Writing Teacher's Sourcebook*, edited by Edward P. J. Corbett, Nancy Myers, and Gary Tate, 3–8. 4th ed. New York: Oxford University Press.

Goldenberg, Robert. 1984. "Talmud." In *Back to the Sources: Reading the Classic Jewish Texts*, edited by Barry W. Holtz, 129–75 . New York: Summit Books.

Goldman, Israel M. 1975. *Lifelong Learning Among Jews: Adult Education in Judaism from Biblical Times to the Twentieth Century.* New York: Ktav.

Gradin, Sherrie L. 1995. *Romancing Rhetorics: Social Expressivist Perspectives on the Teaching of Writing.* Portsmouth, NH: Heinemann.

Gurock, Jeffrey. 1988. *The Men and Women of Yeshiva: Higher Education, Orthodoxy, and American Judaism.* New York: Columbia University Press.

Harris, Muriel. 1999a. "Diverse Research Methodologies at Work for Diverse Audiences: Shaping the Writing Center to the Institution." In *The Writing Program Administrator as Researcher: Inquiry in Action and Reflection*, edited by Shirley K. Rose and Irwin Weiser, 1–17. Portsmouth, NH: Heinemann.

———. 1999b. Email message to the author, 28 April.

Healy, Dave. 1995. "In the Temple of the Familiar: The Writing Center as Church." In *Writing Center Perspectives*, edited by Byron Stay, Christina Murphy, and Eric H. Hobson, 12–25. Emmitsburg, MD: NWCA Press.

Helmreich, William B. 1982. *The World of the Yeshiva: An Intimate Portrait of Orthodox Jewry*. New York: The Free Press.

Holtz, Barry W., ed. 1984. "Introduction: On Reading Jewish Texts." In *Back to the Sources: Reading the Classic Jewish Texts*, 11–29. New York: Summit Books.

Marsden, George. 1992. "The Soul of the American University: An Historical Overview." In *The Secularization of the Academy*, edited by George Marsden and Bradley J. Longfield, 9–45. New York: Oxford University Press.

———. 1994. *The Soul of the American University: From Protestant Establishment to Established Nonbelief*. New York: Oxford University Press.

Perkins, Priscilla. 2001. "'A Radical Conversion of the Mind': Fundamentalism, Hermeneutics, and the Metanoic Classroom." *College English* 63: 585–611.

Persky, Charles. 2001. Personal interview, 21 October.

Rand, Lizabeth A. 2001. "Enacting Faith: Evangelical Discourse and the Discipline of Composition Studies." *College Composition and Communication* 52 (3): 349–67.

Schwarcz, Michael. 1987. *The Kolel: A Study in Traditional Knowledge and Community Life*. Ph.D. diss. University of Pittsburgh and Ann Arbor: University Microfilms International.

Soliday, Mary. 1994. "Translating Self and Difference Through Literacy Narratives." *College English* 56: 511–26.

Tedmon, Susan. [1991]. 1993. *Collaborative Acts of Literacy in a Traditional Jewish Community*. Ph.D. diss. University of Pennsylvania, and Ann Arbor: University Microfilms International.

Trimbur, John. 1999. *The Call to Write*. New York: Longman.

Turner, James. 1992. "Secularization and Sacralization: Speculations on Some Religious Origins of the Secular Humanities Curriculum, 1850–1900." In *The Secularization of the Academy*, edited by George Marsden and Bradley J. Longfield, 74–106. New York and Oxford: Oxford University Press.

Welch, Nancy. 1993. "Resisting the Faith: Conversion, Resistance, and the Training of Teachers." *College English* 55: 387–401.

# 13

# Negotiating Individual Religious Identity and Institutional Religious Culture

Rebecca Schoenike Nowacek

The compatibility of faith and academic writing—in particular, the struggles between fundamentalist Christian students and their writing teachers—has been a focus of recent scholarship. These inquiries have focused on students who use spiritual identity as "the primary kind of selfhood . . . [they] draw upon in making meaning of their lives and the world around them" (Rand 2001, 350). One impulse in this scholarship has been to correct teachers' tendency to trivialize religious discourse by explaining the worldviews of particular religions so that we might better understand what motivates writers.

The students I write of in this chapter are Catholic and Quaker students, individuals of what we might call a more "moderate" or "liberal" (though no less deeply felt) faith, working to reconcile their religious beliefs with their academic work. My portraits of Alan, Betty, and Tigra (pseudonyms the students selected) are based on ethnographic research conducted at Villanova University (see Nowacek 2001). Through my analyses of classroom discourse, written assignments, and interviews I have come to understand that students' individual religious identities are not separable from institutional religious culture.[1] This is not to say that it isn't useful for teachers to familiarize themselves with the values and epistemologies of different faiths; the work of Rand and others provides a great service in that regard. But we must constantly question how those generalizations play out for particular individuals within specific institutional and classroom contexts.

Founded in 1842 by members of the Order of St. Augustine, Villanova University is home to approximately 6,000 undergraduate students. The campus is dominated by the double spires of the Villanova Chapel, an apt architectural reminder of the central role of the church in university life. Augustinians can be found throughout campus, some easily recognizable in their black habits, serving as faculty and administrators (including University president), participating in extracurricular activities, and living in residences alongside students.

Church teaching is incorporated into academic life. Most prominent is the study of Augustine included in the two-semester Core Humanities seminar required of every Villanova undergraduate. Many students go on to learn more about Augustine and Christian theology through their two required religion courses. Others choose to focus on non-Catholic religious traditions and topics in classes such as Introduction to Islam, Feminist Ethics, and War and Morality. Even while taking its Augustinian heritage seriously, Villanova hopes to attract students of other religions, describing itself on its website as "a comprehensive Roman Catholic institution that welcomes students of all faiths" (http://www.villanova.edu/enroll/admission/university/).

## Alan, Betty, Tigra, and the Religious Culture of Villanova University

Alan, Betty, and Tigra were enrolled in a team-taught interdisciplinary course titled Interdisciplinary Humanities II, the second semester of a three-semester sequence of courses colloquially referred to as "Interdisc." Interdisc II is worth nine credits: three for the literature component, three for history, and three for theology. Although the three professors coordinate readings and assignments and participate in one another's class discussions, each is responsible for his or her own classes, assignments, and grades. The syllabus specified particular class periods for each discipline; students kept separate notebooks for each subject and spoke of a given class period as "belonging" to a particular discipline. For that reason I will treat the writing assignments from each course as if they are from three distinct courses, though it is significant that these courses were linked under the rubric of Interdisc II (as my analysis of Alan's writing will make clear).

Although Alan, Betty, and Tigra studied the same materials in the same classrooms, these three students developed dramatically different interpretations of the religious culture of Villanova, which in turn shaped their perspectives on writing.

## Alan: Wrestling with Catholic Doctrine

The product of thirteen years of Catholic schooling, Alan had attended an Augustinian prep school. But there, he explained, the focus had been "religious teaching on behavior and stories as opposed to doctrine and history." Given that background, Alan's first year at Villanova challenged his faith in ways both stimulating and frightening. Alan found the theology component difficult because although he was "born and raised Catholic" and "pretty much believed it," he had never studied the theology of his religion. Studying theology, Alan said, "has challenged me a lot. . . . A lot of things . . . I believed before I still believe, but [now I know that] I didn't have enough to believe in. I found out so much more of the things that I need to believe in order to believe the other stuff that I'm not sure where any foundation for what I had was." Examining the relationships between the intellectual underpinnings and day-to-day practice of his religion, Alan explained, "tore me apart throughout the semester. That was the hardest thing."

Although Alan found examining the practical implications of Catholic doctrine profoundly challenging, he experienced the larger Villanova culture as supportive of his struggle. His Interdisc I class, taken the previous semester, had pushed him to develop an historically rich, archeologically based understanding of early Christianity. Alan also participated in Villanova's first Religion and Postmodernism conference. Sponsored by the philosophy department, the three-day conference attracted participants including Jacques Derrida, Richard Kearney, and David Tracy. (The conference proceedings were subsequently published as *God, the Gift, and Postmodernism* [Caputo and Scanlon 1999].) Sitting in a room with Derrida and others, listening to debates over the possibility of reconciling faith and philosophy must have been a heady experience for a first-year student, and it appears to have confirmed Alan's sense that he was part of a community seeking to reconcile rigorous academic inquiry with a faith-based worldview. Alan also valued his work as a pastoral musician, a program through which students provided the music for masses celebrated in the Villanova chapel. The effort to understand the implications of Catholic doctrine for daily life—as well as the belief that the university culture supported that effort—were recurrent themes throughout Alan's interviews and papers.

This focus on the relationship of faith and academic inquiry appeared overtly in Alan's theology and literature papers for Interdisc II. The first theology assignment asked students to "re-create the way in which, according to Aquinas, human beings achieve salvation." One of the goals of this assignment, the professor explained, was "to deal with Christianity as an intellectual item . . . to think with one of the most rigorous Christian thinkers." At the end of the assignment Alan's professor also invited students to "append your own personal critique as to its failings. What key preconceptions, conclusions, or arguments separate you from Aquinas?" Like his classmates, Alan focused primarily on the concepts of grace, free will, and salvation—but he also devoted two of his paper's seven pages to critiquing Aquinas' *Summa*, more than any of his classmates. He argued that a "lack of passion" in the *Summa* creates "a distance from what his purpose was: the creation of a theology," making it more procedural than inspirational.

What is striking is not so much Alan's critique but his *willingness* to be critical—something that most students were reluctant to do for anything more than a paragraph at the end. They explained that presenting Aquinas' view of salvation was difficult enough; they simply didn't have energy to undertake a critique. That Alan crafted such a critique and that it focused on the theology *qua* theology is not surprising given Alan's interest in doctrine. Alan's theology professor responded with nearly two pages of handwritten endnotes (in addition to voluminous comments throughout the paper), engaging Alan's critique in detail. This thoughtful and thorough response likely affirmed Alan's sense that Villanova encouraged students to engage questions of faith with full intellectual rigor.

More surprising was the overt appearance of the doctrine theme in Alan's third literature paper and its reception by his literature professor. The assignment invited students to write on *The Merchant of Venice* or *Paradise Lost* and offered two potential topics: comparing marriage in the two texts or commenting on whether Eve was created "sufficient to stand." Alan's paper focused instead on questions of Christian doctrine, tracing the theological implications of the debates among the fallen angels in *Paradise Lost*. Throughout the body of his paper, Alan uses close readings of the fallen angels' statements to argue how their conceptions of God and His creation differ.

In the final two paragraphs of the paper, however, Alan shifts into a different mode, introducing the concept of hubris for the first time:

> The crime committed by the fallen angels was hubris. They felt themselves equal to God in nature, deserving of his power, and for this, He threw them into [hell]. . . . The[y] have not learned the lesson of hubris when this discussion begins. . . . While [the fallen angels] perhaps suffer from ignorance of God's supremacy, they must also maintain some form of hope for the future. Though arrogant and impossible, the fallen angels do secure hope for themselves through the inferences made as a basis for this discussion. While they cannot teach one another how to take things for granted, they may foster tranquility through their discussions. However, for true peace of mind, one must single-handedly take these inferences and run with them.

Although this meditation on hubris, doctrinal implications, and the search for religious tranquility certainly resonates with Milton's epic, this conclusion might also be read as going off on a religious tangent—focusing not on literary analysis but on the sin of hubris (the ultimate sin in Augustinian theology). Despite the doctrinal theme and the hubris-focused conclusion—and contrary to what previous scholarship might predict—neither Alan nor his professor experienced the paper as veering into inappropriate territory. Why?

Alan saw the conclusion not as a religious statement but as a hybrid of disciplinary genres. He realized that he wasn't writing a traditional literature paper: in an interview he contrasted literature papers that demand a focus on close textual analysis with philosophy papers where "it's all my thought, forget the quotes." In the body of his paper, Alan grounds his argument in textual evidence in a very "literary" way, but at the end he moves away from the text and argues more "philosophically." Although we hear echoes of Alan's recurrent preoccupation with questions of theological doctrine, he never entirely abandons his concern for meeting disciplinary expectations. Alan sees himself as writing in a hybrid genre, not breaking with academic convention altogether.

Alan's literature professor also seems unconcerned by the focus on religion. In her response to an earlier draft she writes that Alan has chosen an "interesting topic," praises the body of the paper, then encourages Alan to "set out the stakes" and explain "why you're interested/what we'll gain from following this problem through." She never expresses any discomfort with the content or tone of the paper. Given the interdisciplinary nature of Interdisc, she was able to read Alan's paper (and especially its potentially "preachy" conclusion) not as an inappropriate insertion of faith-based writing into academic discourse, but as a moment of interdisciplinary connection.

## Betty: Navigating the Minefield of Religion

Unlike her first-year classmates, Betty was a sophomore transfer from a secular university. One of only three non-Catholic students in Interdisc, Betty was the only one to speak publicly of not being Catholic. If she experienced any religious crisis, she never alluded to it in interviews. Her religious background differed from Alan's and Tigra's, not only because she was not Catholic but also because she had changed religious affiliations. Her parents were born and raised Catholic, but had (in Betty's words) "turned away" from Catholicism. Until she was in fifth grade, Betty had been a member of a Unitarian Universalist church, but after her father decided it wasn't enough of a "real" religion, her family began attending Quaker meeting. "I really like that," Betty said, "and I definitely consider myself a Quaker."

Though she expressed little doubt about her faith, she expressed concern about how others perceived that faith. If Alan was concerned with developing a clear sense of religious doctrine and Tigra (as we will see) felt frustrated with what she perceived as religious hypocrisy, Betty felt as if she were navigating a minefield. Villanova describes itself as a university that welcomes students of all faiths, and certainly Betty had experiences that affirmed her Quaker faith; for instance, the chair of the English department—also a Quaker—had made her acquaintance and offered to bring her along to his meeting house, a gesture Betty clearly appreciated. Other experiences, however, led Betty to view Villanova's religious culture with some suspicion.

Her theology professor became a focus of that suspicion. In interview after interview, Betty made clear that although she liked her professor and thought he was a very fine teacher, she worried that he was trying to promulgate Catholic beliefs. Her concern sprang in part from her confusion over a comment her professor had made at the end of an individual conference held about halfway through the semester. She explained:

> I love [the theology professor] to death but I look at him as really having an
> agenda. One of the things he said to me before I left [was] "most of the people
> in the world aren't religious," or "as religious as we are." Almost like he was
> testing me to see if I was religious enough. And I got the impression from him
> that one of his objectives was to see who was more religious than whom. I think
> it's really important to him and I honestly think he feels that one of his jobs as
> a Villanova theologian or faculty is . . . to instill some belief in us. I don't know,
> maybe I'm totally reading it wrong, but that was the impression I got.

As Betty describes her uncertainty about her professor's motives, she sees
them as linked, almost inextricably, to Villanova itself. Though Betty's beliefs
about her professor's motives grew out of particular interactions with him in
class, in conference, and via his assignments, they also reflect a concern about
the culture of Villanova as a whole.

Significantly, though, this concern about a religious litmus test seems to
have affected her writing in only one of her papers—the first theology paper
on Aquinas. What troubled Betty most about the Aquinas assignment was that
it was designed to "get the Catholic kids learning exactly how a very famous
Catholic theologian says this is how you are saved." Although Betty's interpretation may have been influenced by her conference with her professor, it
was also grounded in the text of the assignment. She particularly latched onto
the phrase, "I want you to be his defense lawyer, get inside his head." She read
through the assignment for the first time during an interview, and after she read
the phrase "I want you to make a case for the reasonableness of Aquinas' theology on this issue," she paused to make the following observation:

> So I guess there I think he wants, he's sure that you find Aquinas reasonable,
> which I think most of us have come to decide. But ah, oh, be his defense
> lawyer. So he wants you to defend Aquinas. See, you can't, he doesn't want
> you to go against him.

In fact, the assignment does acknowledge the possibility of disagreement and
a number of Betty's classmates did include some critique. But Betty seems
most influenced by those phrases that suggest that there is a party line to which
successful students will adhere.

That Betty is wary of testing how much dissent even her classmates will
accept is clear in an excerpt from a group interview conducted with Betty,
Alan, and Tigra. Betty initiates the conversation by asking what the others
thought of the Aquinas assignment. They respond that it was a reasonable,
challenging assignment. Then Tigra asks, "Did *you* not like it?" Betty quickly
answers, "No, I thought it was alright," but then redirects the conversation,
eventually suggesting that their professor may have a personal agenda:

*Betty:* Maybe it's because I come from a bit of a different perspective but
(*pause*) it seemed, it seemed very like (*pause*) Villanova would like you
to think this way so I'll kind of teach it that way. To me.

*Tigra:* Really?

*Alan:* I didn't see that at all.

*Betty:* Like Villanova would like you to know exactly what Aquinas said, to the tee, so I'm going to make sure you get out of your theology requirement knowing this.

Tigra seems a bit flummoxed by this possibility, but after mulling it over, concedes that such an agenda might be possible, and attributes their different perceptions to their different religious backgrounds:

*Tigra:* See for me, a lot of what he says is actually pretty unbiased. Because I come from people pushing it down my throat more. I had seven years of Catholic school so to me he seems very, you know, not like that. But if you're a Quaker it might seem that way.

Alan, however, continues to argue against any hidden agenda, saying:

*Alan:* Everyone has a bias. Everyone has a reason for teaching anything. So they're going to teach you the material that's relevant to whatever their class is. I don't find it a bad thing. You just have to realize you're getting this from a theology teacher. Oh my god they're talking about theology! You know, what would you expect?

Here Alan seems to miss Betty's concern that their professor may have a particular religious agenda. He does not (in this particular exchange anyway) even acknowledge the possible risks of having to write about religious issues.

Based on a semester's worth of observations and interviews, I believe that Alan did not intend to ignore Betty's concerns. Rather I suspect he felt much freer to be critical of a tradition he felt firmly part of: he was the loyal opposition rather than an uncertain outsider. Given that Alan experienced Villanova as supportive of his theological inquiries, inside the classroom and out, it is not surprising that he was willing to critique Aquinas' theology. Betty, interpreting the religious culture of Villanova and of her theology class quite differently, worries that she may be facing an unspoken test—not simply of her academic abilities but of her spiritual condition. In both cases, these students' perceptions of the religious culture of their university likely influenced their sense of rhetorical options.

Rather than adhering to a thesis-driven structure, Betty wrote her paper as a dialogue between Aquinas and a highly deferential student. Betty explained that she chose a dialogue because "If I'm pretending to be Aquinas, I figured that's as much in his head as I can get." But it is also the case that this particular structure allowed Betty to put all questions and answers into the mouths of others without indicting herself.

Despite the fact that Betty described her theology professor as "having an agenda," she does not seem to have worried about the litmus test when writing her second theology paper. At first this may seem difficult to explain since both theology assignments asked students to demonstrate a knowledge of the basic theological tenets of various thinkers and to trace the implications of those tenets. But in fact, the classroom context had shifted significantly by the time Betty wrote the second paper, alleviating her concerns. Betty's second theology paper looked much like those of her classmates: an argumentative paper that supports a thesis with textual evidence. Why not use a dialogue for the second paper? Perhaps she didn't want to overuse a somewhat gimmicky strategy. But the second paper was not as risky as the first, since it asked students to compare ancient and modern thinkers. Betty found the modern views of Hobbes and Locke more congenial than the writings of Anselm, Aquinas, Luther, and Calvin—as did her Catholic classmates, who were raised with the same post-Enlightenment values. Rather than inhabiting a non-Catholic minority, Betty was now one of many post-Enlightenment students, and the litmus test no longer applied.

Based on her reading of the religious culture of the university and her theology classroom in particular, Betty sees the primary challenge in writing about these religious issues as the matter of negotiating her own identity. Those challenges are not dependent solely on a Quaker worldview or Villanova's religious culture, but on a subtle and frequently shifting nexus of individual beliefs, classroom contexts, and institutional culture.[2]

## Tigra: Questioning Religious Hypocrisy

Like Alan, Tigra was preoccupied with religious issues, but her self-described "religious crisis" had started before she arrived at Villanova. Raised by devout Catholic parents, Tigra had attended Catholic middle and high schools, but in her senior year had gone into what she described as a "tailspin about religion." This crisis cast a long shadow over her personal and academic life, and it came up in nearly every interview.

In particular, Tigra was preoccupied with figuring out what was "real" about her faith. Although relatively certain that she would eventually return to her Catholic faith, she felt driven to understand whether that faith represented an "absolute truth, if such a thing exists" or if it is "just a social thing." Tigra believed that people often create a god who suits their own needs, and explained how she saw this tendency at work in one of her own family members:

> What I realized is that . . . he's just doing the same thing as all these theologian guys. The way he lives his life best is by concentrating on the doom and brimstone and fire and hell, so he makes these things up. [He] lives his life best when he thinks about these things, [but they aren't] truths, if those exist. They're just things that help him with a better life and they're truthful for him but maybe they're not for everybody else.

Whereas Alan was working to understand the theology of the church fathers and its implications for his daily life, Tigra was overwhelmed by the possibility that religious doctrine might be nothing more than a self-serving projection.

This concern made Tigra particularly sensitive to religious hypocrisy. She compared her experience in Interdisc unfavorably to her high school English class where people "weren't afraid to question, even if the answer was kind of off the wall."

> Everyone [in class at Villanova] was pretty much sure they were secure with God . . . I'm very distrustful of people . . . who can say "I believe in God" because I don't feel that they've questioned it enough at this point in time. . . . I think it might be part of the university . . . because I find very few genuine people since I've been here. And a lot of them seem very superficial to me. Not really questioning things deeper than what clothes are you wearing? Are they from the Gap or where? Not to say they're not here, but it's hard to find them. It might be the university.

Unlike Alan, who experienced Villanova as supporting his struggle to understand his faith, Tigra wondered if her classmates' unwillingness to wrestle with difficult questions—a type of religious hypocrisy or denial—might be linked to the religious culture of Villanova as a whole, a perception that led her to transfer after she finished Interdisc II.

Tigra's religious themes are visible in her writing, but they operate much more covertly than in Alan's writing. Her history professor's medieval diary assignment, for example, asked students to record "a day in the life" of a medieval European in order to put material details into a larger context. Like many of her classmates, Tigra wrote her diary as a monk. Most students chose this perspective because one of their assigned texts included many details about monastic life. But when Tigra wrote her medieval diary, she did not focus on those material details. Instead, she composed a psychological portrait of a hypocritical monk. As the diary begins the monk recounts how he fell asleep during morning prayers; he later writes, "I found myself doubting as to whether or not I should be here, in your most holy presence, under the pretense of renouncing the world."

This subtle shift in focus—from the material to the psychological—is grounded in Tigra's personal experience. Tigra's experience of writing this text differed significantly from her classmates' experiences in ways that the text itself cannot fully reveal. First, Tigra was writing about the theme of religious hypocrisy that so deeply concerned her. Second, she was writing to a large extent from personal experience, having gone on monastic retreat with her mother.

It would be a mistake to think that Tigra simply got swept up in religious preoccupations, writing about her hypocrisy theme and throwing other concerns aside. She remained aware of her professor's disciplinary expectations, explaining that the diary was hard to write because she wanted to keep in mind something stressed repeatedly in class: namely, that the modern viewpoint is very different from the medieval.

> I was a monk and his thoughts kept coming out very modern. Like things *I*
> thought. I actually visited a monastery . . . so it ended up being things that I
> thought while I was there. Which were kind of good but kind of bad because
> I think it was too modern and [the history professor] wanted something that
> was from a previous time period.

Underneath the surface of this paper, then, are Tigra's religious experiences
and concerns as well as her efforts to write about them in ways that would be
satisfactory in an academic context.

Tigra faced a similar challenge in her theology papers. As her interaction
with Betty indicates, she did not worry about her religious identity being judged.
Instead she worried about meeting disciplinary expectations. Tigra, like Betty,
generally kept her religious preoccupations out of her writing. Even when writing about theological issues for her theology class, echoes of her religious themes
can be found only in the conclusions. This makes sense given Tigra's view of the
discipline of theology, which she felt was not a forum for personal opinions: "It's
nice that we have our own theological opinions, but we're not interested in our
opinions. We're learning the history of what other people have said." Whereas
Alan devotes a significant portion of his Aquinas paper to offering a critique of
Aquinas, Tigra includes only two paragraphs (about one of her paper's ten pages).

Tigra's second theology paper offers an even clearer example of how she
pushed her own religious themes to the periphery of her papers. Her initial thesis, articulated in the paper's opening paragraph, is that "Locke, as a leader of
early modern thought, separates himself from classical [theologians] in his
ideas on religion and the state, toleration and zeal, salvation through works
and/or faith, ceremony, miracles, and humanity's role in the universe." The
body of the paper follows this implied outline exactly, comparing Locke to
Anselm, Aquinas, and Luther on those six topics. Only in the final paragraph
does Tigra finally allow herself a comparison, not included in her thesis, which
echoes one of her religious preoccupations:

> Despite these differences, Locke engages in essentially the same project as
> those who went before him, from Anselm to Luther and Hobbes. He, like
> every other [theologian], simply reinterprets God's character and the role
> God plays in humanity's life. . . . The result is the same: Humanity defines
> God according to what it wants to believe. Whether humanity speculates
> about a deity's role, regarding itself as lowly and insignificant, or openly
> admits to regarding man as all-important, humanity still taints its specula-
> tions of God with its own preconceived notions of itself.

Here Tigra finally includes in her paper a theory she had articulated in interview: that individuals create God according to what they want to believe.
Eager to meet disciplinary expectations by focusing on "the history of what
other people have said," she allows herself to incorporate her religious convictions only in the final two sentences.

In his response to this paper, Tigra's professor identified this last point as key to what she wrestled with in understanding these thinkers. And his written comments suggest that Tigra's effort to keep her religious themes out of her writing may have undermined her argument: "You make many good points but they don't really add up to a finished paper yet. It might have helped if you incorporated some of your conclusion in your introduction and let it drive or guide the discussion that followed." Based on her sense of academic propriety (that in theology "we're not interested in our opinions") Tigra worked to minimize the appearance of her deeply felt religious concerns, which—ironically, given her efforts to be a good student—may have worked against her academic success.

## Conclusions

These analyses illuminate the ways students negotiate the complex nexus among their individual religious themes, the rhetorical demands of particular classrooms, and the religious culture of their academic institution. As my analyses of Alan's and Tigra's efforts illustrate, in our attempts to understand a given religion's worldview we must not overlook significant differences that emerge as students work out their individual religious themes within particular classroom and larger institutional contexts. Betty's experiences further emphasize that those classroom and institutional contexts can shift in subtle but important ways, making religious identity a key issue at one point in the semester and relatively insignificant only a few weeks later.

I am not arguing that we must (or even can) attend to the religious dimensions of academic writing whenever they emerge: after all, as Tigra's papers show, the manifestations of those concerns are often brief and covert. But these cases suggest that we need to be prepared to talk with students about how to draw on religious concerns as they engage in academic work, how religious themes may productively inform their inquiries and compositions. We also need to be prepared to discuss the degree to which they may incorporate those religious themes into their writing. We need to learn from students (and from our religious studies colleagues) how students are being taught to write about religious issues in an academic context. In some cases, students are making interdisciplinary connections that, because of the university's disciplinary divisions, we might not see. Finally, we must open ourselves to the possibility that when we confer with students and read their writing, our students may be trying not to preach, convert, or witness but to negotiate the intersection between religious beliefs and academic work. The more we can be sensitive to that possibility, the better equipped we will be to help students in this very difficult, very important process.

## Notes

1. These analyses are strongly influenced by the work of Prior (1998), who argues that literate activities are situated, mediated, and dispersed. Although a student's

interpretation and completion of writing tasks are linked to times, places, and social identities beyond the classroom, I believe that careful analysis can re-create some of the rich texture of these literate activities. In order to better understand the intersection of students' religious identities and literate activities, I worked to identify—through analysis of student papers, interviews, classroom transcripts, and field notes—three intersecting elements: the moment-to-moment interactions within a classroom; the traditions of reading and writing that students and teachers brought to that classroom; and the religious concerns of individual students. I focused in particular on identifying religious themes resonant for each student. To do so, I first read their papers, identifying elements related to religion or spirituality. I next analyzed transcripts of individual interviews and a focus group with Alan, Tigra, and Betty for comments related to religious belief, identifying for each student a handful of recurrent themes. I then reread the papers in the light of those themes and full class discussions. This final round of analysis confirmed my earlier readings of Tigra's and Betty's papers, and yielded new insights on Alan's papers.

2. After reading a draft of this chapter, the theology professor offered an additional explanation. He explained that a student in a subsequent Interdisc class "remarked that each time I taught a new author they were all convinced that I agreed with [the new author]. If that was also the case during the earlier class, Betty would have seen me do my Luther and Calvin routine by the time she wrote the second paper. That may have taken some of the edge off her suspicion."

# Works Cited

Caputo, J. D., and M. J. Scanlon, eds. 1999. *God, the Gift, and Postmodernism.* Bloomington: Indiana University Press.

Nowacek, R. S. 2001. Writing Instruction in the Interdisciplinary Classroom: Histories, Challenges, Possibilities. Unpublished dissertation. University of Wisconsin, Madison.

Office of University Admission. 2001. "A View of Villanova." http://www.villanova.edu/enroll/admission/university/ Accessed 28 April 2005.

Prior, P. A. 1998. *Writing/Disciplinarity: A Sociohistoric Account of Literate Activity in the Academy.* Mahwah, NJ: Laurence Erlbaum Associates.

Rand, L. A. 2001. "Enacting Faith: Evangelical Discourse and the Discipline of Composition Studies." *College Composition and Communication* 52 (3): 349–67.

# 14

# (Sacra)Mentality
## *Catholic Identity in the Postmodern Classroom*

Jeffrey P. Cain

> Our vision of the face of God is always fragmentary and
> impaired by the limits of our understanding.
> > —Pope John Paul II,
> > *Fides et Ratio*

> God is a Lobster.
> > —Gilles Deleuze and Felix Guattari,
> > *A Thousand Plateaus*

Two major institutions, the Church and the university, share an underlying concern with the imbricated acts of composition and inscription. For the university, writing is a way of generating, formalizing, and transmitting knowledge; for the Church, the act of writing serves as holy writ and ritual codification. Through inscription, Judeo-Christian patriarchs handed down law and creed. Through the mystery of the *logos*, the Word was both deified and made flesh in the person of Christ. Through the scriptures, God—at least putatively—still reveals his Word to believers and unbelievers alike. When a university's mission statement and other public documents attest to a specific religious purpose, it is faith in the sacred text that cuts across culture to connect or to oppose the academic to the spiritual.

As do their peers at secular schools, students at Catholic universities perform the tasks of reading and writing in a shifting and postmodern intellectual setting. The term *postmodern,* however, is by no means static. The advent and subsequent devolution of postmodernism poses much more of a challenge in the Catholic composition classroom than it does elsewhere, because recent conceptions of textuality challenge the belief that inscription—written words—can be imbued with singular or essentialist meanings. While most secular English departments were adapting to the demise of the old new criticism and the arrival of dialogic, deconstructive, and post-colonialist literary theories, Catholic institutions found themselves confronted with a new epistemology that seemed to threaten the very foundations of their existence. So widely revered a Catholic scholar as Gerald A. McCool has characterized deconstructionist thought as having "caused the present-day crisis of meaning, the pervasive despair of finding of any meaning for human life or for the world in which that life is lived" (2000, 97–98). McCool goes on to note that Pope John Paul II regarded this crisis of meaning as the single most important challenge to the Christian faith today (98).[1]

During the last decade a sustained debate has transpired in Catholic higher education, centering primarily on documents such as Pope John Paul II's apostolic constitution, *Ex Corde Ecclesiae* (1990), and an encyclical letter, *Fides et Ratio* (1998). These documents are addressed to the Church as a whole, and they set forth, respectively, the Pope's position on the role that Catholic universities should play in encouraging students to develop a spiritual identity and his opinions concerning the relationship of faith to reason. In both cases, he adjures Catholic intellectuals to maintain philosophical principles consistent with the Church's religious doctrine and epistemological tenets. Because Catholic universities in America function in the same competitive academic environment and face much the same practical financial needs as their secular counterparts, some Catholics oppose parts of *Ex Corde Ecclesiae*.[2] In keeping with the Church's deference to writing as the primary site of authority, this resistance is largely textual.

The epistemological assumptions that undergird *Fides et Ratio* and *Ex Corde Ecclesiae* are important, simply because they affect so many people who are concerned with higher education as an institution. The more than two hundred Catholic colleges and universities in the United States serve thousands of undergraduate and graduate students in every academic discipline. All Catholic universities seek to distinguish themselves from secular institutions by publishing mission statements that connect educational practice with the Church's definitions of spirituality, morality, epistemology, and social progress. Almost all Catholic universities maintain affiliation with a specific religious order, such as the Dominicans or the Jesuits, and all are in some degree answerable to the Church for the beliefs and values that they purport to convey. Catholic universities thus understand themselves in the most basic way as having a definite cultural agenda: to harbor and impart a Catholic identity firmly grounded in Christian theology arising from the Catholic intellectual tradition. To accomplish this task, the Church presumes a metaphysical and spiritual hierarchy, a great chain of being that extends downward from God to the clergy, the institution, the administrators, the professors, and finally the students.

For writing instructors, this hegemonic chain is significant because it pre-scribes certain views regarding the nature of the self and of truth, concepts that have concerned rhetoric and composition theorists for centuries. Therefore, I want to explore the pedagogical implications of Catholic *identity* (the term itself is problematically singular) in three distinct but closely related ways. First, by rereading *Ex Corde Ecclesiae* as a textual artifact, I hope to shed new light on its social and cultural implications, as opposed to its purely theologi-cal import. Second, by deploying the concept of the Body without Organs (BwO) developed in the work of Gilles Deleuze and Felix Guattari, I want to examine the apparent disjunction between the Vatican's epistemological posi-tion and the vestiges of postmodernism that still inform composition theory and practice. Third, I wish to suggest that such an examination might lead to a critical pedagogy that strives to interrogate, as well as impart, moral and the-ological precepts.

It is time for appraisal of the uses of Catholic intellectual tradition. Such a critique should test assumptions about the perceived relationship of the self to the postmodern world. For teachers and students of rhetoric and composi-tion, this analysis will pose particularly challenging questions. Although the dominant epistemological ground of the writing classroom has for some time now been comfortably social-constructionist, exactly *whose* social construc-tions will prevail remains to be seen. The concepts that undergird the BwO illuminate the Church's efforts to contain critical pedagogy, a goal realized primarily through the numinous workings of twin aspects of theological ontol-ogy: immanence and transcendence. The idea of transcendence is the more familiar of the two and is easily recognized in the Church's hierarchical and supernatural view of reality. Immanence, however, is much less spectacular and more localized than transcendence and often renders itself as the trope of organism. *Ex Corde Ecclesiae*, for example, is a text that proclaims its organic origins in its very title. While resistance to hegemony of an absolute or tran-scendental kind has long been the subject of the composition classroom's crit-ical pedagogy, the concept and function of immanence deserves more atten-tion, particularly at the level of student writing. I will show, therefore, that the BwO can deconstruct and demystify the organic without doing violence to immanence itself. I would also contend that this same clarification and critique may ultimately foster the intellectual and spiritual strength of conviction, or faith, that the Church itself intends to inspire.[3] Therefore, a de-territorializa-tion of organism is not so much iconoclastic as it is regenerative.

## The Catholic University as Organism

Catholicism does not, despite its name, occupy a monolithic category. Instead, it comprises a set of highly—though not perfectly—inclusive social, spiritual, artistic, historical, and theological relationships. A range of interpretive polit-ical subjectivities pervades the spaces between and beyond, forming a culture

that the Church simultaneously circumscribes and authorizes in such textual
spaces as *Ex Corde Ecclesiae* and *Fides et Ratio*. Catholic culture encodes its
mysteries in a complex series of tropes that derive their meaning largely from
the idea of a hierarchical and yet "organic" unity that always seeks to transcend the individual in order to ensure the spiritual health of the whole body
of the Church. *Fides et Ratio* therefore argues that the real connection between
faith and reason is specifically an organic one, since it is the body of the
Church that contains both belief and thought.

> Through philosophy's work, the ability to speculate which is proper to the
> human intellect produces a rigorous mode of thought; and then in turn,
> through the logical coherence of the affirmations made and the organic unity
> of their content, it produces a systematic body of knowledge. (Pope John
> Paul II 1998, Introduction 4)[4]

What is organism's role in this context? *Fides et Ratio* also contends that, in
antiquity, philosophy's organic unity with faith was capable of having
"attained the supreme good and ultimate truth in the person of the Word made
flesh" (4.42). The semiotic enigma of the *logos* that becomes an organism (a
man named Jesus of Nazareth) is epitomized by the revelatory character of the
Eucharist, "in which the indissoluble unity between the signifier and signified
makes it possible to grasp the depths of the mystery" (1.13). Here lies the epistemological root of Catholicism's arguments for *organ-ism*, the belief that certain organs maintain a unitary and "indissoluble" connection to being and
meaning. The organic is also the immanent, the face and flesh of God made
observable within the human sphere. Thus the Church's theory of signs is pre-
structuralist, since it affirms an essential and immanent connection between
word and thing, the old semiotic conundrum that argues the seamless union of
*res* and *verbum*. In this sense, Catholic iconography and symbolism are akin
to the sign theory that arose in the classical world from divination, magic, and
the early practice of medicine.[5]

*Ex Corde Ecclesiae* thoroughly elaborates the doctrine of organic unity,
constructing the university as an organism by reliance on the etymology of the
word *university*, whose Latin roots denote a "turning as one," which in turn
implies a coordinated movement of the revolving spheres of both faith and reason. These concentric and symmetrical spheres subsist in an essentialized,
immanent, and mysterious organic harmony that both defines and orders cos-
mology. The model extends itself downward and inward to the heart, in the
well-known medieval and early-modern theory of "man as microcosm." Consequently, the rhetorical and epistemological foundations of *Ex Corde Ecclesiae* support a strongly prescriptive vision of culture, developed according to
dicta first laid down at the time of Vatican II. "Culture," remarks Pope John
Paul, "indicates all those factors by which man refines and unfolds his mani-
fold spiritual and bodily qualities. It means his effort to bring the world itself
under his control by his knowledge and his labor." [6]

This view of culture refers to the human or knowable sphere of an ultimately unknowable cosmos; it begins with the individual human body but includes family and civic community, both of which help to construct the body politic and the body of the Catholic Church, even as they participate in the central trope of the graced communion, the Eucharist, the immanent body of Christ. The function of the university in this paradigm is to search reality for aspects of the transcendent, and to disseminate such discoveries as portals that lead to intellectual and spiritual growth.[7] The perfect university would then be the institutional culture in which the Catholic Church does its thinking; no actual dissonance between the intellectual and the spiritual would obtain.

*Ex Corde Ecclesiae* exploits this same longing of the individual for transcendence and unification by referring epistemology to Augustine's notion of innate joy in "searching for, discovering, and communicating truth"(Pope John Paul II 1990, 1). Furthermore, citing one of his own official writings, Pope John Paul II states that "a Catholic University's task is 'to unite existentially by intellectual effort two orders of reality that too frequently tend to be placed in opposition as though they were antithetical: the search for truth, and the certainty of already knowing the fount of truth'" (1).[8] This declaration simultaneously invokes and denies the binary opposition of truth as humanistic discovery and truth as divine revelation. However, the reconciliation of these two categories depends on the imposition of unity by what *Ex Corde Ecclesiae* specifically describes as "*privileged . . .* intellectual effort" or force (1, emphasis in original). Thus, the purpose of the Catholic university becomes "proclaiming the meaning of truth," and of "researching [its] essential connection with the supreme Truth, who is God" (4).

Such a position demands transcendent teleology. *Ex Corde Ecclesiae* states flatly that a university, and especially a Catholic university, "has to be a 'living union' of individual organisms dedicated to the search for truth . . . [i]t is necessary to work towards a higher synthesis of knowledge, in which alone lies the possibility of satisfying that thirst for truth which is profoundly inscribed on the heart of the human person" (16). The "individual organism" in this passage is a biological trope that (in)forms the physical and spiritual bodies of students and scholars, whose hearts are "inscribed" with a thirst for truth. The title of the document itself, *Ex Corde Ecclesiae*, "Out of the Heart of the Church," appropriately unfolds the authorial presence of a centripetal institutional organ: a sacred heart of perpetual re-inscription that (organ)izes— in an anagogical as well as analogical sense—the symbiosis of the Church's intellectually organic body and cells. The microcosm of this biospiritual text may be read in the inscription on the individual academic's graven heart. Students and professors emerge, not as mere individuals, but as meaningful links in the chain of being, their proper efforts tending always toward the teleological and increasingly unified—although *less* organic—"higher synthesis" of knowledge. An intellectual who willingly identifies with the Catholic Church is, in this sense, an incarnation or repetition of the *logos*. It could be said that all the classrooms and all the courses in a Catholic university also involve continual reiteration of the *logos*, inasmuch as they participate in the immanent and organic body of the Church. Composition and writing classes are especially implicated in the repetition of the word. Critical writing pedagogies, of course, claim to impart an empowering ability of intellectual resistance to models of pure transcendence, essentialism, and hegemonic unity. For any form of this pedagogy to function in a Catholic university, articulation of the epistemology of organism and immanence is vital.

## The Classroom as a Body Without Organs

In a fairly detailed history of the postmodern investigation of being, Catholic theologian Michael Peters has argued that only after Nietzsche's attack on traditional metaphysics could a revaluation of the concepts of presence and immanence occur.[9] For compliant intellectuals in Catholic colleges and universities, the loss of modernist assumptions regarding a transcendent and knowable faith has produced an affective state of nostalgia. Authority no longer appears as a simple and singular force vested in relatively just and benevolent instructors. For years it had been quite possible to construct the space of the classroom as protected, democratic, contemplative, and transparently intersubjective. Instructors could pride themselves on having constructed an intellectual forum where debate and the free exchange of ideas were not only feasible but required. However, the critique of the Western metaphysics of presence by Derrida, Foucault, and others has unfolded and demystified authority, thereby showing that both students and teachers are implicated in the same limiting and hierarchical system. Clearly, this situation is far more deleterious to the traditionally liberal values of democracy and personal accomplishment than was formerly admitted. Yet even if the days of unified and essentialist meaning are gone, it does not follow that the default position is nihilism.

Of the thinkers that Peters discusses, the one seemingly most antipathetic toward Catholicism is Gilles Deleuze. Both alone and in collaboration with Felix Guattari, Deleuze created a series of texts that rethink the terms by which being and epistemology are understood. One of Deleuze and Guattari's concepts, the Body without Organs (BwO), provides a series of useful vantage points from which to critique the composition classroom as an organ in an organization: the Catholic University. The BwO appears in more than one guise and more than one nexus in Deleuze and Guattari's works; like all of their concepts, its meaning is highly fluid and contextual. Nevertheless, we must catch a brief sense of the concept so that we can put it to use here. In *The Two-Fold Thought of Deleuze and Guattari: Intersections and Animations* (1998), Charles J. Stivale remarks that the BwO operates as a set of mutually delimiting tensions:

[F]or every social interaction or situation, a highly complex and collective overlapping of expression of desire is in play, the elements of which are at once dispersed and highly dynamic. Just as this dynamic energy propels desire's expression and production, so too does a counterforce, the body without organs, arrest this movement provisionally, yet also propel this productive energy further. The body without organs functions, therefore, as a key component for conceptualizing at once desiring and social production. (10–11)

The facets of the BwO called into service here are fittingly evoked by considering yet another definition, circulated by Aden Evans in 1996. Evans writes that the BwO is best understood as a limit, because it simultaneously enables and restricts the multiplicities of flux that serve Deleuze and Guattari as both physics and metaphysics. The BwO acts as a recording surface on which all the flows of earth, air, fire, water, people, words, ideas, and culture that constitute reality freely merge and diverge. The need for flows to continue unrestricted is called desire, but on the surface of the BwO each flow is nonetheless interrupted, and it is these breaks in the flow, these striations of the otherwise smooth space of the BwO's surface, that disclose reality to human perception.

Why "Body-without-Organs"? The absence of organs means the lack of organization, or the fact that the BwO is not broken down into parts distinct from each other. It remains a body, though, even if it only ever presents itself as an attractor or repeller, a surface to slip over or bounce off of. For no sooner does a flow return to the BwO, than it is reconstituted as part of another flow. (Evans 1996)

Furthermore, there is no "inside" to the BwO, because it is a folded surface conceived as an infinite limit, a kind of origami of time and space. Analogies might be drawn between the BwO as a thought model and the Moebius strip or the Klein bottle. For the BwO, however, the appearance of physical extension (if it occurs at all) is at best a secondary quality. I would suggest that the BwO might be thought of, for our purposes, as part of the deconstruction of organism, but with immanence intact. Or it might be said that immanence is the aporia, or figure of textual doubt, within which the concepts of the BwO and organism can neither be reconciled nor rejected. Less negatively, the BwO is what transpires during the simultaneous existence of free-flowing desire and infinitely precise limit or striation.

Evans remarks that, because it embodies both free flow *and* interruption, or segmentarity, the BwO makes the idea of complete freedom paradoxical. The only real autonomy appears to lie in death. Hence an acquaintance with the BwO leads to the basically optimistic question, "What would be a limited freedom?" (Evans 1996). This deconstruction of the idea of absolute freedom is not, therefore, something imposed by the critic's mind, as Jacques Derrida has pointed out; on the contrary, it is rhetorically unavoidable, a phenomenon of language that "just happens" (Olson 1990). Again, a pragmatic decentering of the notion of absolute freedom does not necessarily indicate a headlong flight into nihilism. A most important point of definition: the BwO "arrests" or limits *pure* desire and desiring production, but it also sets free the flow of desire for overcoding and striation. Therefore, the BwO is a limit when seen in relation to pure flux, but it is an agent of flow and release when compared to monolithic or opposing binary categories, specifically (for the present purposes) the organism.

As Deleuze and Guattari note in *A Thousand Plateaus* (1987), the BwO is not the enemy of the organs, which are themselves a folded series of interrupted or stratified flows, but *organism*, the belief that certain organs naturally belong together in an autonomous and rigidly segmented structure (158–59). Therefore, the concept of the BwO would appear to oppose itself spontaneously to the idea of the Catholic university as organism. However, "oppose" is far too static a term with which to render Deleuze and Guattari's highly dynamic and versatile concept. To bring the BwO to bear on the university as a site of organized Catholic identity, it is essential to note that for Deleuze and Guattari organism is only one of God's many manifestations, all of which easily sustain a naturalized belief, all of which operate by means of a variably dual mechanism. "God is a Lobster, or a double pincer, a double bind" (40) and thus also the agent of a double articulation, a process of unfolding and folding, that operates constantly to encompass the meaning of the creative actions that take place on the surface of the BwO. Deleuze and Guattari illustrate this concept by means of two separate yet overlapping processes from the academic discipline of geology. "Sedimentation," they write, "deposits units of cyclic sediment according to a statistical order" and therefore functions as a first-order articulation, a kind of unfolding. "The second articulation is the 'folding' that sets up a stable functional structure and effects the passage from sediment to sedimentary rock" (1987, 41).

Deleuze and Guattari thus offer a conception of God as the creator of a twofold process, rather than as a metaphor, myth, anthropomorphic projection, taboo, or fetish. The example of sedimentary rock formation works on more than one level, since the etiological tales told of the earth usually claim the first principles of geology for God.[10] These concepts sort agreeably with the passage from *Gaudium et Spes*, cited in *Ex Corde Ecclesiae*, that calls culture a "two-fold" entity. Deleuze and Guattari's multiple points of view of the Church's relationship to the Catholic university entail neither a strict affirmation of religious doctrine nor its outright negation. Instead, such a perspective allows for further consideration of the flow of possibilities and nuances that merge, emerge, and diverge in the twofold model. Deleuze and Guattari do not reject God or the idea of religious and spiritual culture, but they do contrive to rethink ontotheology, the a priori assignment to a monotheistic deity of the Western metaphysics of presence and transcendence.

The use of Deleuze and Guattari's ideas in a composition classroom facilitates more sophisticated acts of critical thinking than might otherwise be expected. Models such as the BwO would, of course, need to be approached gradually, perhaps by way of the idea of stratification. Rhetorical analysis and close reading skills are the keys to this process, but I would argue that Deleuze and Guattari's basic tenets are no more difficult to grasp than, for example, the finer points of Aristotelian logic. In my own practice, I have found that thinking along the lines of double articulation, flow, becoming, desire, production, segmentarity, and stratification helps students conceive of and map new intellectual space; these concepts also benefit my own work in responding to student writing. Unlike more traditional thought models, Deleuzian epistemology celebrates and analyzes paradox rather than rejecting, containing, or ignoring it.

Reading the iconography of the cross provides a good example of this optimistic approach to figures of apparent contrariety. A certain use of *poesis*, both in its original Greek sense of "making" and its literary meaning of creative inscription, pervades the workings of the double articulation, which is itself governed by the idea of chiasmus. For Deleuze and Guattari chiasmus is no mere rhetorical figure. On the contrary, it serves to "cross" the double bind of God's two-handed process. To an organic body, the cross looks like the symbol of the organism's physical suffering, which for Christians produces an icon of salvation; to a body without organs, that same cross serves as a sign that all dualisms have a connection in-between, a third term that traverses and subverts binary oppositions and makes the whole movement of any event even more fluid than the sum of its flows. As John Protevi remarks, echoing the idea of geological rock formation, "what we really have is organism as the limit of a process, just as a BwO is the limit of a process. The organism and the body without organs are limits of the opposed processes of stratification and destratification" (2001, 38). Epistemology and motion serve as almost indistinguishable aspects of becoming and flow.

The organism thus tends to drag the flow of the organs toward a standstill, inscribing its organized version of them upon the recording surface of the BwO. Once there, an encounter with the BwO simultaneously works to destratify the organs and return them toward pure flux. Thus the organic paradigm that underpins a Catholic university's mission statement might imply that the student's heart is a microcosm of the heart of the Church, and of course this idea is valid in an interestingly anagogic way. However, neither of these "hearts" stands still long enough to make the iconic fixation unified, essential, or whole. Neither limit—of pure flow or perfect stratification—is "really" attainable, which is tantamount to saying that there is no such thing as a pure organism or a perceivable BwO (Protevi 2001, 38). Moreover, each is immanent to the other, so that the opposed double processes of stratification (or articulation) and destratification (or flow) continue in perpetuity. Motion and time are inseparable. Under these circumstances, God appears to be more immanent than transcendent, since singular transcendence is an illusion produced by theorizing a ground of total consistency, something organism always promises but fails to provide (39). God's own doubleness unfolds reality even as it limits perception. Thinking along these lines allows students to doubt transcendence without utterly rejecting it and to observe immanence without losing a measure of critical distance.

The act of rhetorical articulation, for example, has always been regarded as one of the most important aspects of composition pedagogy: by throwing their most important ideas into relief, students experience learning as a restratified sense of focus. This particular concept of articulation affects every stage of the writing process, from preliminary brainstorming to a final revision. However, no student articulates his or her ideas in isolation. In fact, most current critical pedagogies would aver that cultural forces are the most telling influences of all.

As Judith Poxon shows, Deleuze and Guattari do not regard the BwO as a body in the conventional sense; rather, the BwO comprises a set of *practices*: "what is highlighted in the BwO is process, flux, function, as opposed to the static identity of the theological body, the body-as-organism" (2001, 45). Poxon notes that "this is so because, unlike the organism that is unified in its organization, the BwO is multiple, and that multiplicity constitutes the source of its vitality, its force" (2001, 46). Implicit in a traditional Catholic model of spiritual articulation are the comforting tropes of benevolent hegemony, naturalized power, extended familial trust, spiritual transcendence, organism, private intellectual space, open discussion of ideas, and singularity. A re-theorized Catholic classroom would of necessity interrogate these values but not subvert them, and Poxon's remarks about the ultimate utility of the BwO as a set of practices would be affirmed. Whatever emerges after the tracing of cultural influence would still participate in the various Catholic intellectual traditions, although taxonomy of these traditions would become less definite. Nonetheless, students might contact and redeem some cultural forces that have previously been taken for granted. For students of faith, an understanding of the role that organism has to play in delimiting unfettered desire can only prove enlightening.

Obviously, the composition classroom as the meeting site of the BwO and the organism would be a very unusual space. To the BwO, this space is an utterly indispensable architectural machine, one that functions as the smooth surface or expanding cerebral plane upon which writing, reading, thinking, reporting, and dialogue flow, assemble, articulate, destratify, and then re-channel. Nevertheless, despite the Catholic composition classroom's wondrous flexibility when conceived as a reflection of the BwO, it is nothing without a concomitant limit; in this case, organism. It was never a fault of pedagogy in the Catholic intellectual tradition to demand order and stratification; the problem lies in a failure to commend and celebrate flow, desiring, becoming, flux, and even instability. A degree of stratification is not only unavoidable, it is positively healthy. Deleuze and Guattari are quite definite on this point: "The worst that can happen is if you throw the strata into a demented or suicidal collapse" (1987, 161). The proper response to the organism's seemingly oppressive acts of stratification and taxonomy—of which the "search for ultimate truth" mentioned in *Ex Corde*

*Ecclesiae* is an epitome—is to wait for the brief window of chance in which one can "patiently and *momentarily* dismantle the organization of the organs that we call the organism" (161, emphasis mine). This process is a gradual and delicate one, not at all like the headlong plunge into nihilism, non-meaning, or anti-meaning against which the organism always warns as an alarming danger, and rightly so. The idea is to experience the strata and the BwO as an exploratory or mapping surface. By means of a careful interaction with the organism's striations and segmentarity, students discover that they are writing inside the folds of a "social formation" (161). Nonetheless, this formation allows for unfolding, for lines of flight, for mapping in fresh directions. The idea, Deleuze and Guattari write, "is to have a small plot of new land at all times" (161). In sum, the "search for truth" is as much a casualty of heavy and unified stratification as it is of deconstruction and cultural relativism. I can think of no more appropriate venue to view these forces in action than student writings, replete as they are with fruitful moments of awkward insight, glimpses of knowledge, and partially realized stylistic experiment.

## Writing as Unfolding

As an example, I would like to discuss a paper by a student of mine, Stephanie, which concerns the relationship between science and religion, a topic that automatically engages the character and authority of the organism described in *Ex Corde Ecclesiae*.[11] Science has always been a particular source of anxiety to the Church, never more so than today, when the Catholic university views science as an indispensable dimension of the "search for truth." At the same time, scientific research on such potentially discordant bioengineering techniques as cloning constantly threatens to untune the celestial harmony. One part of the traditional Catholic intellect, to be sure, respects science in the most positive and helpful way. Another part or tradition, however, preserves a space for science specifically in order to harness it to the will of the institutional organism. This latter tradition seeks to hold science in check by advocating firmly articulated ethical debate rather than open repression. *Ex Corde Ecclesiae* maintains its precisely balanced cosmological analogy by stating directly that "men and women of science will truly aid humanity only if they preserve 'the sense of the transcendence of the human person over the world and of God over the human person'" (Pope John Paul II 1.18). In short, certain Catholic intellectual traditions study science in order to contain it. From the Church's point of view, anxiety about science is quite well founded, since it is science that works steadily to demystify the organs as well as their organization.

Stephanie begins her work by discussing a reading assignment, "The Relation of Science and Religion," by Richard P. Feynman. Her thesis statement promises an even-handed and reasonable exploration of her topic: "science and religion can coexist and both can be used to help in trying to explain the nature of human existence. Science and religion constitute two pillars of society, and are related." Stephanie adapts the "two pillars" metaphor from the last paragraph of Feynman's essay, a tactic that works well from the point of view of traditional academic writing, because she begins where Feynman concludes, immediately adding new thought and fresh analysis to the discussion (Feynman 2002, 515). She proceeds to historicize his arguments, citing other sources to show that just as Egyptian religion helped shape Islam, Judaism, and Christianity, Western scientific method was heavily influenced by Greek physics and philosophy. The roots of science developed by means of a close examination of the material world and bore their first fruits in Aristotle's work on the relation of matter and spirit. Stephanie notes that religion was nevertheless "the most important aspect of one's life" right through the Renaissance, a time when the "Church, oftentimes so overpowering, persuaded the population to feel that religion remained the only choice they had." In the seventeenth century, science and religion merge in the thought of Isaac Newton, who regarded his scientific discoveries as lessons in "the laws of God." Stephanie sees clearly that religion and science discover reality from divergent epistemological angles: "science," she writes, "asks the 'how' questions and religion asks the 'why' questions." Her tone is calm and detached, and she neatly avoids setting science and religion apart in static or monolithic categories, remarking instead that "as history progressed, sometimes science and religion blended together and during certain times they became more separated." Too, she decenters the idea of science as an absolute authority by reframing the popular conception of evolution: "humans may have evolved from another type of creature, but God still took part in determining how this evolution would take place." In the end, having explored her topic thoroughly, she agrees with Feynman—his remains a strong voice throughout her text—that doubt is essential to scientific study, while religion is based mostly upon belief.

How did I respond to Stephanie's paper? As would most instructors in first-year courses, I regarded it as a genuine success. She makes many of the intellectual and rhetorical moves that academic convention expects and demands at her stage of development: an appropriate and exploratory thesis statement, solid historical development, examples drawn from varied sources, and reasonable analytical models of her own devising. Stephanie wrote an excellent paper, but my responses are based more in composition truisms than in interesting theory and practice.

What if I were to regard the paper from a more sophisticated point of view? Had I been thinking in terms of Deleuze and Guattari's epistemology at the time, I might have helped Stephanie focus on her basically incisive realization that the different descriptions of reality provided by science and religion have formed, deformed, and re-formed over historical time. Both religion and science strive to segment, stratify, or articulate the smooth flow of information and language that oscillates freely across the surface of the BwO. Stephanie sees clearly that belief and doubt are the key terms in this process, and her focus on these twin aspects of the process of knowing might easily be sharpened by suggestions for revision. For example, I could have asked

Stephanie to interrogate Feynman's examination of belief and doubt as categories. Stephanie accepts Feynman's argument that "doubt is a necessary aspect of scientific study," as well as his opinion that religion avoids skepticism at all costs. She quotes "The Relation of Science and Religion" at some length on this point: "although there are scientists who believe in God, I do not believe that they think of God in the same way as religious people do . . . I think that they say something like this to themselves: 'I am almost certain that there is a God. The doubt is very small'" (Feynman 2002, 509). Earlier in her essay, however, Stephanie alludes to ideas of her own, which, if elaborated more fully, would certainly lead her to reframe Feynman's blunt either/or distinction. Science, she writes, is itself a kind of religion, because it "functions in explaining the nature of humankind and people's purpose on earth." Reading this remark within the framework of the BwO clearly displays a move toward double articulation. Stephanie knows that science and religion are in some sense twin aspects of the flow called explanation; unlike Feynman, she senses the different shapes into which faith and uncertainty fold reality. If the master trope of academic writing is authority, I would have done well to help my student resist her source a bit more definitely, thus allowing room for her own thought to manifest itself.

The organism of religion absolutely requires doubt, without which there would be no fall from grace, no test of faith, no teleology. Doubt thus plays a positive role, since uncertainty provides a moment of flight from absolute authority, and it is in this moment that immanence unfolds itself. If transcendence cuts the universe into orderly levels, immanence gathers reality in folds. What would result from considering the role of faith in forming the vast taxonomic organism called science? In a peculiar way, belief and doubt "cross" the discourse of science and religion: the doubt of one inverts itself as belief in the other, but this process transpires without negating the reciprocal flow of perception and language that connects disbelief with full spiritual commitment. This crossing of the text, as we have seen, serves as a Derridian signature, a haunting vestige or trace of the linguistic flows that connect human faith and human uncertainty, whether the language of that faith is inscribed by those who uphold the curious epistemology that favors the scientific method or whether the words are written down by believers who practice the ritual worship of one or more of the strange entities called god(s).

A modernist or new critical reading of Stephanie's paper might take rhetorical pleasure in the eerie poetic traverse signaled by the underlying chiasmic series of doubt to belief, belief to doubt, which in turn could be conceived as analogous to the cross that represents such a multiplicity of values to the Church, or to the $x$ that serves science as the generic symbol for a variable. Some versions of post-structuralist thought would play the cross against itself and attempt to collapse or deny its poignant meaning. But for the flexible, optimistic, and decentering thought of Deleuze and Guattari, the chiasmus gestures toward a profoundly significant event. Neither the static and transcendent symbol of the cross nor its nihilistic erasure are conceptually adequate to the terms with which Stephanie sets up her essay or to the lines of flight toward which those terms point. A rereading of many student papers might yield similar instances, folds of conception and language that could be unfolded in order to reveal "a small plot of new land."

Precisely because of their historically theological context, composition classrooms in Catholic institutions are especially well positioned to adapt assemblages of thought, like the BwO, that encourage lines of flight from the institutional organism, and this is the case even while maintaining a healthy respect for the counter-limits dictated by utter (dis)organization. To the extent that *any* model of invention or language is seen as categorically primary—including those propounded by Deleuze and Guattari—our courses will become less productive, more segmented, more static. For the composition classroom to depart, even on a few occasions, from the scene of inculcated convention, instructors and students alike must attempt to unfold the discursive spaces through which thought ceaselessly migrates.

# Notes

1. An interesting corollary to the anxiety over post-stucturalist thought in the Catholic academy is explored by Alan Wolfe (*The Chronicle of Higher Education*, February 26, 1999). Wolfe describes the epistemological phenomenon he calls "parallelism," which, he says, "is popular among those scholars who are religious believers and who see in the rise of postmodernism a potential ally with their communion of faith. If the academy holds that there is no one road to truth, parallelists say, then just as we acknowledge feminist or African-American ways of knowing, so we can also make room for Christian ways of knowing. Religious scholars already skeptical of the Enlightenment can only take heart when they see reason and rationality attacked—even if the attackers themselves may be leftists, possibly atheists." Pope John Paul II's position, delineated in *Fides et Ratio*, would at first seem to reject parallelism, since he argues in favor of the union of spiritual truth and Enlightenment reason. However, he also compartmentalizes philosophy: "the church has no philosophy of her own, nor does she canonize any one particular philosophy in relation to others . . . even when it engages theology, philosophy must remain faithful to its own principles and methods" (1998, 331). For the Pope, then, reason has a prior and naturalized quality of orientation toward truth, so that philosophy will eventually discover revealed and spiritual verities. The problem with this position is that it assumes a singular and unifying definition of the word *reason*. What of philosophies that function primarily by denying the premises and progress of Enlightenment reason? Such a philosophy, Pope John Paul II remarks, "would serve little purpose" (331).

2. See, for example, *"Ex Corde Ecclesiae* Creates an Impasse," by J. Donald Monan, S. J. (Chancellor of Boston College) and Edward A. Malloy, C. S. C. (President of The University of Notre Dame), 1999. See also Cadegan, et al. (1999); McMurtrie (2000); O'Hare (1999); Wilkes (1999); Saunders (1997).

3. A full treatment of the extremely sophisticated "analysis" to which Deleuze subjects the concept of immanence is beyond the scope of this paper. His last published

work, *Pure Immanence: Essays on a Life* (2001) contains his most detailed and extended examination of immanence as a concept. My present purpose is merely to use aspects of Deleuze's thinking to help position critical pedagogy for interesting and useful resistance to hegemony.

4. References to *Ex Corde Ecclesiae* and *Fides et Ratio* are cited by part and paragraph number.

5. For the early forms of sign theory, see Giovanni Manetti, *Theories of the Sign in Classical Antiquity* (1993). For a detailed exposition of the debate over *res and verbum* see Brian Vickers, "Analogy Versus Identity: The Rejection of Occult Symbolism, 1580–1680," in *Occult and Scientific Mentalities in the Renaissance* (1984).

6. *Ex Corde Ecclesiae*, note 16, citing Vatican Council II: Pastoral Constitution on the Church in the Modern World, *Gaudium et Spes*.

7. Cf. *Ex Corde Ecclesiae*, 1.15: "A Catholic University, therefore, is a place of research, where scholars *scrutinize reality* with the methods proper to each academic discipline, and so contribute to the treasury of human knowledge."

8. *Ex Corde Ecclesiae*, citing John Paul II's 1980 Discourse to the "Institut Catholique de Paris," 1 June 1980: *Insegnamenti di Giovanni Paolo II*, Vol. 3.1: 1581.

9. In an article titled "*Orthos Logos, Recta Ratio*: Pope John Paul II, Nihilism, and Postmodern Philosophy," Catholic theologian Michael Peters regrets the Pope's consignment of all postmodern and post-structuralist thought to the limbo of utter relativism and nihilism. For Peters, the most significant proposition in *Fides et Ratio* is that it regards Nietzsche's announcement of the death of God as pure nihilism. Peters insists, to the contrary, that "it is the imperative of Nietzsche's figure of the philosopher-artist, in the face of nihilism—of suicide, pessimism, cultural dissolution and fragmentation—to create new values. It is also the case that those who follow in Nietzsche's footsteps—Martin Heidegger, Jacques Derrida, Gilles Deleuze, Maurice Blanchot, and Michel Foucault—are fundamentally concerned with the history and meaning of being (as the history of Western metaphysics) and with the question of value" (Peters 2000). For these philosophers, as well as for Nietzsche, it is precisely nihilism that must be overcome by cultural and intellectual critique, even if the outcome is something less perfect than a seamless and unified metaphysics. Peters' detailed history of the postmodern investigation of being shows that, without Nietzsche's exploration of the failures of traditional metaphysics, there could be no subsequent re-valuation of presence and immanence, concepts essential not only to postmodern epistemology, but also to theology.

10. For Deleuze's analysis of the relation of organic matter to the forces of folding and unfolding, see Chapter One, "The Pleats of Matter," in *The Fold: Leibniz and the Baroque* (1993).

11. I am grateful to Stephanie Shulder for her kind permission to use her writing in this essay.

# Works Cited

Cadegan, Una M., et al. 1999. "Dear Bishops: Open Letter on *Ex Corde Ecclesiae*." *Commonweal* 5 (November): 16–18.

D'Arcy, Bishop John. 1999. "Achieving *Ex Corde Ecclesiae*'s Goals." *Origins CNS Documentary Service* 29 (23 September): 15.

Deleuze, Gilles, 1993. *The Fold: Leibniz and the Baroque*. Translated by Tom Conley. Minneapolis and London: University of Minnesota Press.

———. 2001. *Pure Immanence: Essays on a Life*. Edited by John Rajchman and translated by Anne Boyman. New York: Zone Books.

Deleuze, Gilles, and Felix Guattari. 1987. *A Thousand Plateaus: Capitalism and Schizophrenia*. Translated by Brian Massumi. Minneapolis: University of Minnesota Press.

Evans, Aden. 1996. "BwO Definition." Online Posting. 3 June. Deleuze-Guattari Mailing List. 5 July 2001. http://lists.village.virginia.edu/~spoons/index.html.

Feynman, Richard P. 2002. "The Relation of Science and Religion." In *A World of Ideas*: *Essential Readings for College Writers*, edited by Lee A. Jacobus, 503–16. 6th ed. Boston: Bedford/St. Martin's.

Manetti, Giovanni. 1993. *Theories of the Sign in Classical Antiquity*. Advances in Semiotics Series. Translated by Christine Richardson. Bloomington: Indiana University Press.

McCool, Gerald A. 2000. "The Christian Wisdom Tradition and Enlightenment Reason." In *Examining the Catholic Intellectual Tradition*, edited by Anthony J. Cernera and Oliver J. Morgan, 75–101. Fairfield, CT: Sacred Heart University Press.

McMurtie, Beth. 2000. "Vatican Backs Rules for Catholic Colleges That Spur Concerns About Academic Freedom." *The Chronicle of Higher Education* 8 June. http://chronicle.com/daily/2000/06/2000060801n.htm.

Monan, J. Donald, S. J., and Edward A. Malloy. 1999. "*Ex Corde Ecclesiae* Creates an Impasse." *America* 30 (January): 32–38.

O'Hare, Joseph A., S. J. 1999. "The History of the Issue." Association of Catholic Colleges and Universities Business Meeting, 3 February.

Olson, Gary A. 1990. "Jacques Derrida on Rhetoric and Composition: A Conversation." *Journal of Advanced Composition* 10.1. http://jac.gsu.edu/jac/10/Articles/1.htm.

Peters, Michael. 2000. "*Orthos Logos, Recta Ratio*: Pope John Paul II, Nihilism, and Postmodern Philosophy." *Journal for Christian Theological Research* 5:1 pars. 6–14. http://apu.edu/~CTRF/articles/2000_articles/peters.html.

Pope John Paul II. 1990. "*Ex Corde Ecclesiae*: Apostolic Constitution of the Supreme Pontiff John Paul II on Catholic Universities." *The Holy See: The Vatican*. Accessed 21 September 2002. www.vatican.va/holy_father/john_paul_ii/apost_constitutions /documents /hf_jp-ii_apc_15081990_ex-corde-ecclesiae_en.html.

———. 1998. "Encyclical Letter *Fides et Ratio* of the Supreme Pontiff John Paul II to the Bishops of the Catholic Church on the Relationship of Faith and Reason." *The Holy See: The Vatican*. 4 June 2002. www.vatican.va/holy_father/john_paul_ii /encyclicals/documents/hf_jp-ii_enc_15101998_fides-et-ratio_en.html.

Poxon, Judith. 2001. "Embodied Anti-Theology: The Body Without Organs and the Judgement of God." In *Deleuze and Religion*, edited by Mary Bryden, 42–50. London and New York: Routledge.

Protevi, John. 2001. "The Organism as the Judgement of God: Aristotle, Kant, and Deleuze on Nature (That Is, on Biology, Theology and Politics)." In *Deleuze and Religion*, edited by Mary Bryden, 30–41. London and New York: Routledge.

Saunders, Paul C. 1997. "The Vatican, the Bishops, and the Academy." *Commonweal* 26 (September): 11–14.

Stivale, Charles J. 1998. *The Two-Fold Thought of Deleuze and Guattari: Intersections and Animations*. New York: Guilford Press.

Vickers, Brian. 1984. "Analogy Versus Identity: The Rejection of Occult Symbolism, 1580–1680." In *Occult and Scientific Mentalities in the Renaissance*, edited by Brian Vickers, 95–163. Cambridge: Cambridge University Press.

Wilkes, Paul. 1999. "Catholic Spoken Here: A Report from the Academic Front." *America* 1 (May): 13–18.

Wolfe, Alan. 1999. "Catholic Universities Can Be the Salvation of Pluralism on American Campuses." *The Chronicle of Higher Education* 26 February: B6.

Woltering, Mo Fung. 2002. "Shopping for a Catholic College with Pope John Paul II." *Human Family Foundation*. 21 September. www.rc.net/org/humanfamily /shopping.html.

# Contributors

**Jeffrey P. Cain** is an assistant professor of English at Sacred Heart University in Fairfield, Connecticut, where he also serves as Director of Communications across the Curriculum. His research interests include postmodern and post-structuralist literary theory, early modern literature, the history of semiotics, environmental writing, and literary nonfiction. He lives in Clinton, Connecticut, with his wife, Noel, son Tommy, a basset hound named Gracie, and three cats.

**Douglas Downs** is an assistant professor of rhetoric and composition in the Department of English and Literature at Utah Valley State College. When not studying the role of faith in writing classrooms, he researches conceptions of writing among students, faculty, and the public through ethnography and critical discourse analysis. His work focuses on improving the public image and status of Writing Studies in higher education.

**Lauren Fitzgerald** is an assistant professor of English at Yeshiva University where she directs the Composition Program and the Writing Center at Yeshiva College. Her work in composition studies has appeared in *The Writing Center Journal*, *The Writing Lab Newsletter*, and, with Denise Stephenson, *The Writing Center Director's Resource Book* (ed. Christina Murphy and Byron Stay, LEA). She has a forthcoming essay in *Judaic Perspectives on Literacy: Contexts for Rhetoric and Composition* (ed. Andrea Greenbaum and Deborah Holdstein, Hampton Press).

**Kristine Hansen** is a professor of English at Brigham Young University, where she has directed both the English Composition Program and the Writing-Across-the-Curriculum Program. She frequently teaches undergraduate courses in Advanced Writing and the History of Rhetoric as well as graduate courses on theory and research methods in composition and rhetoric. She has published chapters in several volumes and articles in *WPA Journal*, *CCC*, *English Journal*, and *Language and Learning Across the Curriculum*. Her books include *Resituating Writing: Constructing and Administering Writing Programs*, coedited with Joseph Janangelo (Boynton/Cook) and two textbooks, *A Rhetoric for the Social Sciences* (Prentice Hall, 1997) and *Writing in the Social Sciences: A Rhetoric with Readings* (Pearson, 2003). A member of the Council of Writing Program Administrators, NCTE, and CCCC, she served as a member of the Executive Committee of WPA from 1994–97 and currently serves on the editorial board of the *WPA Journal*.

**bonnie lenore kyburz** is an associate professor of English at Utah Valley State College. Her teaching interests include writing and rhetorical theory, and introductory critical/literary theory. She directs the Communication across the Curriculum Project (CXC) and serves as Chair of the Advisory Board for the Faculty Center for Teaching Excellence. Her work involves valuing ambiguity and complexity in the classroom, in writing, and in communication. She also volunteers with the Sundance Institute, fulfilling a desire to work with/in film as well as to better understand film communities, discourses, and production.

**Elizabeth Vander Lei** is an associate professor of English at Calvin College where she teaches courses on writing, linguistics, and writing pedagogy. She continues to research the intersections of rhetoric, particularly African American rhetoric, and religious belief.

**Keith D. Miller** is the author of *Voice of Deliverance: The Language of Martin Luther King, Jr., and Its Sources* and many essays about the civil rights era, including one about Malcolm X and alternative literacy that appeared in *College Composition and Communication* (*CCC*) in December 2004. With James Baumlin, he also recently coedited *Selected Essays of Jim W. Corder.* He is a professor of English (and former WPA) at Arizona State University.

**Mark Montesano** is currently a faculty associate teaching in both the English and Religious Studies departments at Arizona State University. His research interests include applying rhetorical and philosophical theories of language to religious discourse and the implications of these theories for ethical practice. Before teaching at ASU he was a psychotherapist for twenty years.

**Rebecca Schoenike Nowacek** is an assistant professor at Marquette University, where she teaches courses in rhetorical theory, advanced composition, literacy studies, and writing for the professions. Her current research focuses on the intersection of writing across the disciplines and interdisciplinary studies, and she is at work on a manuscript about writing instruction in interdisciplinary classrooms.

**Brad Peters** is an associate professor and founder of the University Writing Center at Northern Illinois. He teaches courses in rhetorical theory, nonfiction writing, and gender studies. His recent publications include chapters in Gilyard's *Race, Rhetoric, and Composition*, Nagelhout's and Rutz's *Classroom Spaces*, and a coauthored article on online learning among LGBT students in *Computers and Composition.*

**Duane Roen** is a professor of English at Arizona State University, where he serves as Head of Humanities, Fine Arts, and English on the East Campus. He has published six books in rhetoric and composition and authored or coauthored more than 170 chapters, articles, and conference papers in the field. His current project, *Views from the Center: The CCCC Chairs' Addresses, 1977–2005* (Bedford/St. Martins and NCTE), is scheduled to appear in 2006.

**Jennifer M. Santos** is a graduate teaching associate at Arizona State University, where she has taught a variety of composition classes in online, hybrid, computer-mediated communication, and face-to-face settings. She is currently working on her Ph.D. specializing in Gothic and Romantic British Literature. Aside from this area of specialization, her other interests include teaching writing and literature.

**Juanita M. Smart** teaches Composition and Literature at Clarion University of Pennsylvania. She does her best thinking about writing and teaching while tromping through local game lands with her two "special edition" dogs, Shiloh and Stormy.

**Bronwyn T. Williams** is an associate professor of English at the University of Louisville. He is the author of *Tuned In: Television and the Teaching of Writing* as well as articles in several anthologies and journals including *College English*, *College Composition and Communication*, and *The Writing Instructor*. He is the editor of the upcoming collection, *Composing Identities: Literacy and Power in Higher Education* and the coauthor, with Amy Zenger, of the forthcoming book, *Written on the Screen: Representations of Literacy in Popular Culture*. He also writes a regular column on issues of literacy and identity for the *Journal of Adolescent and Adult Literacy*.